AF413226

ADVANCE PRAISE

With *Burying the Ghosts* Sonia Case has joined the group of second generation, writing their parents' Holocaust story as a novel. She has ensured her mother's legacy will continue to be remembered and can be used to help teach today's young people about the dangers of racism and hatred through her well-written and engaging book. – **Debra Barnes, Association Jewish Refugees Next Generation Manager and author of *The Young Survivors***

The Holocaust is hardly an unknown story. But Sonia Case brings fresh eyes, great clarity and warm personal feelings to her family memoir, making us feel in the grip of something quite new. It is an appealing reminder that nothing is as gripping as the history we thought we knew – but didn't. – **Robert Winder, Deputy Editor of Granta, Trustee of The Migration Museum, London and best selling author of *Bloody Foreigners: The Story of Immigration to Britain***

While such accounts as Burying the Ghosts exist, we won't forget the lives and fates of people like Hedda Israel. Sonia Case has based this novel on her own mother's experiences and brings to life not just the sweep of historical events, but the detail of sometimes fraught relationships and the texture of everyday life. She has fashioned her mother's accounts into a gripping and vivid story, whose message is as necessary as ever. – **Adele Geras, Author**

Holocaust memories can be extremely difficult for those of us born after the awful events of WWII. As someone who lost no one of close family, such accounts are to some extent at a distance.

But that distance must be crossed if we are to prevent a repetition – a likelihood sadly growing as we see once again the rise of antisemitism and Jew hatred from both left and right. Sonia Case's novel, based on her mother's testimony, is an important reminder that human stories are far more complex and difficult when lives are torn apart by hate. The fact that it is based on fact reinforces the ties that bind and the ties that must be let go. – **Jennie Kreser, Solicitor/Administrator and Community Coordinator of Bromley Reform Synagogue**

BURYING THE GHOSTS

SHE ESCAPED NAZI GERMANY ONLY TO HAVE
HER LIFE TORN APART BY THE WOMAN SHE
SAVED FROM THE CAMPS: HER MOTHER

SONIA CASE

ISBN 9789493322127 (ebook)

ISBN 9789493322103 (paperback)

ISBN 9789493322110 (hardcover)

Publisher: Amsterdam Publishers, The Netherlands

info@amsterdampublishers.com

Burying the Ghosts is part of the series WWII Historical Fiction

Copyright © Sonia Case 2023

Cover design by Kate Malecki

CONTENTS

PREFACE

Back in 2020, between COVID19 lockdowns, my nephew sent me an email. He told me that the link to my mother Ruth's online video testimony would soon expire and that we would no longer be able to view her recordings online. What was this testimony?

When filming *Schindler's List* on location, Steven Spielberg had the idea of capturing the stories of as many Holocaust survivors as possible from all over the world. He established the Shoah Foundation whose mission is to develop empathy, understanding and respect with those who have survived the Holocaust. He recorded their spoken testimony on video and it was then stored within the archives of the University of Southern California. The collection, recorded in the late 1990s, covers 56 countries and 32 languages.

I had left my parents' home in the late 1970s. Busy with my work, husband and later my children, I showed little interest in the recordings my mother made. And following my mother's death in 2007, I was too upset to watch them, knowing that I would spend most of the time sobbing.

When I knew that time was limited, I downloaded the four tapes and over the next weeks watched with growing amazement. Her story of how she managed to leave Germany in early 1939, and how she got her mother out of the Nazi labor camp to make a new life in London, was remarkable. She was one of the lucky ones, as were the many other survivors who gave equally compelling testimony.

My mother and father did not talk about their experiences with their children. Did they want to forget? Was it their guilt for surviving when so many others had perished? Or did they have a completely different reason?

Burying the Ghosts is my mother's story of survival told as fiction. The story begins in 1934 at the start of Hitler's rise to power and follows her journey to England. Part 1 draws closely on her video testimony. Part 2 takes flight into the stories she never told and answers some of the questions we never asked. Part 3 is based on my childhood memories and Part 4 provides the "Happy Ever After" essential for all good love stories. Thanks to Spielberg's determination to give voice to the survivors' silence I was able to make a profound connection to my mother nearly 15 years after her death. I am hugely grateful to him and the team of intrepid interviewers who captured their stories, in particular Lesley Nathan who patiently listened to my mother and asked all the right questions.

For the purposes of the story, I have changed some but not all names, and Ruth becomes Hedda.

Sonia and Ruth

PART I

1

TAKE BACK CONTROL

SAARBRÜCKEN

December 1934

Once upon a time, many years ago, in a small coal-filled, black-roofed town on the border of France and Germany, lived a husband and wife, and their two lovely daughters. Edith was the elder, and Hedda her younger sister. Their parents owned a shiny glass-fronted store where they sold skirts and dresses, bags and bows to the fine people of Saarbrücken, who pressed their noses to the windows eager to admire the latest fashions on display.

But, as in all good fairy stories told by the Brothers Grimm, things would soon take a turn for the worse. And, as we would expect, a wicked spell cast over the kingdom meant our main characters' lives would change – and not for the better.

Of course, as you have already guessed, this story is not a fairy story. It is true. It happened. To real people. Real families. Real children. To my mother: Hedda.

* * *

SA Israel and Co, purveyor of fine clothing and accessories, had been a familiar sight on the streets of Saarbrücken for many years. Loyal and passing customers streamed through the elegant shop doors, enjoying the abundance of goods imported from all across the continent. The owners, Paul and Alice Israel, employed well-paid staff in the shop and in their home, and enjoyed a comfortable lifestyle: holidays on the Dutch beaches in the summer and in the Swiss mountains in the winter. But things *were* changing. Increased competition from trading rivals RothEngel had affected the cash registers, as well as Alice's temper. Dinner-time conversation had descended into painful parental arguments, Alice keen to point out her husband's lack of financial acumen.

"But business is good," Paul would say. "We lack for nothing. The car, the apartment, our furniture. The children's toys and clothes. We have staff! How many people can say they have their own chauffeur? Their own cook? What more do you want?" and he would look to his daughters for support.

"Mutti, the shop is doing well," Hedda would reassure her mother. "The shop is always busy. People are loyal. They're not going to shop elsewhere."

Edith would stay out of the talk, focused on the plate of food in front of her, shifting the boiled potatoes slathered in creamy butter from side to side. Her mother had a habit of turning on her older daughter, her choice of boyfriends coming in for the sharpest criticism. Alice had loved Ernst, the first serious one, so handsome and from a similar Jewish background. In his second year of a law degree, he would have been a perfect son-in-law, but Edith had found him dull and lacking in spirit. When she was introduced to Marc Steinberg, a theatrical impresario with dark flashing eyes under caterpillar eyebrows, she was smitten. Ernst was yesterday's news, she told her mother.

It was Hedda who mediated family debates and today Edith was hunting Hedda down following yet another mother and daughter disagreement, this time in the shop in front of customers. Her mother's face had colored crimson with embarrassment.

Edith found Hedda lying on her bed lost in a book and

slumped down noisily. The younger sister reluctantly sat up and closed her book. "Honestly, Heddi, I've had enough. She's impossible. I've tried to tell her so many times and she just won't listen. I told her in front of Frau Richter: 'It's definite this time!' I don't care. I'm 19. Old enough to make my own decisions. It's a chance of a lifetime: Berlin, the theater. If I don't do it now, I never will. You understand, don't you?"

And Hedda, 14 years old, awakening to the world beyond her parents, a world of girlfriends and boys and new adventures and staying out after school to go to the park and chat and giggle, did understand. And while she thought Edith's plan to go off with this ancient man was revolting and ridiculous, she imagined her sister's future would be filled with thrilling adventures and she envied her just a little. The political events taking place in her hometown and in the wider country seemed scary and unpredictable, just like her own existence shifting from childhood pleasures to something she couldn't quite describe.

"I'll go down, Edie, and see what I can do. I know Vati's on your side. He trusts you. And she'll come to accept it. She will. Honestly."

In the shop below their apartment, Alice was bending over the counter to assist two well-dressed ladies in cashmere coats examining the soft silk blouses. As Alice saw Hedda, she waved her over. "Darling, these ladies," she whispered, pulling Hedda away, "say they've seen identical blouses at RothEngels but considerably less expensive. I said to them that the quality is bound to be inferior since these are pure silk."

Hedda looked over to see the items being examined in forensic detail, the ladies rubbing the delicate green fabric between their gloved hands as if softness could be felt through leather.

"Please, darling. Go and check for me?"

Hedda looked at her mother. "But Mutti, it's beginning to snow."

"I know, but you'll do this for me?"

As Hedda left the store, the first morning flakes floated downwards, settling white on the blackened lampposts, flat tram roofs, slush pavements, and her fur-topped head. She was thinking about Edith and Berlin and her new life as the only child, alone with the endless bickering of her parents, when she rounded the corner into Hauptstrasse, and heard a steady droning, cheering, and clapping, mixed with the rhythmic sound of determined steps. Lines of men and women, children and even babies in arms, wrapped in thick coats and hats against the winter chill, filled the pavements. With that many people jamming the way, there was no possibility of going further. Even if she could have pushed through, the shops in the main street were closed as if it were a Sunday.

It looked like the whole town had gathered to gaze upon the sight appearing in the street. Something special was happening and it was thrilling: the swelling noise and the exhilaration of the crowd. Hedda felt an energy, an excitement, that made her bubble inside.

Rather than turning straight round to report back to her mother, she squeezed through the umbrellas and managed to get to the street corner where a school party of neatly organized children was overseen by a woman who towered far above them. Frau Fischer? Hedda thought. She didn't know any other teachers that tall. The children smiled and pushed at one another at the front. One small boy echoed the passing parade and raised his arm into a 45-degree salute. The other children laughed at their daring classmate, and not wanting to be outdone, copied the leader until 15 little arms waved in the air, accompanied by shouts of "*Heil Hitler,*" followed by giggles at their bravery.

The teacher looked at their bare hands extended upwards. "*Ah, meine Kleine,*" she whispered, her face filled with maternal pride.

Hedda called out to her. "Frau Fischer, it's Hedda Israel. How are you? What's going on? I had no idea that this was a special day."

A solid line of soldiers in shiny black boots and wide-belted jackets marched past as Hedda elbowed herself forward until she was beside the teacher, who turned at the light touch on her arm. Her face broke into a wide beam of recognition. "Hedda! How lovely to see you. You look so much older and all grown-up, even with a touch of lipstick. It suits you," she said, reaching out to stroke the cheek not covered by Hedda's hat and scarf.

Hedda felt stupid. She had forgotten she had reddened her lips before leaving, borrowing Edith's latest Rubenstein in an effort to look more sophisticated, and here she was not even knowing the purpose of this giant parade.

"Isn't it marvelous?" Frau Fischer said. "Not long now till the vote. I'm sure your parents will be using theirs?"

Between discussions about the shop, and lengthier ones about Edith and her boyfriend and general family business, there had been some talk in the Israel household about the plebiscite, a vote about whether Saarland would unite with Germany. Everyone in Saarbrücken spoke German, not French. They were born in Germany, proud German citizens, holding German passports. There was a sense of missing out on the new government under Hitler and his National Socialist party. Despite some real worries about what he said about Jewish people, he was putting the country back together again. People had confidence in him. They believed his promises and Hedda tried to see his attraction, even though she couldn't understand why the Nazis said horrible things about Jews. After 17 years of being under French control, this referendum gave Saarbrücken and the surrounding land the opportunity to return to Germany. Alice had already decided it would make little or no difference to her family and their future. As long as they continued to sell the best Parisian-style coats, fresh from the capital's catwalks, the most sumptuous ribbons and buttons to adorn their children's party dresses, and parfumerie from the lavender fields of Grasse, then why not?

Hedda's mother generally avoided the subject altogether, preferring the contents of *Modenschau–FashionSchau* to reading the newspapers that Paul devoured. Due to Alice's lack of interest, Paul had tried to explain the political realities to his younger daughter. Of course, she knew about Hitler and some of the things he was saying, Hedda would say to Paul. Yes, she was aware that some laws had been passed that barred Jews from some jobs, she wasn't stupid. She and her friends had talked about him in school. They couldn't see his appeal. His mustache was ridiculous. He wasn't the slightest bit handsome. He had a horrible voice. He probably never read books. Almost certainly, he'd never had a girlfriend. He was a joke! But Vati thought differently. "Heddi, you must know this man is not a joke. He is a danger to us. He blames us for everything, everything, even the war! We didn't lose the war. The Germans lost the war. I was there! I should know. I joined up and fought like everyone else!" Paul would explain that she should be concerned, even if her mother was not, and Hedda tried hard to listen to her father's anxious lectures about what lay ahead.

"I think my father will vote but Mother doesn't take much interest in such things. But looking at all these people, it will be a 'Yes', I'm sure, they're all so…" Hedda tailed off. There was something about the noise, the adoring faces, the cheering crowd, which made her stop for breath. She noticed the washing-line bunting hanging from shuttered window to shuttered window, the smaller flags decorating every second-floor balcony, and the pieces of cloth printed with a black swastika. Women of all ages leant out of windows, shouting endearments to the youthful men marching by. The women's faces were flushed and not from the cold. Some threw bunches of flowers bought from the flower shops with romantic offers attached. Hedda wondered if she would ever feel like that: that adoration, that blind love. She wasn't sure whether she felt envy or contempt for their lovesickness. It was clearly powerful. Was that what Edith felt for Herr Steinberg? Was that what being in love felt like?

"I must go. It's been so nice to see you again. I enjoyed your lessons very much," she said, shifting back to reality. "Thank you."

The children still held their arms up high as Hedda turned and pushed her way back, cutting across the path of the synchronized troops kicking their legs and saluting the crowd.

Paul Otto Israel sat behind the small table, sipping his soup and carefully turning the pages of the *Saarbrücken Zeitung* to avoid marks from his greasy fingers marring the print. In the background, his treasured wireless played light melodies. Crumbs from the *Kaisersemmel,* so delicious when dipped directly into the soup, littered the desk and steamed up his round glasses, perched on the end of his nose. Studying the small advertisements was a useful and undemanding distraction from the current family friction: his wife's inability to accept their elder daughter's decision to leave the family home to chase the bright lights of Berlin, dreaming of a career on the stage. Edith was never going to follow in her parents' footsteps and having her out of the house meant fewer arguments.

Edith and Alice's relationship wasn't easy, and Paul would often leave the room rather than listen to their unkindness. He had realized long ago that both women were incapable of showing an interest in anyone but themselves. With Edith gone, they could concentrate on the shop. Business, its success or failure, was never far from his mind. The need to make the money that would ensure his wife's happiness, the staff were paid, and his daughters saw him as a responsible father.

His children could be proud of the success of Herr Paul Otto Israel, and who knew, Hedda might even inherit the family business when he decided the time for a comfortable retirement had come. This idea filled him with a deep pleasure – to provide for Hedda, who loved her father so completely and utterly. She looked to him for protection and kindness, and in return bathed him in genuine love.

He failed to understand why his wife seemingly could not demonstrate maternal love for both the girls. He loved his wife but didn't like her much, and that morning had woken up with a headache and unpleasant aches in his chest which he wondered if they were symptoms of his contradictory feelings. Maybe he was uncharitable to Alice, who was doing her best even if that was hard to detect. She had enjoyed Edith and Hedda when they were younger, when they could be cooed over and dressed in pretty dresses and have their hair tied in ribbons and bows. But as they grew older, when they were less keen to be put on display, and their skin bore the occasional blotch or spot, Alice found it harder to play the role of loving mother.

Above the wireless, broadcasting a lunchtime concert live from Berlin, hung a large portrait of Alice herself. She had a blunt-edged bob, the horizontal cut dividing her face into two parts, a fashionable style when the picture was painted eight years ago. Her head was tilted to one side, flirtatiously. Bold splashes of yellow, blue and green amongst the pale flesh-colored hues signaled the artist's modernity. He had been up and coming when Alice sat for him and made quite a name for himself since then. The picture was worth quite a bit, but there was no question that it would be sold. A portrait of Alice took pride of place and was more important than money.

Paul finished the last mouthful as Hedda burst into the room, flung off her snow-wet hat onto the nearest chair, and wrestled with the sleeve of her coat. She gave her father a cold kiss on his cheek, moved to the wireless, turned the dial until it clicked off, and then threw herself into the seat beside Paul. "The shops were shut. It's completely mad out there. No one's shopping. Everyone's watching the soldiers, and I saw young boys there, from the Party. Why didn't we know?"

Paul wiped his mouth with a large white napkin. He had forgotten that today was that day. There had been much talk in cafés, shops, on the radio, and in the newspapers for weeks and weeks, predicting a great vote in favor of the German government and their slogan of "Take Back Control." "What did you see? Were you scared, my Sputzie?" he said, imagining his Hedda being shoved and jostled.

"To be honest, it was exciting!" She stood up to describe the scene more vividly, pacing out the participants in the drama. "There were so many young boys marching together, followed by men in uniforms. There were men in top hats who waved at the crowds. It was really exciting, like something special would happen. I know it's awful, really, and the way the crowd were joining in with their salutes, that was horrible, but it still felt... well... different from just normal every day!"

Paul closed the newspaper and wrapped his arms around her. "You know, it's not good news." He paused, unsure whether to stop there. His lunch was delicious and he wanted to digest it properly. His headache was just beginning to lift. "I will of course vote next month, but it seems that whatever I do will be useless. People have made up their minds. They want what the rest of Germany has – the little man shouting his promises to the nation. 'Oh, he will do so much, he will make everyone's lives so much richer and happier, and Germany will be great again.'"

"But Vati..."

Paul continued as if addressing a town hall audience and not his own daughter "And who can he blame for our woes? Yes, he still blames France and England for how they punished Germany. But that's not enough, is it? You can't villainize a whole country. You need defined villains and a clear hero."

Hedda wasn't sure she understood, and this registered on her face.

"People, people you can see and hear, people that are close by, people you can reach out and touch! Let's blame the Jews again. They're the ones when we need someone to blame." He paused for just a moment. "It's never gone away, however much we try to fool ourselves. Always us. History loves a repeating pattern."

Hedda had heard her father's views before, but this was different. The way he spoke frightened her.

"We know what they look like with their hooked noses, and their crooked backs, and their long beards and their stinking breath. They are the ones with the money, and the banks, and the power. The Jews! They are the problem." His face was blotched and he was breathing heavily. She knew he was miserable when business was bad, but this angry and upset?

"I did my bit for our 'Beloved Country.' Beloved Country was clearly not what Paul was feeling right now. "When I arrived at the Recruiting Officer's desk that day, you know what he said? 'Just our luck to get the Jew.'" Paul laughed. "It never goes away. I thought things would turn out alright for us all, and maybe they still will, who knows? Maybe Herr Hitler is just a one term chancellor, and the people will come to their senses. Maybe. But who am I fooling, really?"

Paul was interrupted by the shouts of Alice ascending the stairs from the shop below. The door was flung open and she appeared, clearly on the warpath. "I was expecting you back in the shop at least half an hour ago. Have you seen Edith? Has she told you? She's leaving next month, she says!" Alice's interrogation stopped short as she noticed Hedda squashed up beside her father on the arm of the chair. "You're back already? How did you get on? Were they selling the same blouses?"

Alice's tone of voice changed as she addressed her daughter. The nagging irritation ceased and she adopted a sweeter, oilier style. It was unpleasant, Hedda thought, her mother too capable of turning on and off her feelings, depending on who she was talking to, and what she wanted to gain. She had frequently heard her mother' s voice become cloying and childlike, when she wanted to persuade a reluctant customer to purchase an overpriced item.

"All the shops are shut in Hauptstrasse. And I don't think there will be many customers for us this afternoon, judging by what I've just seen. Everyone's watching this huge parade. Everyone! Edith is so excited about Berlin and she'd love it if you would give your blessing. She said we can come and see her perform once the show opens."

Hedda couldn't bear the idea of having to describe her morning for a second time. Nor did she want to stay for another family argument about Edith's planned departure. "Anyway, I'm completely behind on my letter writing. I promised faithfully I would reply to Betty weeks ago and still haven't put pen to paper. I think today would be a good time to get this done, and I have lots to write about."

Picking up her hat, the last of the melting snow still dripping, Hedda grabbed her coat and started composing the words that she would send to her pen friend:

Dear Betty, I hope you are well.

The struggle of putting pen to paper, even when you've been writing to each other for nearly two years, she thought. It was too formal. Too like writing to a great-aunt.

Dear Betty, Well, there's so much to tell you. Where shall I start?

That was better. Betty had become a dear friend despite the challenges of Hedda's written English and Betty's even more limited German. English was so illogical and hopeless at following the rules, unlike the straightforward German language.

Hedda had first started writing to Betty when she was 12, encouraged by her teacher, Frau Schmitt. All the pupils had been given a pen friend of similar age from an English school in a nice area to develop their written language skills and build 'cultural relations'. She had been told she had a natural aptitude for languages and was thrilled when her first report from the secondary school had awarded her 'Pupil of the Year' for English.

Her father was delighted too, and even Alice had wrapped her fleshy arms around Hedda in a perfumed hug, rewarding her daughter with a creamy lace blouse and matching fitted jacket and skirt in deep maroon, selected from their own shop. When she tried these on and looked at herself in the full-length mirror, she was shocked. She could pass for a sophisticated young woman! She was definitely taller than she remembered and had lost the puppy fat of childhood. Her round face was pretty rather than chubby, and if her mother would allow her a new haircut, she would look a good three years older. She could even attract the eye of the mysterious Walter, the boy who had recently joined the school in the class above her.

Well, I'll start with some questions!

How are your mother and father? You said that your mother had been unwell. I do hope she's better.

What about Peter? Is he still in medical school? It must be wonderful to have an older brother who can tell you about grown-up things and teach you about what boys like and don't like. Edith leaves

Hedda tailed off as the images and sounds of the morning
returned in sharp focus. Seeing those soldiers and officers and
hearing the adoring cheers of the crowd made her wonder whether
she should feel similarly elated. But of course not. None of today's
events were for her family. Nothing in particular had happened to
them and life seemed as normal despite Hitler's words. The shop
was doing well, and Christmas meant more customers.

Still Hedda felt uneasy. Maybe her father did have reason to be
worried. He and Alice argued constantly. If it wasn't about what he
read in the newspapers, it was about the state of the business and
how they were constantly on the edge of collapse, even when the
customer numbers had broken all records. She knew they had once
loved each other and enjoyed leafing through the family albums
which showed her parents laughing, holding hands and, in one
memorable picture taken on their honeymoon, kissing. These days
her mother rarely showed her husband much kindness or affection.
When I get married, I will make sure my husband knows I love
him, thought Hedda. I will smother him with kisses, and hold his
hand, and tell him how handsome he is.

By the time the letter was written and rewritten, the afternoon
light was fading. The large wooden dolls' house, an expensive
present for Hedda on her seventh birthday, still took pride of place
amongst her bedroom possessions, its brooding presence taking up
too much space in the room. Next to it were her dolls: Lottie, Liese

and Leyna, and a collection of books, some now too childish, but still containing the pictures that made her feel warm and cozy and secure. Switching on her bedside lamp, she picked up her pen, stretched out her legs which were falling asleep under her, and started again:

I really enjoyed those pictures you sent me of the Jubilee. Your King George looks very handsome. I wish we had a king instead of our chancellor! Have you seen him in your newspapers or heard him on the radio? Honestly, not everyone likes him. We don't but I don't think it's a good idea to say too much out loud. We might get into trouble!

I don't really have much more news right now. There's a boy I like called Walter. He seems nice although I've not spoken to him since he arrived a few weeks ago. I don't think he's Jewish but that doesn't matter. We're not very strict really. We're looking forward to Christmas and next week will be decorating our Christmas tree which is something I love. Mother ensures we have freshly baked Lebkuchen. They're delicious: full of honey and ginger and cinnamon. Do you have special biscuits at Christmas time?

Anyway, I think I had better end this letter now before Mother comes. She will want me to help her shut up the shop.

Please, please, please write soon.

Your very loving friend, Hedda.

Hedda leant over to open the drawer of the small bedside cabinet and pulled out a fresh envelope. She carefully folded the paper in half and then half again, tucked it in, and licked the envelope shut, which left an unpleasant fishy taste in her mouth. A letter finally completed! She wondered whether to post it now in the fading twilight, or wait till the sky had blackened and the electric street lamps would be switched on. Then the Christmas illuminations would cast red and green splashes onto the settled snow-covered pavements of Neukirche Strasse.

2

THE WILL OF THE PEOPLE
SAARBRÜCKEN

March 1935

The plebiscite held two months previously had been a resounding success. Over 90 percent had voted in favor of Saarland's happy return to Germany. The people had braved the freezing cold, gloved hands clutching stubby string-tied pencils, to make their marks and post their decisions into the tin boxes placed centrally in the halls and buildings requisitioned for the vote.

And what a pleasure and what a thrill for Saarbrücken when Herr Hitler had rewarded those voters with a visit! There he was in the flesh as his motorcade drove slowly through the main streets, his hand raised in the familiar salute, smiling at the cheering crowds. The whole town had dressed up and turned out that day, and every newspaper headline proclaimed, "The Pride of the People." The police, bodyguards, storm troopers and Deutsche Front were magnificent when they marched, but to have the man himself ride through the town, even visiting the local hospital, where he met elderly patients wheeled out to shake and kiss his hand, was close to spiritual. He embodied the human touch.

Since that day, the flags and bunting had remained hanging

from sill to sill, lamppost to lamppost, leaving no doubt of the will of the people. Who would want to stay under French control when the good townsfolk could be full members of the German recovery, the country back in its rightful position at the beating heart of Europe? Proud to be German again.

***

The Gymnasium playground was a dull open space, bounded by wire fences and dotted with largish plane trees, providing shade during summer months. Now they stood bare of leaves, and only occasionally visited by the ever-hungry town pigeons or cheeky sparrows. Despite "March 10" scratched in white chalk on school blackboards, muddy snow still lay in patches on the ground where the groundskeeper had missed scattering the salt.

The older students chattered outside. For the more studious, the topic might be the latest science lesson or their mathematics homework, and the less so would focus on teenage preoccupations – girls or boys, clothes and crushes. Some were keen to talk about the news, the latest events in their town and the wider country, and especially about whether to join the Youth Movement now actively recruiting. All were pleased it was the last day of term.

In one corner, beside the fencing that separated the school from the ordinary streets, stood a small group of young boys, idly kicking the remains of the snow with their metal-tipped boots. Their hands were in their pockets and their scarves were wound tightly round their necks. Martin, tall, skinny, and blond, was wearing an ill-fitting cap that seemed to be pointing at an older girl who was leaning against the school wall, lost in her thoughts. Hedda Israel.

Continuing to shake his arm in her direction, his friends responded with muffled sniggers and more animated kicking of the ground, turning away to face the fencing, then back again to stare at the target. Martin broke from the group and swaggered across the schoolyard.

"Hello Martin," said Hedda, surprised by his arrival.

The school was small enough for everyone to know the names

of most other pupils and Martin's brother, Dieter, who was even taller and skinnier and blonder than Martin, was in her class. The boy shuffled his feet. He wasn't expecting Hedda to acknowledge him in such an unassuming, friendly way, and it threw him off balance.

"Is everything okay? Dieter's inside, catching up with some work, I think, if you're looking for him?" said Hedda.

Martin turned to check on his friends. All eyes were on him. He couldn't back out now. Pulling his right hand, gloveless, out of his pocket, he raised it, took aim and, before Hedda could pull away, slapped it down hard against her left cheek. It helped that, despite being a couple of years younger, he was at least four inches taller. "You bloody Jew!" He made a thumbs-up gesture then promptly sprinted back to his friends, who were all now clutching their faces in recreation of the blow.

At first Hedda felt no pain, merely shock and disbelief. But a sharp stinging soon spread across her cheek and down her jaw and she felt her eyes fill with tears. What had just happened? She had been assaulted! Hit by a child! Her skin and bones hurt – the boy had a powerful punch. But now, something worse – those three words spat at her, as his hand completed its journey from pocket to face. You. Bloody. Jew.

This was a school where Jews, Protestants, Catholics, and non-believers sat side by side in the classroom, shared desks arranged by register order, where religion played no part in daily education, where no one had any interest in your birth certificate, only in where you fitted into their social circle, because you liked the same books or listened to the same music. How could this happen? There were at least four or five other Jewish students in her class alone, so why single her out? None of this made sense.

Walter, the new boy, had been standing by the door that led back into the school when Martin crossed the playground. He was too far to hear anything, but close enough to see the slap and Hedda's response. He walked over to where she was planted, not moving, head facing down, cold hands still clutching her cheeks.

"Oh, my goodness. I saw that! Are you okay? Do you know that boy?" Walter's questions poured out in a rush. "I'm Walter, by the way. Walter Dabek. I'm in Mr. Storl's class." Having introduced himself, Walter was unsure what to do next.

Hedda was silent in response, hardly raising her head.

"Seriously, are you alright?" Walter persisted, reaching out his hand to touch Hedda's arm gently.

At the feel of Walter's hand on her, she looked up. This was unbearable. The boy she had wondered about from afar since January, to whom she'd been writing romantic love notes in her diary, carefully locked away, who occasionally entered her night-time dreams to hold her hand and look at her lovingly as they walked through the city park, had witnessed her humiliation. This was not how their first meeting was meant to go.

"Yes, I'm fine," said Hedda. "Honestly, I am. What an idiot."

"I think he said something to you too. It didn't look nice."

"Oh, nothing really. Sticks and stones and all that – just words." But as soon as she said it, she knew the cliché, so often spoken by adults to brush away a childhood nastiness, was untrue. "Actually he did say something. It's really horrible. I don't really know what I should do. If I report it, I could just make things worse."

"Do you want to tell me what he said?" Walter asked.

Hedda shook her head. She wasn't up to repeating the three words. Bringing them into her mouth and speaking them out loud was allowing the emotional filth to become physical.

"Look, why don't you and I go in now and speak to the principal. I can be your witness. We can't let him get away with it. After all, he might make a habit of this – get a taste. Tomorrow there might be someone else, or he might try it on again with you." Walter started to walk towards the school building. "Come on," he shouted. "Oh, and I don't even know your name."

"Hedda. Hedda Israel."

Immediately Walter guessed what was said by the skinny, blond boy to the dark-haired girl.

"This is absolutely unacceptable, Hedda. I'm so sorry that one of our pupils behaved in this manner. Believe me, this will not happen again and I will be writing to his parents. Why do these things always happen on the last day?" she said to no one in particular. "Martin Muller, you say? I'm surprised."

Frau Theiner sat across from Hedda and Walter behind a large oak desk, covered with papers, writing implements and folders, the paraphernalia of schoolteachers. On the back wall was a picture of her and the local mayor shaking hands with some of the graduating pupils. The previous year she had been awarded a Special Recognition certificate for the outstanding results her students had achieved, particularly in science, with record numbers transferring to the University of Heidelberg.

As she talked, Frau Theiner fiddled with her glasses, taking them off to breathe warm air onto the smudged lenses before replacing them. Hedda had always liked her, her appearance a sharp contrast to that of her mother. She was tall and angular where Alice was small and comfortably fleshy and had a face devoid of powder and lipstick, in contrast to her mother's pink powder that sometimes collected in the creases around her nose and mouth. The principal's graying hair was tied in a simple bun at the nape of her neck. There was a straightforward honesty to Frau Theiner, and as she spoke, Hedda felt the relief of confession, even if this was of another's sins.

"And Walter, you saw this. But didn't hear the boy?" she asked.

"I was too far away but I saw him look back at his friends and laugh, so I thought it was something they dared him to say. Hedda's told me now, though. She didn't want to but I guessed." Walter spoke quietly but clearly; in the witness box, even the most doubting jury would believe him.

"Thank you both. Leave it with me. There will be a few things I need to do, but please don't think I've forgotten about it. Now, you have missed far too much of your lessons. Blame it on me if your teachers complain!"

Hedda and Walter pushed back their chairs, leaving Frau Theiner to search amongst the desk debris for the school logbook containing the names and addresses of all the pupils' parents. She would write that letter immediately.

As she walked home, Hedda chewed over the slap, Walter's light touch upon her arm, the meeting with the Principal, thoughts swirling around in a stewy mess in her head. Gray dusk was just settling on the streets and houses. Rounding the corner and approaching the shop, she stopped in her tracks outside Grubbers' large hardware store. Up ahead were two uniformed figures stationed either side of their shop entrance. Hedda wondered who they were and why they were standing there. She had been looking forward to getting home and washing her face clean of the day's events. These men would delay her return, she thought.

They were dressed in brown uniforms, belted at the waist, and wore peaked caps and from what she could make out, were chatting loudly to each other as they watched the late afternoon customers leave the department store. They seemed to point out certain people, the younger ladies in particular, and it was obvious that their comments were crude and their gestures cruder. She watched, unsure of what to do next.

Removing her glove, she put her hand to her cheek and felt the raised skin where Martin's nails had opened up a dark-red scratch about two inches long. Yes, it was still there. It wouldn't scar and would disappear in a couple of days, she thought, unlike those words as unforgettable as her own name. She would have to tell her parents. The small mark was an obvious clue, but the larger lump at the back of her throat was a greater one, and she knew her tears would prevent her from keeping this secret. Her mother would find it difficult to say the right thing. There would be an implication that somehow Hedda had brought this upon herself. Maybe she had said something to upset the boy? Her father would hold her and let her know how adored she was. He would listen patiently, and she would feel safe again.

"Shop's nearly closing, Fräulein," said the young, uniformed man to the right of the door as he raised an arm to prevent her entering.

She had seen men like this appearing on the streets ever since the French had left town, strutting and swaggering in small groups, throwing their new weight around.

"You don't want to shop there anyway. It's run by the Israels. Know what I mean?" He sniggered and looked at the other young Brownshirt who was yawning and making signs to move.

"I live here," said Hedda. "I've got to go in, go home. I live in the apartment above."

"Oh, that's funny. Do you work for them then?"

"No. I'm their daughter. I'm just home from school."

"Hilarious. You don't look like one. You could have fooled me," said Right-Door Man. "You're lucky. No nose on you!" He made a gesture in the air of an upturned six.

"Still, you can't get rid of that name so easily, plastered all over your shop!" Left-Door Man added. "Come on, Jürgen, we're done for today. See you tomorrow, Jew-girl, all being well." Slapping each other on the back, the two young men strode off, vulgar laughter leaving a discordant trail.

Hedda watched as they passed the Grubbers and rounded the corner, their shapes merging into the gloom of the evening. Once out of sight she entered the hallway and climbed the concrete stairs, avoiding the central lift that she'd once been stuck in as a young child.

As she opened the apartment door, she could hear her parents arguing again. Her mother's voice was definitely the louder one, the more insistent one, the voice that was accusing, prodding and poking. In contrast, Paul was placating, only occasionally pushing to make a point, however unsuccessfully. Hedda wished Paul would fight back, use the same tactics as Alice, but those times he did raise his voice, Hedda hated it – her stomach would churn, and her skin would prickle with fear.

"There's nothing I can do. It will only make things difficult right now," Hedda heard her father saying. "We need to get used to it and for all we know it might just be a temporary state of affairs."

"That's ridiculous," Alice spat back. "Temporary? Why would it be temporary? They're going to put off the customers, and that's the idea, isn't it? No one will want to shop with those – those 'boys' standing outside like orangutans!"

Maybe if she entered now, her mother would calm down. Pretending not to have heard their raised voices, Hedda flung open both the double doors. "I'm so sorry I'm late home. I hope you weren't worried."

Her pretense of stone deafness was enough for Alice to turn the volume right down and compose herself. She smiled.

"Hello, Liebchen," she said. "You must be so hungry. Dinner will be ready soon. Your father and I were just talking about the young men outside the shop. SA men. We were just discussing what we could do about it. It's going to put people off, don't you think?"

Paul sat back down in his favorite armchair and took out a pouch of pipe tobacco. Pleased his daughter had returned and the hurricane of an argument was downgraded to a light breeze, he could finally start his evening wind-down. Hedda crossed to a table by the window, where a collection of pipes and smoking paraphernalia was arranged and picked up the Dutch one, a blue-and-white ceramic bowl at its end. It was her favorite, a souvenir from a trip to Holland when she was little. It brought back memories of the warm evening walks along the canals that sparkled in the reflected glow of the streetlamps, holding her parents' hands tightly as she skipped between them, a feeling of perfect contentment and family love. How different from now.

"I don't know," said Hedda to her mother as she gave the pipe to Paul, catching his eye and exchanging a look. "Maybe it's best to ignore them? Or be polite? We could find out their names and bring them hot chocolate."

As she spoke, Hedda knew her suggestions were naive and frankly ridiculous. She wasn't stupid. These young men delighted in their new roles and responsibilities, ensuring their part of Germany would become properly Germanified, if there was such a word. They weren't stationed outside the Grubbers' hardware store or any of the other shops that Hedda had passed on her way home.

Paul lit his pipe, breathing in and puffing out like a bellows. On the successful exhale, he looked up and noticed Hedda's scratched cheek. "What happened to your face?" he asked with paternal concern.

Immediately Hedda felt the tears come and quickly wiped her eyes.

Alice walked over to examine the damage. "That looks nasty. Shall I bathe it and apply some rosewater? That will reduce the redness." She gingerly reached out her hand and touched Hedda's cheek.

Now was the time. She hesitated, then spoke: "We were playing a game of rounders, a special treat as it's the last day of term, and when I wasn't concentrating, the ball caught me, slap, on the side of my face! I was just lucky it wasn't a little higher. It could have been my eye! Anyway, Dieter was so apologetic and the teachers were really kind and it's no problem really. That rosewater sounds lovely. And then dinner?"

3

SUNSHINE AND CLOUDS
SAARBRÜCKEN

March 1935

The sun shone through the bedroom windows as Hedda woke up late on the first day of the Easter holidays. It was the first warm day of spring, a beautiful start to the two-week break. Here was the opportunity to forget about yesterday and luxuriate in time for herself, her books, meeting up with her friends in the local park, writing her letters, dreaming of walks under the stars. It was past II o'clock before she was fully dressed and downstairs for breakfast. With both her parents working in the shop, Saturday being one of their busiest days, Hedda was free to do exactly what she wanted. A whole ten days ahead of her! Freedom!

Once she had cleared the table of the coffee jug, butter dish, and plates of hard-boiled egg, and shaken the crumbs for the sparrows perched on the window ledge, she took stock.

"Sometimes in life, we have horrible days, even horrible weeks and if we didn't, well, we would never appreciate the happy ones... We need the bad to allow us to feel the good, black versus white, night versus day," she philosophized, pleased with her intelligent perceptions of human experience. "Why, today wouldn't feel half so

25

joyous if yesterday hadn't happened. Look at the weather! I can enjoy the sunshine so much more today because yesterday was cold and gloomy. And today I can feel full of hope because yesterday I met Walter properly! If Martin hadn't done what he did, Walter would never have spoken to me. It was meant to happen!"

Hedda decided she would stay happy all day. She was in charge of how she felt, no one else, and would make sure she handed on her 'happiness' to her parents and especially to her mother. Sometimes she wasn't kind to Alice, rarely giving her a hug or a kiss. Maybe that's what her mother needed, more cuddles from the remaining daughter.

Alice was working in the ladies' dresses and skirts section as Hedda came into the shop. It was busy with women of all ages strolling amongst the merchandise, picking up items that weren't stored in glass-fronted cabinets and fondling the detachable fur trims that would not be necessary until the following autumn. "This costume is definitely one that would bring out your peach skin tones and hair color, madam," Alice was saying to a rather bulky woman in her early sixties, whose aging face and graying bun were not necessarily features to be highlighted.

The woman fingered the silk-lined skirt and inspected the hemming, checking whether there was surplus material inside to allow for later alterations. "It is extremely tempting, I must admit," she said. "Do you think it will still be available if I don't purchase it today?"

"But why wouldn't you?" Hedda's mother replied immediately, trying to close the sale. "This is an original. We only brought in five of this particular design. All in different sizes of course, so I can't guarantee it will remain in stock for any length of time. It is your color, and this size would fit you perfectly."

The woman was silent for a moment, clearly considering the imminent removal of around 40 Deutschmarks from her leather purse. "Very well, you have persuaded me and it's beautifully tailored. And of course, the shop may not be here next week," the woman said.

Hedda's mother either didn't hear or chose not to hear, so

delighted to have made such a lucrative sale. But Hedda heard. Was she going to allow this one silly statement to ruin her plans for a day of happiness? Absolutely not! She watched as Alice folded the jacket sleeves towards the central buttons, then placed a thin sheet of green tissue paper on top, then a horizontal fold of jacket edge to collar, a turn through 90 degrees, and placed to one side. Another sheet of green tissue paper was positioned on the skirt, folded once also horizontally, hem touching the waistband. Finally, both were slipped into a large white and gold paper bag emblazoned with the shop name, and pulled together by green, finely twisted drawstring.

The woman handed over the note, waited for her change, and left the shop, stroking other clothing on display. Watching her leave, Hedda was able to see that Jürgen, Left-Hand Man, and nameless Right-Hand Man, were not stationed in the main doorway.

"Where are the men from yesterday? Have they been here?" Hedda asked her mother.

"No," Alice replied, still holding the money in her hand. "I think they're already fed up with their duties and have gone off to bother another shop or household. Good riddance is what I say! They were just sent to scare us, much good it did! Look around. The shop's full of customers all wanting to buy new clothes now the sun is here. Out with the old, in with the new, that's what I say."

Her mother positively glowed with the pleasure of the cash registers ringing. The lovely melody of customer chatter harmonized with the jingling bells from the tills and the whoosh of suction machines that sped the bank notes through glass tubes above the customers' heads. A symphony of commerce.

"Why don't you select a new outfit to celebrate? Celebrate that the school holidays have started. Choose something, anything, and we will go out this evening to the *Biergarten,* the one next to the park, and show off your new dress. Choose what you like, my darling. Price no object!"

The dress was perfect: not childish, no ribbons or bows, but not frumpy or matronly. Made from a deep-yellow crepe cut on the bias, it hung perfectly from slightly padded shoulder to waist, from waist to just on the knee. The sleeves were caught in a band at the wrists where there were two small covered buttons. Subtle pleats of folded material fell gracefully downwards to add interest, but not too much interest, to the bust. Not only did it look perfect, it fitted perfectly too.

<hr>

Hedda was excited to hear the brass band from the open back window of the family car. *Vati* sat bolt upright in front, steering wheel held firmly in two gloved hands, whilst the scent of Mutti's strong perfume filled the interior, despite the evening air drifting in through the half-open windows. As they turned the corner beside the park, the music became louder still. Approaching the main gate, they saw great garlands of white, pink, and golden lights hanging from the eaves of the wooden buildings and studding the branches of the trees. What a beautiful sight! And this was where their evening meal was being prepared for them: Hedda could already taste the salty sausage and the sweet apple. Now closer, Hedda recognized the band's tune to be a song sung to her on nights when she couldn't sleep by her mother, or was it her father? It triggered a warm, childlike memory of when she and her sister would creep into each other's bedrooms when their parents were downstairs entertaining guests. In the dark, they would share scary stories to see who could frighten the other more. Maybe it was her sister who sang the song? Memory was fragile and Hedda was unsure whether thoughts in her head of earlier days were real or the stuff of fairy tales.

Paul drove slowly along the curb until he found a convenient place to park his beloved Mercedes. The car needed sufficient space to accommodate its impressive size, and it was important to park away from overhanging tree branches in case one should, God forbid, drop and scratch the shiny waxed surface of the roof. Finding the perfect place was complicated by the need to be close enough to the entrance to avoid Alice having to walk too far in her

Italian leather shoes, as precious to her as the Mercedes was to Paul.

A pretty waitress, wearing a green skirt and bib partially covered by a crisp white apron, greeted them. The place was already full with families enjoying the early Spring warmth and the start of the holidays. Following a quick scan of the seating that stretched under the plane trees and along the beech hedges, Paul spotted a table and pointed it out to the young woman.

"We seem to have arrived just in time," Paul said to her with confident charm. "I'm glad we didn't leave it any later. That one?" He pointed to one of the last to be filled.

It was close to the kitchen entrance and servery, where bustling waiters and waitresses issued back and forth, arms piled high with oversized trays carrying plates of steaming sausages, potato salad, gherkins, and of course large tankards of ice-cold beer.

After they were seated, Alice wiping the bench with a large handkerchief she had pulled from her handbag, Hedda had a chance to look around more closely. It really was beautiful. The colored lights cast magical glows on people's faces, smudging them with small caresses of green and pink, of red and blue and yellow. The chatter was loud, people speaking noisily above the thumpty-thump of the music, so that when the band stopped playing for their well-deserved sausage and beer break, the voices were required to re-adjust. There were no menus, food choices being limited to six variants of sausage, served with accompaniments, and either beer, *Glühwein* or a fruit drink for the children. Another waitress, older and broader this time, took their orders.

"This really is delightful," said Alice, fiddling with the small pot of mustard on the table, and smiling sweetly. "I'm so glad we decided to do this." She turned to her daughter. "You look marvelous! Please eat carefully to avoid any nasty food stains on you – we wouldn't want to spoil the dress!"

"It won't matter if it's the mustard though," Paul joked. "The color will just blend in!" He brought out his slightly soiled handkerchief to stop his chuckles, which made Hedda giggle.

Alice's face was not giggling. Luckily, at that moment, the waitress arrived with two large beers and an *Apfelsaft*.

"Prost," said Paul, holding up the tankard.

"Prost," said Alice, raising her glass and clinking it with her husband's and daughter's.

"Prost," said Hedda, all feelings of yesterday gone in this gorgeous moment of family unity.

As their glasses came together, Hedda spotted three people standing at the entrance of the beer garden, the young waitress clearly explaining the full occupancy of all the tables and waving her arm around to indicate that there was no room at the inn. The tallest one, a young man, looked incredibly familiar – it was Walter! She felt a tickling feeling of anxiety, fear and anticipation in the pit of her stomach.

"I know that boy!" she said to her parents, pointing to the entrance. "That one with the man and woman. He's new in our school. It looks like there's no space for them. Could we ask them to sit with us?" She spoke fast, terrified that they would turn and leave and find somewhere else to go. She wanted Walter and his parents to meet her parents and for them all to like each other immensely, and for them to all become lifelong friends before the day of the wedding...

"I'm not sure. This table isn't really big enough," Alice replied, but was clearly curious and squinting her eyes towards them.

"I'm sure if we all squeezed up a bit, we could fit in. I think that would be a lovely thing to do. Run over and suggest it," said Paul, who was already moving from his side of the bench to sit next to Alice.

Rather inelegantly, Hedda sprinted between the other diners, dodging high-held metal trays, to arrive at the archway just as Walter and his family were leaving. "Walter! Walter! Stop!" she said, breathlessly.

They turned to see who was calling his name. "How funny to see you here!" said Walter, looking pleased. "Mother and Father, this is Hedda. She's in my school."

Now that she had their attention, Hedda felt even more nervous and was sure her hair was a mess and her dress crumpled. "My parents have said that it would be lovely if you could join us. They've already moved up to make space." Hedda paused, waiting for their response.

"Well, how kind of your parents. Pawel?" asked Walter's mother of her husband, an older and even more handsome version of Walter.

"How could we possibly refuse such a generous offer, and from such a beautiful young lady," he replied.

"So, Pawel. What line of work are you in?" said Alice, making the first move.

"I'm an engineer. We've only been living in Saarbrücken for three months and are still finding our feet, but it seems like a delightful community."

"He works for a company that manufactures and installs pipelines," said his wife, Barbara. She was an elegant, understated woman in her mid-thirties. "We're from Poland, but you've worked that out from our accents, no? Fortunately, our schools are excellent in their teaching of the German language. This has opened up many opportunities."

Hedda was delighted that conversation between the grown-ups was flowing freely – those wedding bells were already tinkling in the background.

"The firm knew it was inevitable, so they started preparing for the German office and factory quite a time ago."

Pawel spoke with a stronger accent than his wife, and Paul wondered whether that would cause some future difficulties for the man – after all, there was no love lost between the Poles and the Germans. He was interrupted in his speculations by the other man asking after Paul and Alice's occupations.

"Well, you may have already shopped in our department store. Wouldn't that be marvelous?" Alice laughed in that simpering way which so annoyed Hedda, who tried not to show it. "And if you haven't, you really must. We are very proud of the shop. But we don't think Hedda will follow in our footsteps. She wants to be a doctor. Don't you?"

She smiled a familiar smile at Hedda, one designed to signal a mother's pride in her clever daughter but to also invite her daughter to respond in kind.

"A doctor?" Barbara said with genuine interest. "You and I may have something in common. I'm working in the children's department in the hospital."

Barbara looked like the very doctor who would cure sickly children instantly, setting them on the course for a future life filled with health and happiness. She was the doctor Hedda wanted to be.

"Would I ever be able to visit you on the ward?" Hedda asked shyly.

"As long as we make a proper appointment and fill in the right paperwork, I can't see why not."

Hedda knew this day could not get any better. The happiness she had promised herself earlier had arrived in so many unpredictable ways. Nothing could happen to improve the day. Nothing.

Under the table, Hedda felt a foot nudge against hers. She shifted away, avoiding further embarrassment. The foot nudged again and this time, Hedda knew it was a deliberate move. She looked at Walter who offered the smallest of smiles. She smiled back, loving their shared intimacy.

"So how do you two know each other?" Alice asked.

Walter looked at Hedda before replying. There was something in the way her eyebrows furrowed and her lips curled down which indicated how he should answer.

"We both like science and just got talking one day about the biology teacher. We think he's very boring in his lessons. No wonder the pupils play up."

Huge relief spread across Hedda's face; he had read her right. His foot found hers again and this time she held it there, not moving, just touching, still buzzing.

"Excuse me, could I have a word?" The older waitress was standing at the end of the table, looking directly at the Israel bench.

"Of course. Our order does seem to be taking a long time," Paul said.

"No, it's not that. This is awkward. I'm sorry." The woman's lips were pinched together, moving as if she were muttering words recently memorized.

"I'm sorry," Paul echoed. "I don't understand."

"We don't serve here," she said, the words now out in the open.

Paul felt a familiar wave of anxiety.

The waitress repeated herself. "We don't serve you, Herr Israel. I'm really sorry. It's the orders of the management. Your guests can remain. Their food is on its way. It's only yourselves that we are discussing. We would be grateful if you don't make a scene and disturb our customers." She stood there for a minute to ensure the message had been received, then turned and left their table, moving more swiftly than might have been expected back into the kitchen.

Even over the band's vigorous oom-pah-pah tune, the Dabeks had heard. It was Barbara who broke the conversational silence. "That's just terrible. Is there anything you would like us to do? I feel absolutely dreadful." Genuine concern flooded Barbara's face. It was how Hedda imagined she would look at her tiny patients and at that moment she prayed that this doctor would perform a medical miracle and make Germany well again.

Alice had already swung her legs from out of the confines of the bench and was picking up her handbag. She was trying not to cry. "It's been so lovely to meet you," she said in a sickly voice, "you know where we are. Please come and visit us in the shop. And Walter, it would be nice if you and Hedda could spend some time together over the holidays. See you all again."

The Dabeks were still standing and watching the departure of the Israels as their steaming bockwurst, mayonnaise covered potatoes, juicy cucumbers and sweet apple sauce arrived on shiny trays. The pot of mustard in the middle of the table provided the finishing touch.

After that, the remaining days of the holiday passed, neither good nor bad; they just passed. Hedda met with Walter on four occasions, each time for a walk in the park, where the trees were bursting into flower, the pink and white blossoms decorating the previous bare branches in a gorgeous promise of summer.

Against all expectations, Hedda's feelings for Walter were underwhelming. On their first park visit they discussed in detail the event in the playground and the awful embarrassment in the *Biergarten*. Walter allowed Hedda to talk. He was a good listener, a perfect gentleman. By the end of that first meeting, he had reached for her hand, taken it in his, and the walk had continued for a further ten minutes in that manner, neither of them commenting on the fact that their hands and fingers were now interlinked. His hand was considerably larger than hers, and slightly clammy to the touch. The handholding felt awkward, and she was glad when the walk ended and they could break contact. Could they meet again tomorrow? Of course, she said. That would be lovely – and of course it would be. By tomorrow she would have overcome her feelings of physical awkwardness.

The second time round, Walter took Hedda's hand from the start and this, she hoped, would allow more time to get used to flesh on flesh. But when he placed his arm around her waist her awkwardness and self-consciousness re-emerged. This time they talked about their home lives, brothers and sisters, and their parents. Hedda explained that though she loved her mother, she found her unpredictable and not very nice to her father and sister. She explained that Edith had moved to Berlin and was treading the boards in a small theater that no one had heard of. Hedda described how her mother could turn on the charm, especially in the company of young men, and definitely when she wanted something: a sale in the shop, a request to be granted from Paul. She would employ that oily, higher pitched voice. At other times, Alice would be livid with anger over some minor infringement of domestic routine. Paul would say nothing when his wife was in full flow, always in the hope that when the screaming would cease, the apology would emerge. Sometimes it did.

Walter, meanwhile, seemed to have been born into a family of marital bliss where mother and father treated each other as true equals – both respecting the other's professional as well as personal expertise. Dinner-table conversation meant sharing news and views of the day, each adult excitedly describing the happy and demanding parts of their work to an appreciative audience. Walter loved to hear about his parents' work; the hospital with its tremendous tragedy and great medical triumph, and the factory full of oil, grease, and great moving parts of machinery. And Walter would talk about cell division in plants, or the causes of the Napoleonic wars, or how Beethoven set about writing his symphonies.

Hedda was envious, not only of this portrait of wedded love, but also of Walter's parents' love of their work, filled with purpose and pleasure. So different to Alice and Paul's friction and arguments over the shop.

On their third walk, in late afternoon, sitting on an ornate metal bench opposite the large duck pond, Walter kissed her. It was after a long conversation about religion. He was Catholic but his parents were uninterested in the more fanciful practices of the Catholic church, and she a Jew, but her parents uninterested in the intricacies of the Torah, the Talmud and keeping Saturday free of work. Why would they? Saturday was the best trading day of the week. Hedda rarely went to synagogue; Walter rarely went to church. The Saarbrücken Jewish community didn't welcome the Israels into their bosom, and the dislike was mutual. For Walter and his family, they had been in the town for too short a time for the devout Catholics to sniff them out and decide if they were worthy Papists.

Their kiss was not unpleasant. Walter had waited for a pause in the conversation, and then reached out his hand, gently touching Hedda's jaw and chin and, with a light touch, angled her head in such a way that he could bring his lips to hers and hold them there.

"Oh," Hedda said.

"I hope that was okay, to kiss you, I mean," Walter replied.

"It was. Thank you."

An awkward silence followed, and then Walter kissed her again, this time holding the kiss that little bit longer. During the second kiss, Hedda again felt that sense of awkwardness, a sense of standing outside herself watching the goings-on. Maybe she wasn't meant to enjoy this, maybe it was something that you just, well, did? It wasn't as she had imagined in her dreams of romance. In the setting sun, orange flares reflecting in the calm water, Hedda could see a swan nesting in the middle of the lake, and she wished that she was back home, nesting in her bedroom, surrounded by her old toys and her favorite Grimms' fairy tales.

The final meeting before school resumed combined handholding, arm-around-waist and more kissing, this time underneath a large oak tree. Standing allowed for greater physical contact, with chests as well as lips pressed closely together, with arms round waists and hands clamped against backs. If only Hedda could remove that feeling of watching herself from the outside and allow herself to be within the experience. They both agreed that they wouldn't discuss the events when they returned to school next week, that they would be "friends." It would be easier if they avoided each other's company in the breaks, in the corridors, or anywhere else where other pupils might notice. This plan of secrecy and subterfuge added a sense of danger which Hedda found exciting.

4

CHANGES TO THE TIMETABLE
SAARBRÜCKEN

April 1935

Typical. The first day of the summer term and it was pouring. The sky was a mass of darkened clouds, and rain was bouncing off roof tiles and into overflowing gutters. Despite the gloomy weather, Hedda felt relieved to be returning to routine, the pressure of the hand holding walks removed, replaced by lessons and essays. It also meant less time to spend with her parents, particularly her mother, who had responded to the event in the *Biergarten* by throwing herself even more fully into shop life, standing outside the shop and engaging potential customers in conversation, encouraging them with offers of "good discounts" and "attractive prices."

The two SA guards had returned midweek, and although Hedda tried to avoid them they would always manage to find something to say to her: "Hi Hedda! You're looking good today – for a Jew-girl! Off to meet the new boyfriend?" How did he know?

"Hi Hedda, tell your mother we enjoyed the *Apfelkuchen*! More please!" Hans, the older of the two, would add.

The rain was finally stopping when Hedda arrived at the gates,

37

the pupils avoiding the playground puddles and drifting into classrooms where alongside the start of the new term's syllabus, she was looking forward to catching up with her two best friends, whom she hadn't seen during the holidays.

Entering the form room, wet coats and headscarves hung in the corridor beside the solid radiators, Hedda was surprised to see the wall displays quite rearranged. Where there had been pictures of famous German writers and musicians and artists, along with a map of Germany's political regions and geographical features, there was now a detailed map of Europe. A new larger map of Germany was beside it, and in the left-hand corner of each was a swastika. A prominent picture of Herr Hitler replaced the previous portraits. The furniture had been moved and it took Hedda a while to find her desk, now located right at the back, furthest from the blackboard, in-between Monika's and Christine's. The three girls took their seats as a new teacher entered. She wore a dreary brown suit and there was no mistaking her political affiliations; a wide armband covered most of her upper arm, displaying the Nazi insignia.

Facing the class, she raised her arm in a salute and spoke two words. She waited. First one student, then another, cautiously replicated the teacher's words and movement.

"Young people," she said, examining all the students. "My name is Frau Fochs, and I am your teacher. I have traveled from another school in Germany where I have left my own hard-working pupils to be with you. They were very sad to say goodbye to me, but understood that you, the students of the Saarland, have been deprived of a proper education. From now on, I will be teaching your lessons, to educate you about Germany and its magnificent future under our brave chancellor, Herr Hitler. Each day will start with a recognition of how lucky and privileged we are to be living in these unique and historic times. We raise our arms to welcome our Leader."

She circled the room again, ensuring all eyes were looking at her. "*Heil Hitler!*"

This time, all hands raised in salute including those at the back and a synchronized *"Heil Hitler"* echoed the teacher's clear command.

During the break, Hedda, Monika and Christine gathered under one of the playground trees, dodging the occasional drips from the branches above. After the quick holiday catchups, Hedda describing hers as "nothing much, dull really," conversation moved to the new teacher and the humiliating greeting required of them.

"My father said he thought something like this would happen," said Monika, her feet shifting the gravel from side to side. "He predicted this. It's been happening in other schools and was only going to be a matter of time, he said. We're making plans, though."

"I'm so pleased it's not just us then," said Christine, clearly relieved at this major news. "We think we might be off to stay with my mother's sister in Utrecht," she went on. "We can move in for as long as we want, and she's got the space. They have a really big house outside town and it's just a matter of sorting out what we'll do with our furniture and valuables."

Hedda was shocked. Here were her best friends making active plans to leave the country. But despite the many changes to the laws, and the daily disgusting portrayals of Jews as "rats," her parents were either deaf or deliberately sticking their heads firmly in the sand. "Really? You're really going to move?" Hedda asked both girls.

"Definitely!" Christine replied, "and you should too. I'm sure your parents will listen when you tell them what's just happened."

"I'm not coming back tomorrow. My parents won't want it anyhow, and we can sort out a new school once we get to wherever my parents are planning, hopefully France where there's some distant cousin that might be able to put us up. I won't be sad to go," Monika added.

Hedda wasn't sure. The stubbornness of Alice meant it would be an uphill struggle persuading her mother to leave. Alice was able to clamp shut her eyes, citing the success of their business as a reason to stay. And where would they go? Hedda wasn't aware of any convenient relatives in Holland or France and following Edith to Berlin was only shifting the problem from one town to another.

At lunchtime, Hedda saw Walter in the dining hall; they waved at one another but didn't speak. Last week already felt like another lifetime, and although she wanted to ask him about his new teacher, she was embarrassed by the morning's events. Their teacher had pinned a large picture to the blackboard: a grid of faces, four by four, showing "worthy" and "unworthy" facial types. Students had been called to the front of the class and asked to point out those they considered worthy by selecting forehead shape, size and curvature of nose, and other defining features. Hedda had been dreading the call-up, but fortunately the teacher had not selected anyone from the back row.

Later that afternoon, the Jewish girls were asked to leave the classroom one by one to pay a visit to the principal. Hedda was the last to go. Standing outside the wooden door with glass panels in the upper half, she could make out the shapes of two large figures, one of whom was seated behind the desk, and the other who appeared to be walking the room, left to right, right to left. Hedda gently knocked and waited.

"Come in, please," summoned a voice. Frau Theiner's desk had been tidied. Gone was the former clutter of pens and papers, files and general debris, and in its place was a large open book, which looked like a new pupil register. To the right of this book was a neat pile of white envelopes displaying handwritten names and addresses.

"Good afternoon, young lady. Your name?"

"Hedda Israel, Miss..."

The new principal checked off her name in the book. "Good. Hedda Israel. No siblings I see. I'm sure you noticed the difference in the lessons today. No, please remain standing!" the principal barked.

Hedda had foolishly pulled out the chair in front of the desk.

"We have a letter for your parents. It concerns our thoughts about your educational future. We are firmly of the opinion that you would thrive in a school which specializes in education for young people like you. We don't believe that this institution best meets your needs. We are content for you to stay on until the end of the week if that is what your parents decide, but after that, we will be closing our register and removing you from the school roll."

Hedda said nothing. The tiniest part of her had been hoping for the call to the principal's office was to inform her that the dreadful name-calling incident before the holiday break had been dealt with, that Martin Muller had been punished and the Mullers had apologized profusely; their son would never do anything like this again. How ridiculous. At this very moment, Martin Muller was probably being awarded some special honor for his bravery and loyalty to the German state.

The principal nodded to the pacing assistant, indicating the letter on the desk. The assistant stopped, picked up the top envelope and as Hedda took it, she noticed that the picture of the smiling Frau Theiner had been replaced. Instead, above the new principal's head was a framed photograph of the Führer in an alpine setting surrounded by beautiful blond children, some with long plaits, some with golden curls, hands joined in a wonderful circle of German purity.

For the remaining week, each meal was either taken in grave silence, accompanied by the sound of chewing, swallowing, coughing, slurping, or was the continuation of stormy arguments that consumed family communications since the start of term. Having read the letter that Hedda had thrust into their hands that first day, Paul and Alice had listened, asking only occasional questions.

"So, all the teachers are new?" asked her father.

"And they are all dressed in party member clothing? They are all Nazis?" continued Alice.

"It seems so. I didn't see everyone," Hedda replied.

"And your lessons were different to usual?" Paul asked gently.

"That's what I said."

"You're sure of this?" asked Alice.

"Oh for goodness sake, you've read the letter – of course I'm sure!"

They had decided that Hedda would remain till the end of the week so as not to appear intimidated, although Paul had said Hedda would have left that very day if it was up to him. But for Alice it was important they should not be bullied, and this philosophy dictated all her decisions.

On Wednesday evening, following Hedda's urging, Paul had tried to discuss the possibility of leaving the country. It was a painful session, with Alice becoming increasingly sure of her own arguments, convincing herself that events were exaggerated, that good upstanding German Jews like themselves were not the targets of Hitler, that he was after the less well-off, the less well-educated, the less well-cultured. Those from a different social standing. Did she have to spell it out? Raised voices grew louder as Alice rejected each of Paul and Hedda's ideas that might persuade her otherwise, throwing them aside with superior contempt. When Hedda heard the change in Paul's breathing, she knew it was time to close the conversation.

Thursday evening over braised beef served with rice and carrots was a silent affair; the Friday meal in which they were now engaged, a meal of smoked trout, boiled potatoes and a side salad, was loud and heated.

"We haven't found an alternative school. Hedda has no school to go to from Monday. We must start planning our departure. The sooner we do, the sooner she can restart schooling. I know you've never been fond of them, but we could try your cousin in Holland. We must do something. The problem isn't going away, you know that. We can organize some closing-down sales over the next weeks, sell off the stock, and let Herz know we will be arriving with money in our pockets. Please."

"You're not hearing me. We're not going. The shop has never been better. We have some beautiful items for sale. You're a coward. You always were."

Hedda was horrified at her mother's cruelty. "Herz and I haven't been in touch for years. How could I speak to him now? It would be demeaning. Is that you want? That we go crawling to our cousin, with a begging bowl…" Alice spoke in a whiny voice: "'Oh please, Cousin Herz, can you help me and my poor husband and daughter?' You must be mad!"

Paul was the angriest Hedda had ever seen him. He spoke slowly, carefully, each word its own singular emphasis. "You are wrong. You'll have all of us dead before you wake up to what's happening. We must make plans to leave while we still can. Don't do it for me. Do it for your daughter!"

Hedda was sobbing, gulping for breath, overwhelmed with the sadness of her parents' conflict, her father's desperation and his paternal love, and her mother's inability to do what was right for the family. It was so unfair that she had to bear this on her own, Edith having escaped months ago without a care in the world. "Please, Mutti, listen to Vati. Please," she managed to say between sobs.

"You are both against me. I will have to think about this. Now leave me alone. Both of you." Alice pushed back her chair from the table, nearly hitting the dresser behind. She stormed out, and it was obvious to Hedda that her mother was also choked with tears and anger.

Hedda watched her mother go, then turned back to Paul and placed her hand over his. "Maybe she will change her mind now. The closing-down sale is a good idea. Maybe then she'll change her mind?"

Paul gently put his other hand to Hedda's cheek and stroked it gently. "I hope you're right, *meine Kleine*, I do hope so."

Alice stood outside the store, bright morning sunshine casting a confident glow on the newly polished entrance which led to the sharply discounted dresses, suits, skirts, and blouses hanging from every rail. Hedda remained in her room. The family arguments had left her feeling empty and sick, with no desire to leave her safe space and risk a chance encounter with either parent. Another letter to Betty was long overdue as it was, and although she would have preferred to stay in bed, she began to consider what stories to share with her pen friend.

Paul was working on the week's accounts in the back office, a small well-organized room at the back of the shop, when a rap on the door broke through the numbers he was carefully adding up. A sharp rap, not likely to be one of the shop employees.

"Come in," Paul said, putting down his pen, and standing up as soon as he saw who it was.

Jürgen, Right-Door Man, stepped into the office, a strange smirk on his face.

"Herr Israel? My name is Herr Heitmann, and I am assigned to ensure the security of your shop. I act on behalf of the German government, in my capacity as an SA Officer. Your wife is under arrest. Our commander will put the charges to her then decide on any consequences. Do you have any questions?"

Paul stood frozen, the fear of antagonizing the young officer preventing questions as to why Alice had been arrested.

"Ah, that's good then." Jürgen Heitmann turned to leave.

Paul stuttered, his hand reaching for the corner of the table to stop himself falling off the mountain on which he now stood. "Can you tell me why? What did she do?"

Jürgen smiled and was clearly delighted to extend the pain of the meeting. "What was she doing?" he snapped. "What was she doing?" He sighed loudly. "She was shouting at our noble German citizens who were simply trying to enjoy their Saturday morning. She was rude, crude, and loud, demanding customers enter her store because: 'Her shop was the best, the cheapest, the most luxurious'. She was embarrassing the population. They were embarrassed, no, shocked by her boastful ways. She was without shame. Your wife needs to be taken under control."

"Where is she now?" Paul managed to ask.

"As I said, the commander's office on Heinrich Heine Square, where she will be formally charged. It is fair to say, Herr Israel, that your wife needs to ensure that she does nothing else to disrespect this Great Nation. As I'm sure you are aware, further infringements would result in more serious consequences!"

After the SA officer had strutted out, Paul sought refuge in the high-backed chair. He sat there staring into space, his head empty of useful thoughts. He knew his wife was hot-headed and it was likely the argument that had provoked her, but the consequence of her temper made him sick with fear. He would tell Hedda and then they would wait for Alice's return. His wife had to learn from this.

Paul and Hedda saw her at the same time, rounding the corner into Neukirche Straße, sandwiched between Jürgen and Hans. She was carrying something in front of her but from where they stood, they couldn't make it out. As Alice came closer Hedda's young eyes deciphered it first. It was a cardboard sign, hung around her neck by some coarse string. Words were scrawled on it.

"So that wasn't so bad, was it Frau Israel?" Jürgen smirked, as he allowed Alice to approach her husband and daughter. "Tell them what you're required to do to show regret for your actions." Turning to Paul, he added, "Your wife has got off lightly: the kindness of the German state."

"They want me to walk up and down the street, wearing the sign. I am so ashamed."

Hedda had never heard her mother's voice like this: quiet, gentle and genuinely sorry. She reached out to her mother and took her hand. "I am so sad for you, but just do what they ask, do what they say. It will be over soon and then we can plan what we do next."

"C'mon, Alice. Let's get going," said Jürgen. "The quicker you start, the quicker it will be over. Up and down the street now, until we call time."

A small crowd had gathered, mainly of women, curious to know what was happening and amused by the well-dressed shop owner wearing the crude cardboard sign. "Go on, love, do what you're told!" shouted a young woman in the group, already growing in size. "We want to see what you're modeling – a new piece of neckwear?"

The woman screamed with laughter at her own wit and others joined in: "It's such a pretty necklace. All the fashion in Paris!"

Hedda watched as her mother started up the street, away from the crowd and towards the Neumarkt.

A little boy broke from his mother's grip and followed Alice, veering in front of her, running backwards, and pointing at the sign. "It says... it says...." the boy panted as he ran in reverse, reading the scribbled words. "'This Jewish sow disrespects our Führer!' Mother, mother, she's a pig! She's a Jewish pig!"

Alice had reached the corner of the street. She turned slowly, her head drooping, and started the long walk back. The crowd was loving every moment, thrilled by the cheap entertainment.

"Only another five laps to go," Jürgen said to Paul. The SA officer had taken a position between Hedda and her father, preventing the smallest act of family support. "Then she can prepare lunch. I'm sure she will have worked up an appetite after this."

5

PROTECTION OF GERMAN BLOOD
SAARBRÜCKEN

April 1936

During the following year, the Israels kept their heads down, stayed out of trouble, and concentrated on keeping the shop going despite dwindling sales. Under the Führer's command the country had seen rapid changes and almost a year after Alice's humiliation, hundreds of jackbooted soldiers now marched into the Rhineland to cheering crowds, met with feeble protests from France and silence from Britain. "Why do they say nothing?" Paul had asked. "Why does no one see what is happening and challenge the man?"

Meanwhile millions of true Germans celebrated the Rhineland's return; it had been an unnecessary punishment, imposed by vengeful enemies and should never have left the Homeland.

A new motorway joined towns north to south and jubilant Germans sped down the *autobahn* enjoying town and country life, visiting far-flung relatives, and breathing the fresh mountain air as their chancellor recommended. What a role model he was! Leather wallets bulged in the pockets of the men, filled with *Deutsche Marks* from well-paid jobs in construction and factories, churning out steel and motor parts and aircraft engines. Women focused on serving the Motherland, giving birth to beautiful blond children, and rearing their ever-larger families. Hope had returned. A sense of purpose flushed the shabby nation clean. Life was good and the people had every reason to celebrate their Führer. And if there was a darker underbelly to the increasing success of their country, why should they care? The people had no interest in the new laws that prevented some less desirables from holding certain jobs or marrying real Germans. If they were no longer allowed to be German citizens – well that was their fault. No, why should the good Germans care when preparations for the Olympic Games filled the newspapers and were discussed in every *Bierkeller* in every town. German ears were firmly covered.

Paul's health had not improved in the last 12 months, but neither had it worsened. Since the horrors of the cardboard sign, husband and wife had agreed to a relative state of peace. Thanks to the *entente cordiale*, Paul's blood pressure remained out of the danger range, and Hedda was able to reduce her visits to the pharmacy for the stronger gastric medicines. She had secured a school place in the only Jewish school left in the town, where she was taught Hebrew for an hour a day and was required to study the Talmud. The arrangement was not to their liking. The Israels had never felt part of the Saarbrücken Jewish community and knew the more observant held dark opinions of them. Once in school, Hedda was relieved to find others like her, there to get an education of any sort. On her way to the new school, she had to pass her old *Gymnasium* and now the Nazi eagle and swastika flew proudly from a flagpole that had been erected outside the main entrance. She would see the boys practicing in full Hitler Youth uniform, marching up and down the yard, unified cries of *Heil Hitler* coming from Martin and Dieter Muller.

For a while, she had stayed in touch with her non-Jewish school friends. At Christmas she'd looked forward to the traditional ice skating outside Saarbrücken, where young people from local villages arrived for a magical fairy tale. Ice would cover the lake enclosed by tall pine trees, their dark branches heavy with snow, and lights would sparkle and fragment into a thousand stars in the reflected blue light of the frozen surface. The girls, donning their white laced skates, would show off their shapely legs in short flared skirts, drink *Gluhwein*, and get tipsy. Edith always returned with stories of handsome boys, speedy skating and festive music. Hedda would listen, her eyes wide, not quite believing that one day she would be old enough to attend this Winter Wonderland. An old girlfriend reassured her that all would be fine because she didn't really look Jewish. Hedda declined.

The phone call from Walter was a surprise, coming straight after a long and important telephone conversation with Edith. She hadn't spoken to her sister in months. It was the end of the Passover school break and Hedda was in her room leafing idly through an old photograph album when the telephone rang in the hallway. Alice and Paul were both in the shop, so this call was all hers.

"Hello, the Israel household. Who's speaking, please?" she said in her most formal voice.

"Hedda, it's Edith! Your very big sister. How are you?"

Hedda was both pleased and cross at the same time. She knew she was about to be deluged with the news of her sister's wonderful life and there would hardly be any time left to share her own less happy experiences, but on the other hand, she loved to hear about Edith's exciting adventures. It gave her hope that things could get better. She made herself comfortable on the hall chair and listened.

"Hedda, we're leaving! Marc is taking us all, the whole company, to the Argentine. We'll be sailing in a few months. It's so very exciting!"

Hedda knew something even bigger was about to be announced so didn't attempt to fill the short gap.

"And Marc and I are engaged to be married! You should see the ring! I'm going to be his wife. What do you think Mother and Father will say? Do you think they'll be pleased?"

There was now a genuine pause and Hedda seized the opportunity. "That's wonderful news! But why so far away? What will you do there? Is that where you'll get married?"

"The whole theater company is going. He's organizing

everything. We're doing really well and they love our musical shows, and we're booked to perform for a month from August! It will be really hot. The sun never stops shining in Buenos Aires. It's the capital, and they are encouraging Jews like us to emigrate there. They want us! Isn't that something? Do you think Mother and Father would consider moving?"

Hedda's hand shook at the thought and she lowered the mouthpiece into her lap. Edith was providing the answer. A way out.

"Are you still there? What do you think? You'd like to go, wouldn't you? There's the tango and the South American men are so handsome! Oh, but I won't have a roving eye! I'll be Frau Steinberg before the year is out but we're considering changing our name anyway – to something more Spanish sounding."

"It's marvelous, honestly. Is it definite then? Does he know people there?"

"His brothers moved to Buenos Aires years ago and they love it! They're in business with beautiful homes. I've seen pictures! We'll look for our own place, once we're over there; we're packing crates and cases now. They're shipping from Hamburg and Marc's sorting all the paperwork, visas, exit documents, you know, that sort of thing. What about if I tried to visit before we leave and speak to them?"

"Would you be able to? Vati's not so well and Mutti is... she still thinks everything's going to be alright, and we're better off just staying put and quietly getting on with things. It's difficult, you know." Hedda felt that teary lump stuck in her throat and didn't want to spoil her sister's happiness with her own sadness.

"I'll ask Marc about a visit before we go, but I'm a big part in the current show and we're fully booked for the next few weeks. I'm just not sure..."

"It would be wonderful if you could. Please?" Hedda urged her. Surely Edith would see the importance of a visit back to the family home?

"I'll try, honestly. But can you tell them *for* me? Break the news? It will sound better coming from you."

There was a desperate quality that was familiar to Hedda, Edith still reliant on her little sister to be the messenger and suffer the consequences. "Tell them what, Edie? The engagement? The move? The idea of all of us going there too?" Hedda knew the answer.

"If you would, please. Oh my goodness, this call will be costing Marc hundreds of Deutschmarks. I'd better go! I'll phone again in a week."

There was a click on the end of the line. The call was over. Hedda sat still trying to absorb the quantity of new information teeming through her brain. Fragmentary images of South America swirled in her head: exotic animals swinging from vine-covered branches, wooden canoes slowly drifting down the Amazon, tree-lined boulevards with whitewashed buildings, brightly colored umbrellas and Spanish squares filled with tables and chairs. Glorious sunny pictures that contrasted sharply with the gloom of her current location. She would happily live in the Argentine tomorrow if given the chance, but would she be able to convince her mother? Or even Paul, whose ambition only extended to moving in with Cousin Herz in Holland; no water to cross on that journey. Her tumbling thoughts were interrupted by the phone ringing loudly again. It was probably Edith calling back with even more vital news she'd forgotten to mention.

"Hello Edith?" Hedda said, not bothering with niceties.

"Hello Hedda, it's Walter. Were you expecting to hear from your sister? You answered so quickly," he said in that kind voice which always made Hedda's heart flip over.

She hadn't spoken to him for at least two months. They had retained a friendship of sorts, meeting very occasionally in the park to share thoughts about parents, school, politics, and the future. Hedda was pleased that Walter rejected the Nazi propaganda so forcefully. It was fed to the pupils on a daily basis – lessons about Jewish conspiracies and plans for world domination, the Jews' racial inferiority and the threat to all decent Aryan people.

"It's nice to hear from you. Yes, Edith and I were just talking on the telephone. She's become engaged to Marc Steinberg. Do you remember him? She's got this engagement ring and she's emigrating to South America! The Argentine! It seems so far away. They have it all sorted, all packed and tickets booked. She's going to try to visit before she leaves, she said, but I don't think she'll manage that. It's too far and I'm not even sure it's such a good idea. My parents will be happy and sad all at once; they don't even know she's leaving yet. I'm telling *you* before *them!*" Hedda suddenly felt disloyal sharing the news, but secrets were good between friends.

"What a relief, leaving Germany. She's doing the right thing, you know."

"I know. I'm envious," Hedda replied. "I think this might be the time to start 'The Conversation" again. We don't talk about anything these days, just how the shop's doing, what we're having for dinner, what I'm learning in school." There was an awkward silence which Hedda filled. "Anyway, were you calling for a reason?"

There was another silence. Then Walter said, "There's a dance being organized this weekend in the Neumarkt and I was wondering if you might want to come with me?"

Hedda felt herself blushing, an entirely strange response given she couldn't see him, he couldn't see her, and she didn't have that sort of feelings for him anyway.

"That's such a nice idea, but I'm not sure if it's a good one."

"I think it would be fine, honestly." He paused, and she wondered what was coming next although the tone of his voice had already given it away. "It's just that you–"

Hedda interrupted. "I completely forgot! I promised to help my father out with the accounts this weekend and knowing him, it will take all day and all night..."

Another silence at his end which this time, she didn't fill. Finally, he said, "Another time. Please give my regards to your mother and father. Goodbye for now."

"Goodbye," Hedda said, forcing some jollity into her voice. She considered what had just happened. Probably best now if she stopped all further communications with him. Irrespective of their park walks, the steady drip, drip, drip of the Nazi narrative had finally begun to infect his thoughts. Best now to stick to your own as far as possible. A lesson learnt.

The man was breathing heavily, his face taut with tension, and from the rapid turning of his head, he was clearly in a hurry to be somewhere else. Hedda was helping her mother on the front counter. It had been a quiet morning. Customers had been decreasing in numbers and each week's takings were less than rent, heat, light, paying the wages of the remaining shop staff. From helping her father with the accounts, Hedda knew they were just a few months away from making those final decisions.

The man was young, with dark slicked-back hair parted in the middle, darting black eyes, and sharp features. He was not their usual type of customer, dressed in a drab raincoat and carrying what looked like a small suitcase.

"I wonder if you could help me?" he wheezed, leaning both sticky hands on the counter housing the ladies' blouses, far fewer now on display. Stock was running down and not being replaced. Hedda stared at his trembling hands and gave him a hard look to which he responded by standing straight, leaving sweaty finger marks on the glass.

"Yes, of course," Alice answered, just pleased to have a customer. No one had entered the shop in the last half an hour, and anyone, however down at heel, might be prepared to make a purchase if Alice turned on the charm.

"I need to know the way to the border," he said. "I'm not from round here, you see," he continued, taking short sharp breaths as if recently running. "I'm in a bit of a hurry, you see." His query was not what Alice was expecting – travel directions rather than advice on ladies' fashions.

Hedda grabbed her mother's arm. "He's odd," she whispered. "There's something funny about him."

"Sssh. That's unkind," Alice responded, and turned her

attention towards the young man who was looking nervously at the front doors.

"May I ask," Alice said, "whether you're well? I don't mean to be nosy but if there's anything we can do to help..." she continued.

"I just need to know whether there are buses or trams that would get me close to France. I need to leave Germany," he replied.

"Has something happened?" Alice persisted.

"Mother, just tell him what he needs to know," Hedda said, increasingly uncomfortable. She didn't quite believe this man, the way he paced, the way his darting looks could be mistaken for furtive glances at their reactions.

"I've got to leave. *You* will understand. I had a relationship with a woman. She was German. I'm German, of course. But not the same as her. You understand what I'm saying? You of all people must understand. It's not allowed. We've been found out. She's alright. Her father works for the Post Office, and he holds a very high position. She'll be protected. But me? I must leave. Now!"

He needed to say no more. He was a law-breaker. No Jew was allowed relationships with those of German blood. From the rising color in her cheeks, Hedda could see Alice was excited by the drama, more animated than she had been in a long time.

"You must take the number 11 tram, going west, as far as Volkingen." She spoke clearly but softly, mouthing out the words, her lips rounding and stretching to emphasize each syllable. "From there, there are buses that take you into France. I don't know which ones, but there will be people to ask. The stop is close to Johanneskirche. Go right from here, then left and you'll see it. Good luck!"

"I can't thank you enough," the young man said. "You have saved a poor boy's life." He held out his hand to Alice who squeezed it, with maternal concern.

"Now you see, Mother, how things are going. Now you must see. We've got to make plans to leave too. It won't get easier for us."

Alice did not reply. Instead, her gaze was fixed on the two men now entering the shop, dressed like Jürgen and Hans in SA uniform, but older, and definitely more serious in intent. Hedda knew immediately. She looked at her mother, frozen to the spot, eyes fixed on the men who had paused at the glass doors, as if posing for a photograph. They adjusted their peaked caps and marched towards them.

"Frau Israel, you are under arrest, charged with conspiring to provide aid to a Jew. The Jew has broken the laws of the Great Nation, has contravened the law designed to protect good German people from defilement of their pure German blood. Come quietly. The charge will be put to you when you appear before the magistrates and make your plea. Following this, you will be sentenced. Any previous convictions or misdemeanors will be taken into account."

As the officer spoke, Alice sobbed, her chest rising in gulps; the realization that Hedda had been right was too much to bear. The young romantic, fresh from central casting, with his dark hair, brooding eyes, and sharp jawline, escaping from his darling love, forced to catch the No II tram to the French border to escape the clutches of the SA, was nothing more than an agent provocateur, playing a part to induce the foolish Jewess to break the law – yet again.

Hedda watched the small, stooped figure of her mother leave the shop, sandwiched between two tall officers. They didn't touch her. Alice didn't look round, didn't speak, and had nothing in her hands to carry. When they were out of sight, Hedda locked the shop doors, turned *Offen* to *Geschlossen,* told the last of the staff to go home, and headed to the back office.

Alice had been placed in "protective custody" from the "'wrath of the German people," imprisoned in a jail outside Saarbrücken following her conviction. The courtroom displayed large Nazi flags and the judge was dressed in full uniform, seemingly a high-ranking Party member from the many decorative items displayed on his jacket and lapels. Hedda and her father had sat silently in the public gallery as Alice was sentenced. She had pleaded guilty as advised, and the Gestapo officers had investigated her previous actions. She had been held in cells for over a week and remained surprisingly cheerful through a stubborn refusal to allow even this experience to dampen her blind belief that things would turn out fine in the end.

Hedda had brought her a suitcase of clothing, toiletries and makeup including Dior Flaming Red lipstick, and a compact of Rubenstein powder. On seeing those items, the police showed a keen interest. "For our wives, you understand."

Hedda provided the small gifts, an excellent way of ensuring Alice's incarceration was a little more comfortable. The six-week prison sentence was coupled with a signed statement: if she were to commit any further acts against the German government, she would be sent to a concentration camp for education and punishment. Alice signed the document in her very best handwriting, with every intention of abiding by its contents.

6

A DECLINE IN CIRCUMSTANCE
SAARBRÜCKEN

Autumn 1937

Since Alice's imprisonment, Hedda had known it was only a matter of time before the authorities would make their next move. Following a four-month period of incarceration, her mother had been released and the three Israels had kept out of sight of the authorities, their lives reduced to a series of small routines.

Dabs of early autumn sunshine streamed through Paul and Alice's bedroom windows, as they were woken by loud banging on the front door. Paul instantly felt his heart rate double. Hedda heard the noise, grabbed her dressing gown, and followed her father down the central stairs, the concrete cold under her bare feet.

"Herr Israel! Open the door immediately!" an official voice bellowed outside. The loud knocking continued.

"Vati, will we be okay? Has something happened? She noticed Paul's eyes, puffy and red rimmed. He seemed to be gasping for air, his mouth opening and closing like a fish on land.

"I have no idea," he gulped as he turned the key in the heavy door and it slowly clanked open.

Three peaked cap members of the Gestapo stood outside, the tallest one holding what looked like a set of official papers, their leather coats exuding an unpleasant smell.

"Good morning, Herr Israel. We have a warrant to search your home. We believe your wife continues to engage in activities in direct contravention of her signed undertaking. Allow us to conduct the search."

The officers pushed past and ran up the stairs two at a time, to be met by Alice. Hair hanging loose and sleepy-eyed, she looked a mess and sounded one too. "What's going on? This is so disrespectful, officers." Her face tried to disguise the mounting fear. "It's the first day of Rosh Hashanah. This shouldn't be happening. Today of all days."

Her mother had no religious feelings, didn't read the texts, or keep a kosher kitchen. Hedda was surprised she knew what day it was.

Inside the living room, the officers separated out. The youngest one was probably not much older than Hedda, she thought, as she watched him from the corner of the room. He picked up a china ornament from the table that held Paul's pipes. It was a little girl dressed in typical folk clothing of red headscarf and apron, another souvenir from a family holiday. He examined it carefully, turned it upside down, shook it for imaginary hidden secrets, and placed it back amongst the holiday mementos. Officer Number Two was staring at the portrait of Alice, noted something down in the small notebook he was carrying, then looked behind it in case it hid a safe full of gold and jewels.

The tallest Gestapo officer, with a skinny neck from which a giant Adam's apple protruded, was examining Paul's beloved wireless. Loose wires and bulbs hung from the back where Paul had been tinkering with it, trying to improve the sound quality of the live broadcasts of Wagner operas. His adaptations and rewiring resulted in an "altogether better listening experience", in his words and even Alice had commented upon it. Hedda watched as the officer called the others over and pointed to the back.

"Herr Israel. The wireless. Why?" He waved his gloved hand. "For what purpose are you using this wireless?"

Hedda reached out to Paul who was still struggling to breathe and gently squeezed his hand to encourage him to answer.

"We listen to music. I'm a wireless enthusiast. My daughter and I have been working on better reception by rewiring the connections at the back."

"It's true," Hedda said. "The music sounds much better. We listen to concerts together."

The lead officer walked towards them, his hands now thrust into his coat pockets, ready to pull out a weapon at any moment. He was clearly not convinced.

"We have reason to believe that you or a member of your family are engaged in sending messages abroad and that you are spies working on behalf of a nation sympathetic to the Jewish race. Your wife, Herr Israel, has a history of disobedience, and this is certainly not the first time she has been in trouble with the authorities. We have no choice but to arrest you. Dress yourselves now."

Alice let out a yelp of pain. Paul said nothing.

"Please do not waste our time. We will document all items in the room and produce an inventory. As you know, there are regulations in place itemizing what Jews may retain."

As Paul and Hedda prepared to leave, a high-pitched voice spoke up: "I'm so sorry. Please understand, this has got nothing to do with my husband who is a highly respected member of the community or my daughter. The wireless is mine. I didn't appreciate that my actions could be misconstrued. It was all my fault."

Hedda watched as her mother fumbled in the pockets of her thin nightgown. She pulled out some hair grips and began stabbing loose strands of hair to the back of her head.

"That's not quite true," said Hedda, misunderstanding her mother's purpose. "We were all playing with the wireless."

"Yes, but it was me, darling, that was hoping to speak to my cousins in Holland, over the radio. Not you. I think that's what the officer is interested in, not Wagner or Mozart. Am I right?"

The long-necked officer's face was stern. "Get dressed, Frau Israel, and pack a bag of overnight items." He sounded angry and didn't wish to prolong the visit. "Men! Please start the inventory. We will confiscate the wireless, of course. Herr Israel. Fräulein Israel. You will remain here. Only your wife will be taken into custody today."

Alice walked through the room. As she passed her husband, she lightly brushed her fingers against the back of his hand but said nothing. Her quiet dignity shocked Hedda and she ran after her, throwing her arms around her mother's waist.

"Mother! Please don't be sad. I will look after you, I promise! I will do anything!"

Alice carefully loosened Hedda's grip. She watched her mother enter the bedroom and drop her head into her upraised hands, before quietly pushing the door shut. The officers circulated the room, scrawling onto sheets of paper, counting and describing items that would be later valued. Paul sat on the sofa staring down at his slippered feet.

"She's so calm," Hedda said. "Will she be alright, do you think?"

"She didn't have to do that," said Paul quietly. "That was not like Alice. She did it for us. She's brave."

When Alice reappeared, her hair was tidily pinned in a neat bun at the nape of her neck, her face powdered and her lips red. She was wearing an elegant bottle-green skirt and jacket and a cream blouse. A gold brooch, a small red stone at its center, was pinned at the neat collar. She looked so smart, as if off for an important job interview, and Hedda burst into tears.

"Bye for now! I will see you very soon," Alice said.

Paul watched the main giraffe-necked officer lead her out. Although she had managed the last word, accompanied by a small smile, her confidence was misplaced.

For over two weeks Hedda and Paul had heard nothing. The apartment had been dreadfully quiet. In the first week, Paul had tried to keep the shop open, but without his wife working her charm, there were few customers and even fewer sales. He shut the shop completely at the start of the second week, paid the last two staff a final week's wages, and told them they would be better off seeking alternative employment. Hedda stopped school and she and Paul spent the next days packing the remaining stock into categorized boxes, intending to sell it to wholesalers for next to nothing.

Hedda had spent little time in the kitchen, apart from when very young and when the Sunday bake took place. Then, she was allowed to run her fingers around the two mixing bowls, one containing vanilla dough, the other chocolate. She loved to see her mother, a large apron on, pouring first the chocolate, then the vanilla in vertical layers. *Gugelhupf*, *Apfelstrudel*, and even a *Schwarzwald Kuchen* might be made, although Alice was the first to admit that afternoon coffee and cake at *Kummermann's Konditorei* was preferable to slaving over a hot oven. Shopping and meal preparation now fell to Hedda, and that evening she was attempting a more complicated dinner of *Wienerschnitzel*, served with rice and spinach.

Her mother's old cookbook was open at the meat section. Hedda was pouring over the instructions describing the flour dip, the egg dip, and the breadcrumb dip, and she wished she had chosen a simple stew instead. But her father needed cheering up. With Alice gone he was struggling, and Hedda was finding it hard to witness his descent into a dark depression. He spoke little, unable to focus on future plans of exodus. He was reading the newspaper for hours on end whilst Hedda ran the household. She worried about his constant coughing; his breathing was definitely getting worse. He had no one to talk to about the endless punitive laws. When he read that Jews could no longer work as vets, he shared that piece of news with Hedda. How would a sick animal know the difference? Animals don't judge. Animals don't know who you are, where you come from; all they want is love and attention. How dreadful this Führer was.

Paul's favorite meal might pierce his gloomy mood, Hedda had thought if only she could master the recipe. She cracked the eggs into a wide dish, dipped a metal spoon into the flour jar and shook that into another bowl, adding some salt and pepper. This wasn't so bad, she thought as she found an old packet of breadcrumbs at the back of the cupboard. I just need to dip the thin meat pieces in the right order and fry them.

The smell of the melting butter filled the kitchen, followed by the wonderful sputtering sound of the breadcrumbed veal as each golden slice hit the hot pan. This is going to be a culinary masterpiece, she decided, swishing the *Schnitzels* from side to side to avoid the crumbs from burning. By the time the meat was cooked, the rice upturned into neat little turrets upon the plate, and the spinach drained of all water and sprinkled with caraway, Hedda had decided that a new career awaited her in the grand kitchens of Paris; when not preparing dishes with the finest ingredients, she would be dancing and romancing with handsome French men.

Paul was already sitting at the dining table when Hedda entered with his meal. Behind him, where the wireless had stood, was a dark square on the woodwork. Hedda placed the tray on it and checked that Paul had laid cutlery and napkins for them both. He had.

"Good evening," she said. "I'm so glad you booked a table at Maxims!"

"Maxims! How wonderful," Paul said.

"We have no lobster or oysters, sir, but I do hope you will enjoy the meal I've made. It's your favorite: Schnitzel." Hedda watched her father smile and she felt good inside.

"You are such a wonderful daughter," he said, tucking the napkin into his collar. "Your cooking gets better and better every day. Maxims have employed only the very best!"

Hedda knew this wasn't true, but it was typical of her father to praise her regardless. Her last meals had been lacking in seasonings, and they had only managed to eat half. Paul picked up his knife and fork and carefully cut a small piece. He chewed slowly. Maybe the meat was a little tough or overcooked? When he put the cutlery down neatly across the plate, she was disappointed that he hadn't enjoyed the meal. She pushed her plate aside too. "It wasn't good?" she asked.

"It was delicious, really. But I'm not feeling so well. Today I have no appetite. Would you mind very much if I go to my bed?" At that moment, Paul began to cough, one hand covering his mouth and one holding his chest as if easing a pain lodged within his ribs. He looked pale and bloodless.

"Of course," Hedda said, grabbing his arm and guiding him away from the discarded plates towards the bedroom. "I'll help you."

Paul's coughing continued, and as he slumped down heavily on the bed, Hedda began removing his clothes to speed things up. She unbuttoned his shirt, pulled his arm from the sleeve, and then maneuvered around to pull the garment from his back. As she did so, she noticed what looked like a small red lump at the base of his neck. It looked sore. When the whole shirt was off, Hedda saw the true extent of the problem and let out a cry of horror. Paul's back was covered in pus-filled boils of various sizes and degrees of poison. Some were isolated, others clumped together in angry groups, forming a horrible landscape of yellow and red hills and hillocks. There were boils with scabs, and new boils just starting to fill with toxic matter.

"Vati!" Hedda cried. "What's wrong with you? Your back! How long has it been like this?"

Paul was silent. What could he say? He was grateful to his wife who had tenderly applied night-time poultices to drain the poison and relieve the constant throbbing. The small secrets between husbands and wives behind closed doors; Hedda was touched that her mother had never complained of her nursing duties. Paul couldn't see what she or Alice saw. He did not know the extent of his condition, other than feeling increasingly unwell.

"We must call a doctor – no wonder you are sick. Why didn't you say anything?"

"Why would I want to add to your worries, when you already have so many? You have been such a good girl, looking after your silly father who has lost his wife, lost his shop and can't even enjoy a delicious *Schnitzel*. What can a doctor do? Besides, no one will treat me any longer, you know that. Doctor Arstein closed his practice years ago now, and we are lucky not to have needed his replacement's services. If you really feel it necessary, could you clean my back? Would you do that for your silly old father?"

Hedda tried her hardest not to cry. "Of course I will, of course. But let me help you into bed. Tomorrow, I will visit the pharmacy and ask their advice. Please – no more secrets."

Hedda hung the shirt on the back of a chair and opened the drawers in search of nightclothes. She looked away as her father undressed, replacing his day clothes with the cotton pajamas she had found. She then helped him into bed, drew the curtains to block out the setting sun, and picked up the stained shirt to take downstairs for tomorrow's wash.

"Tomorrow will be better, won't it? I can help make things better," she said at the door. She hoped he couldn't hear the choke in her voice, but he was either already asleep or unwilling to deny her hope of a brighter future; there was no sound, not even coughing, from the darkened bedroom.

7

NEW YEAR RESOLUTION
SAARBRÜCKEN

January 1938

Hedda held the trowel and fork in one hand, wiping away the wet soil on her cheeks with the other. Her knees hurt from bending over the sodden earth and a sharp nagging ache had settled in the small of her back. A worm squirmed its way across the mud. She picked it up between her fingers, something that would have previously revolted her. A decent creature, she thought, responsible for churning the soil, ensuring it was full of healthy air. She placed it back on top of the new-turned patch and watched it wriggle underground, then allowed herself to sit down and think about the events of the past six weeks: her mother, transported to a labor camp and her poor father dead. Her sister had returned for the funeral, hugging everyone and sobbing loudly, returning to Berlin as soon as politely possible to make arrangements for the wedding and the crossing to South America.

On a listless afternoon, a few days after Hedda had discovered how unwell her father was, she was startled by a loud knock. Ever since Alice's detention nearly five weeks before, the door that led to the street remained unlocked on the orders of the Gestapo,

65

allowing easy access to their apartment. Hedda ran to open up to another uniformed man, this one holding a large brown envelope. Like all the party officials they had encountered he was ugly, with a face lacking in any humanity.

"Are you the daughter of Alice Israel?" he asked, and when she said yes, he thrust the letter into her hands before marching noisily down the stairs.

The envelope had printed type on both sides: on the front was Paul's name followed by their full address, and on the back was the printed stamp of the sender, accompanied by a large swastika. The letter had come from the offices of the Gestapo in Berlin. Hedda wondered if it contained the details of Alice's release. The wireless would have revealed no evidence of crimes against the state, so they would have to let her go. This was the news she and Paul had been waiting for.

Written in neat handwriting on headed party paper was the address of the camp to which Alice Israel had been taken on October 16, 1937, a week after her second detention. Starting at Saarbrücken railway station, the journey ended at Moringen, a distance of approximately 500 kilometers and a journey time of around ten hours. The camp housed women only and the letter stated that Frau Israel would be detained there until further notice. It said that she would be expected to perform all reasonable work duties suitable for her age and sex. Now that Herr Israel had an address, he would be allowed to write and she could write back if she so chose. All letters would be read on receipt and before posting.

Hedda took the envelope to Paul and sat on his bed, watching him closely as he digested the contents. She knew it was bad news. Then he read the letter out loud, coughing drily between every phrase.

"Well, we must write and tell Alice what a good cook you have become," he said eventually.

After that day, he left the bedroom only to visit the toilet. Meals were left untouched.

On her father's last Friday morning, she called out his name and hearing no response, went to his bedroom. To begin with, she was unsure whether he was still sleeping, his large bulk unmoving but well-covered by the bedclothes.

"Vati?" she called, reaching out her hand and gently shaking the eiderdown. "Vati?" she asked again, already knowing he was no longer alive from the absence of any rise and fall of the blankets. "Vati!" she screamed, but he couldn't hear.

Paul's death from septicemia occurred three days after the arrival of the envelope. Hedda had tried to persuade him to seek further treatment but it was too late. A combination of poisons, the poison that had flowed through his system for all those months as well as the poison in his mind, killed him.

She sat there on the side of the bed, not looking at him, staring blankly at the dressing table opposite, with no idea of what to do. Half an hour passed before she left the apartment and knocked on the door of the Scheuermanns, who had been friendly until two years ago, when all social interaction had ceased.

Frau Scheuermann opened the door and an initial smile turned into a frozen grimace when she saw it was Hedda. "Goodness me. I haven't seen you in a very long time," she said, as if there had been no deliberate avoidance of the Israels, no neighbors crossing the road to walk on the other side, heads down, pace quickened. "Is there anything wrong? You look quite..." She stopped, unable to describe what she saw in Hedda's pale features.

"It's my father. I think he's dead." Hedda knew he was dead, but it was hard to share such finality with this neighbor.

Frau Scheuermann's right hand flew to cover her mouth as if suppressing an urge to vomit. "*Gott in Himmel!*" she screamed. "How? Has he done something wrong, like your mother?"

So the neighbors had known the whole time that Alice was no longer at home, that she was a prisoner of the Gestapo. They must have known that Hedda had become the housekeeper, caring for her father, shopping, cooking, and cleaning, and despite this none had offered anything. No help. Not a single kind word. Nothing at all. And now? Here was a clear implication that Paul had brought death upon himself for some wrongdoing.

"I found him this morning. I think he died in his sleep. He hasn't been well. He has worried terribly about Mother. I don't know what I should do."

The neighbor had managed to compose herself. Her nausea gone, she removed her hand from her face and with a small wave indicated for Hedda to enter. "Well, come in, come in, and I'll call Herr Doktor."

Hedda hovered in the hall whilst a call was made in the next room. She could just catch "young girl," "no mother," and "Jewish family," whispered down the phone and wondered if the last piece of information might prevent his visit. It occurred to her that she should have called their old doctor. Reappearing with the news, the neighbor spoke in a voice suggesting that huge appreciation should be shown for the considerable trouble caused.

"Herr Doktor will be with you in the next hour. He is very, very busy, he said, and wouldn't normally do this. It means leaving his other patients, but I explained how difficult things have been for you." The neighbor paused to receive Hedda's grateful response for her words and her deeds. Hedda was ungratefully silent. Frau Scheuermann twisted her lips. "If your father is dead..."

He is dead. Was Frau Scheuermann suggesting that Hedda was unable to distinguish between life and death?

"If your father is dead," she continued, "the doctor will issue a death certificate stating approximate time and cause of death. You will need to take the death certificate to the funeral director who will then remove the – remove your father and make the arrangements for the cremation. I hope I've managed to be of some help."

"Thank you, you have. I am most grateful to you." She turned to leave. As she turned over the conversation on her short walk home, she realized not one word of sympathy had been spoken.

The next patch of soil was tougher to dig; its proximity to the larger trees of the cemetery meant it received less light and water and was dry and dusty despite the rainfall. Probably fewer worms around here, she thought, they must prefer the rich soil closer to the newly dug graves where the ashes of the recently dead were buried. No Jews though. A small area within the cemetery was reserved for non-Christian ashes: Jews, Roma, and other undesirables, and Paul's ashes had been laid there. There was no headstone to mark the spot, but Hedda had found some abandoned pieces of stone amongst the Christian graves, picked out the smoothest and most pleasing, and placed them in a vertical arrangement close to her father's ashes. She would soon start digging a small flowerbed that would be filled with crocus and daffodils. No one would notice. She earned enough to buy her weekly food. The work was offered to her during the burial, partly to cover the costs of "providing the arrangements to dispose of Herr Israel," and partly because she was required to offer the community "appreciation for their support." She would buy the bulbs from her wages.

Surprisingly, Moringen, the concentration camp where Alice was held for her "Derogatory Comments and Crimes against the State," had let her attend the funeral and even allowed her to stay with Hedda for a further two weeks. She had wept throughout the simple service, her daughters either side of her, holding each arm tightly as the tears flowed. She had returned to camp life on a freezing day in December, escorted from the apartment and to the train station by the usual Nazi guards.

Edith's stay was brief. She arrived the day before and left the day after, just long enough to say her goodbyes to her mother and sister before starting her new life abroad. Hedda wasn't sad to see her go. She had hoped that Edith might have changed: shown more sympathy and readiness to listen to the horrors of their last year in Saarbrücken. But despite a childhood spent enjoying the same toys and books, and some wonderful family holidays, they had never really been close. Hedda wondered whether her sister would even bother to stay in touch once she'd settled thousands of miles away.

Voices from the main path leading through the cemetery broke up her thoughts. Did she recognize them? There was something familiar in those foreign vowels and consonants. She looked up and could make out two winter-dressed figures, a man and a woman walking hand in hand, who seemed not to have spotted her crouching amongst the graves. She rolled herself into a woodlouse ball to avoid detection, but as they came up beside her, the female spoke:

"Hedda? Hedda, is that you?"

It was Barbara Dabek, the wonderful doctor, mother of Walter, unseen since that dreadful meeting in the beer garden. Hedda unwound herself and stood up, wiping her filthy hands on her work overalls. Barbara hadn't changed: she was still as elegant and refined as before.

"Hello, Frau Dabek! Hello, Herr Dabek," she stuttered, her words covering the acute shame she was feeling, "How are you all?"

Barbara looked surprised to come across their son's former friend on hands and knees in the graveyard. "We're fine, we're fine. But more importantly, how are you and your family? It's been so long. Walter told us you left so suddenly. Aren't you at school any longer?"

Hedda hung her head in shame. "Not at the moment."

"How awful for you. And your parents? We've been so busy with our work but should have been in touch. I'm so sorry that we haven't," Barbara went on. "These times are not good. Not for anyone."

Hedda was unsure what to tell them. It was all too much to share, standing there amongst the bones and ashes of the dead, the white winter sun half-heartedly warming the cold air.

"And why are you here? This is very strange," Barbara said, looking to her husband to make further enquiries.

"These are difficult times for you and your family." Pawel spoke in his distinctive voice. "The company I work for has removed all Jewish employees, however skilled they were. Some left before they were asked, and as far as I know got out, left Germany. To be honest, I'm surprised that you and your parents are still here. Surely it would be better to leave?"

Hedda bowed her head and studied the patch of earth below her feet. "My mother is in a labor camp miles from here. Moringen.

You probably don't know about it. She's been there for nearly three months." Hedda noticed their puzzled faces. "They arrested her, the Gestapo, and we didn't see her for ages, until the day of the funeral. It was my father's – he died in December. He'd been ill for a while, but I think losing my mother made him much worse. He's buried here." Hedda pointed across the cemetery.

Barbara pulled Hedda towards her and wrapped her in a warm hug. She wanted to stay like that forever and for Barbara and Pawel to take her away, back to Poland, back to tenderness and comfort and safety.

"You poor, poor girl," Barbara said, still holding Hedda tight. "You have suffered terribly. We are so very sorry. What does your mother say? Will they be sending her home soon?"

"I have to sort out the right documents. It seems so complicated. The Gestapo say they can release her if I can get emigration papers. They said they were sending her papers to Berlin, so I think that's where I need to go. But my sister's left there now, she's gone to the Argentine, and I haven't much money left. They took away anything valuable."

Describing her circumstances out loud brought home her horrible reality. She was trapped and her mother was trapped and maybe she would have to join Alice in the terrible camp she could picture so clearly from the details in her mother's letters.

Barbara turned to Pawel, who looked ready to burst into tears himself. "What can we do to help her? Do we know anyone in Berlin?"

He frowned, deep in thought, sifting through past and present acquaintances, Finally his face brightened and he turned to his wife. "Do you remember our old neighbors when we were living in Poznań? The Kaleckis? They moved to Berlin a few years ago for their work, didn't they? He left us his address, but what with one thing and another, and then our move, we didn't stay in touch. Goodness – I'm sure I still have it." Pawel reached into his inside jacket pocket and pulled out a thin address book. "Yes, here!" He looked delighted at his detective work. "Kalecki. 35 Olivaer Platz." He faced Hedda. "They moved about eight years ago so I don't know if they're still there or even if they're still in Berlin. Look, I've got a telephone number listed here!"

Pawel was waving the book in the air but suddenly stopped. Looking straight at Hedda he said: "I haven't explained, have I? They're scientists at the university in Berlin, that's why they moved. And..." He paused. "The point is, the Kaleckis are Jews. I'm sure they'll welcome you."

For the first time in weeks, Hedda felt hope. To be here, in this place, on this path, at the very moment the Dabeks had decided to take a winter stroll on this particular Sunday afternoon: well, maybe there was a God, a God who lived amongst the graves and headstones, watching over the dead, yes, but also watching over the living and looking out for Hedda Israel.

"I will phone the number," Pawel was saying. "I will explain the situation. They cannot say no. Please leave it with us."

They both gave Hedda one final hug before walking away in the direction they had just come, their tall figures, hand in hand, passing through the cemetery gates and disappearing as magically as they had appeared. She sat down on the dug earth and cried. She cried for her dead father, her imprisoned mother, and for herself, a future now possible thanks to the Dabeks. Then she picked up the trowel, the fork and the rake, placed them in her bucket and followed the path back to her silent apartment. Beneath the soil, close to the newly dug graves, the worms tunneled deeper, untroubled by human cares and future worries.

8

IMPORTANT LETTERS

MORINGEN, SAARBRÜCKEN, LONDON

January–February 1938

January 12, 1938

From Alice Israel, Moringen, Germany

Dear Hedda

I'm in despair. I don't know how much more of this I can stand. You must help. I have to be careful what I write. They read the letters.

The place is full of women and they are almost all from the religion called Jehovah's Witnesses. They are here because they are not liked. They are nice enough but I've got nothing to say to them and they all stick together. I avoid the communists and the other politicals because they get us all into trouble and I don't want that. I just want to go home. They've told me that if you can sort out my emigration papers, then I'm free. That can't be too difficult? We both need to leave the country and maybe we can go to the Argentine with Edith.

What do you think?

I know you will sort it all out. You are such a good girl, my darling. I

73

know that I've not always been easy and you must be feeling so lonely but it is dreadful here and I need you to be very brave and rescue your poor mother.

With adoring love – always.
    Mother xx
    PS A happy 18th birthday for the 19th. I'm only sorry I cannot be with you.

January 29, 1938

From Hedda Israel, Saarbrücken, Germany

Dear Herr and Frau Kalecki

Thank you so much for your very kind offer of employment with bed and board in your home in Berlin. I am extremely grateful and very relieved. You said that I could come immediately, so I am making final arrangements and packing up my remaining belongings.

As we said on the telephone, I am happy to undertake all duties you request, cleaning, changing the bed sheets, and anything else you require. I hope to arrive on March 5 and will be taking the train which leaves Saarbrücken about ten thirty in the morning and arrives in Berlin in the late afternoon. If you could let me know which bus or tram I catch from the station to your apartment, I might be able to get to you at about six in the evening?

Thank you so much.
    Yours, Hedda Israel

February 17, 1938

From Betty Carter, London, England

Dear Hedda

I received your letter a few days ago and was shocked by your news. I didn't know what I could say or what I could do, so it's taken me a long time to reply. I spoke to my parents about all the terrible things happening and we all feel so sorry for you. Peter said I should tell you that we all think that now Hitler has gone into Austria, our government is confident that's an end to it.

Your poor mother! How dreadful. And I don't know what I can say about your father's passing. You must feel terribly alone. What will Berlin be like? Write to me once you're settled in. All my fingers and toes are crossed that you can sort out the boring paperwork.

My new job is quite fun. I'm working in an office in a really nice part of London – it's called Chelsea and is very smart and swish. The job isn't too exciting at the moment – just sorting lots of papers into order and then putting them into filing cabinets – do you know what those are? When I'm not at work, I've been meeting up with my new friends and we've been going out for afternoon walks in the park and occasionally going out to dances on a Saturday night. I haven't met anyone special yet but I'm still hoping! Peter's got his first position at a hospital called the Maudsley where he can practice his special interest in how our brains work. He has to see people who are having mental problems – I think it's all a bit grim! He's ever so dedicated though. He's managed to find himself a flat not far from the hospital in a place called Camberwell. I'm still living at home.

Anyway, I'm sorry I've not been in touch for so long. Will you write back and let me know how you're getting on? Who knows? We may actually be able to meet up when you get over here – you will, I promise!

Lots of love, Betty

9

THE KINDNESS OF STRANGERS

BERLIN

March 1938

Hedda stared at the panel of buttons beside the door of 35 Olivaer Platz, an apartment building facing a neat tree-lined park and more well-heeled than she had imagined during her long journey to Berlin. There were just two bells to choose from: 1. Dr Kalecki and 2. Dr Schaeffer. A small piece of painted wood was nailed at about head height beside the door frame. She hadn't seen one of those in a very long time: a mezuzah, which held a rolled-up prayer. The Kaleckis were more observant than she had expected. Another readjustment. She rang the bell and waited.

Leaving Potsdam Bahnhof she walked down Linkstrasse clutching two small suitcases. The sights and sounds of Berlin rush-hour were a swirling delight. Everywhere people hurried from one side of the road to the other, walking arm in arm, chatting, laughing, or deep in their own thoughts. Buses crossed tramways, black well-polished cars hooted their horns at passing pedestrians, and not a single street corner was without activity. Looking up, the buildings stretched skywards, vertical lines of perfection – a vision of a future Hedda could never have imagined.

The scale! Berlin was going to be an adventure, she was sure of that.

Hearing no movement from inside, she rang the bell again and this time a young girl put her head round the door before flinging it open. She was sweet looking, Hedda thought, with long dark hair in two neat plaits that fell over each shoulder. She was wearing a simple green shift dress, heavy brown cardigan, thick stockings, and slippers. Her face broke into the broadest of grins when she realized this was her new companion.

"Hello! You're Hedda? We've been waiting for you! Mother and Father aren't home yet. They told me I should let you in." Anna's words tumbled out in a high-pitched voice of childhood. She jumped up to touch the mezuzah with her right hand and gestured for Hedda to enter. In the hallway, covered with red patterned wallpaper, Hedda noticed another. They were clearly serious in their beliefs.

"Mother said I could show you round. Would you like to see your room first?" Anna said, grabbing Hedda's arm, so she had little choice. This was clearly a young girl brimming with sweet confidence, an endearing energy that Hedda envied. She had been forced to grow up too fast.

"Yes, please. And also where I might wash?" Hedda replied.

Anna went ahead, pointing out what looked like a spacious living room to the left, a further dining room to the right, and then onto a large kitchen filled with shiny pots and pans, a huge number of utensils, and an enormous cooking range. At the far end was another door.

"This is where you will be sleeping," Anna said, opening the door to a small room containing a bed made up with clean white bedlinen, a wooden chair, and a chest of drawers on which stood a small mirror. "Do you want to unpack, or shall I show you the bathroom?"

Although all Hedda's clothes were contained in her two small suitcases, she still wondered where she might put everything. The chest of drawers was tiny.

"The bathroom, please."

When she came out, she realized Anna had been waiting outside, on sentry duty like Hans and Jürgen. It felt like both yesterday and a million years ago, the sneering voices of the youths still ringing in her head. How life had been turned upside down in the space of just three years!

"Shall I tell you about our home?" Anna asked without waiting for a reply. "Mother and Father both work at the university. They say they're lucky. I don't really understand. We all leave together in the morning, before eight o' clock, to catch the bus. I go to Goldschmidt School. It's for Jewish pupils. I like it there. Shall I tell you more?"

Hedda nodded.

"On Saturday we go to synagogue, but it's not like it used to be." Her face filled with childlike worry. "Some of our friends have moved away and we're thinking about moving home as well. It's all getting worse, Hitler and the horrible, horrible things he says and does. But it's difficult. We love Berlin and I love my school and we don't really want to move when we have such a nice place to live."

Hedda wondered what Anna knew or didn't know. On her bus journey to the Kaleckis, she was surprised by the lack of flags and visible signs of Nazi success. It was strange given that Berlin housed the beating heart of the party. Were Berliners not experiencing the same changes in daily life as they had in Saarbrücken?

A key turning in the door interrupted both Anna's monologue and Hedda's thoughts.

"She's here! Hedda is here!" Anna shouted and ran down the hall, throwing her arms around her mother's waist. "She's really nice!" she added. Oh, to have such enthusiasm openly expressed; she hadn't experienced such appreciation for years. She stood still waiting for Anna's parents to come through, holding out her hand in greeting rather awkwardly, as if this were her house and they were the new arrivals.

"Hello, I'm Hedda Israel," she said as they finally approached. Both Kaleckis were on the short side with dark hair, dark eyes and an olive complexion, the physical opposite of Hitler's master-race ideal. The mother was well-dressed in a simple gray dress belted at the waist and the father wore a brown suit with a white shirt and a neat bow tie. Neither looked anything like her parents, but why should they? Their only commonality was their religion and even that was a thin connection. The Kaleckis were observant followers of tradition, unlike her own family.

"We're so delighted to meet you and can only apologize for not being here to greet you when you arrived. You must think us very rude," said the woman. "I'm Hanna, so we mustn't get confused with our names." Hedda liked her immediately. She turned and said something to her husband, not in German but in Polish, which felt odd to Hedda, as if she shouldn't be there.

"Forgive me, we still tend to use Polish when we are at home. A terrible habit I know, and not so good for integration into the community. We also speak Hebrew." She paused. "Do you?"

Hedda told them that not only did she not, neither had her family kept a Jewish household: no Friday night Shabbat, no synagogue attendance, no kosher kitchen. If the Kaleckis were shocked, they chose not to show it.

"Well, I hope you don't mind that we're traditionalists, and we follow custom and practice. But I'm sure you will learn."

Borys Kalecki, clearly a non-traditionalist when it came to kitchen roles and responsibilities, prepared a light dinner of soup and challah bread with some delicious salmon to follow. The pleasure of being cooked for! Hedda offered to clear the plates but was told that on her first night in Berlin, she was to relax and enjoy herself. They sat at the dining table, beautifully covered in an expensive damask cloth and fine crockery, and Hanna explained the domestic duties that she expected Hedda to perform in the coming weeks. It was nothing too demanding, just some shopping and occasional cooking, some cleaning and dusting and washing and ironing, while they were at the university.

Their days were long, filled with important scientific research, although they admitted that recently they had been removed from lecturing and tutoring. There were some colleagues that had left, but the Kaleckis had been reassured that their positions were secure. Hedda was not to worry; she would have considerable time left over for making arrangements that would secure her mother's release from Lichtenburg, the new concentration camp in which Alice was now housed. Hedda had written to her mother informing her of the Berlin address, and the authorities had responded with news of her mother's relocation, but that was it. Nothing from Alice. Hedda tried to avoid imagining her mother's existence, the sleeping arrangements, the washing facilities, the lack of any personal space. It was unbearable.

On a large map of Berlin, spread out on the dining table now the plates had been cleared away, they pointed out the offices Hedda would need to visit. There was the Centre for Refugees where she would sort the visas and the papers to leave the country as a legal refugee, and there was the main street, Friedrichstraße, home to the Gestapo's offices, where she would secure her mother's release. Hedda made a list of buses and tram routes, and wrote down the names of the shops that the Kaleckis used for dairy, for meat, for vegetables and for general groceries, They were all a walk away, thank goodness.

As she pulled the duvet closer around her night-gowned body, the flesh on her arms cold to her own touch, she whispered a prayer unspoken since Kindergarten which had entered her head – maybe because she was in a proper Jewish household for the first time:

Fill me with strength, God, and I will fight for my life. Fill me with health, God, that I may live. They who hope in God shall renew their strength. They shall mount up with wings as eagles. They shall run and not grow weary. They shall walk and not grow faint. Amen.

Oh and another thing, God. I am sorry I haven't paid you much attention until now. I'm going to try a bit harder. Thank you, God. Amen. Again.

The Center for Jewish Refugee Resettlement was housed in a run-down building on a treeless street on the east side of the city. Plaster hung off its outer and inner walls like the decaying bark of a birch tree. Hedda's journey required a change of trams but at least she would cross the River Spree. She enjoyed seeing the painted tugboats pulling the long trawlers, carrying unknown cargo to unknown destinations.

There was no knocker on the front door, so Hedda balled her hand into a fist and banged loudly. A few bits of dry paint flaked off and floated to the floor. After a few seconds, a gray-haired man appeared and requested to know her business. He then pointed at another door through which she was to wait. Seeing his turned-down mouth and the dark shadows under his tired eyes, Hedda decided not to ask him any questions. She entered a room where about 15 others sat and stared, mainly young men wearing thick overcoats and hats. Their breath formed freezing clouds despite the small sputtering fire occasionally breaking the silence. An older man coughed and cleared his throat noisily but those waiting kept their thoughts to themselves. She held the carbon copy with her name and number written on it, found a seat, and sat down.

After an hour, a voice called: "Hedda Israel. Next please!"

"Sit yourself down," said a pleasant-looking young woman behind the table, sitting next to another of indeterminate years, "and explain your situation and your needs." They both seemed genuinely interested and Hedda hoped her story would be sufficiently compelling for them to take immediate pity. She took a deep breath.

"I'm hoping that you might help me. I traveled from Saarbrücken two weeks ago and am staying with a Jewish family near Kurfürstendamm. My father is dead. He died only a few months ago and it's not been easy." She stopped for a moment as images of her dead father filled her head.

The young woman gave her an encouraging look. "I'm so sorry, this is very sad. Do go on. What about your mother? Is she with you?"

"My mother is in a concentration camp, not too far from here. You may have heard of it? Lichtenburg. She was in another one, Moringen, but they moved her."

The women looked at each other and scribbled down the

information – clearly this was going to be challenging Hedda thought from the frown on the older woman's face.

"How old are you, my dear? Why is your mother in a camp?"

"I turned 18 in January. My mother is 45. She was arrested about five months ago. She'd been in trouble with the police in Saarbrücken. They took a dislike to her. She hadn't really done anything, but she doesn't always say the right thing. She didn't want to leave our shop or our home. We kept telling her, but she wouldn't listen. She said that everything would be alright if we just stayed put. That it was all a storm in a teacup."

Hedda stopped, not wanting to cry like a baby.

"That's been hard for you, I think? I'm sorry, my dear," the older woman said. "And losing your father? These are difficult times. You must be brave for your mother. She needs you to stay strong. There will be much to sort out. You haven't mentioned which country you are hoping to emigrate to, but we are having the most success with the British authorities right now. Do you speak any English?"

Hedda nodded. "My English is good and I can read and write it well. I won a special prize at school."

The older woman smiled tenderly. "That's really going to help you. I imagine you were an excellent student. Does your mother speak English as well?"

Hedda shook her head.

"Ah well, no matter. I think that you're the one that will be doing the work, not your mother who is currently otherwise engaged!"

Hedda smiled. A joke even in dark times.

"You will need to obtain an entry visa from the British consulate. The easiest way is if you can secure work. That will be true for your mother as well. Most employment being offered to females in Great Britain is domestic service. It's not the easiest of jobs, especially if this is something you're not used to, but at least it's a way of leaving."

Domestic service – washing and cleaning and cooking like she was for the Kaleckis. She could manage that. She was practicing right now.

The younger woman continued: "We can prepare the necessary papers to liaise with our counterparts in London, the Jewish Refugee Committee, who will look for positions of employment. Are you fussy where you go? London? Manchester? Birmingham? Glasgow?"

Hedda had only heard of London; she opted for the capital.

"We will need to know more details about your mother's situation including her expected release date. You need to speak to the Gestapo about their plans."

Hedda looked appalled.

"Don't worry, dear," the older woman piped up. "They're as keen for you to leave as you are. And not surprisingly, their offices are in a much more attractive part of Berlin, with carpet and heating." She gestured at the bare floorboards and smiled again.

Another sweet attempt at a joke, Hedda thought.

"The difficulty is the British Consulate will only be able to grant you and your mother visas to travel once they have seen evidence of the job offer from an English employer."

She paused to see whether Hedda was following the hoops she would need to jump through. Hedda's furrowed face suggested that she was.

"And then you will need papers from the German government stating that your mother is free to travel immediately. You understand?"

The lines between Hedda's eyes visibly deepened.

"It's burdensome, I know, not easy. Have we explained everything that's ahead of you?"

Hedda nodded and her gloved hands clenched tighter.

"So, considerable work ahead. Fill out these forms, bring them back to us in the next week or so. Meanwhile, make an appointment to speak with someone in the Gestapo about your mother. Once you have sorted that, we can proceed to the next stage."

The older woman got up and showed Hedda to the door, placing one comforting hand on her shoulder while handing over a ream of official looking papers with the other. Hedda was grateful to both for their kindness but seriously doubted her ability to achieve what was needed. She wondered whether these women would be off soon, securing their own safety.

"Good luck," said the younger one. There's lots to do, but you can do it. We can both see, you're a devoted daughter. Your mother must love you very much."

10

A GRIMM FAIRY TALE

BERLIN

July 1938

A soft thump on the doormat signaled the arrival of the film magazine *Kino*, wrapped in sensible brown paper. Anna ran down the hallway, discarded the other items that were of no interest and tore at the wrapping. Inside were pictures of film stars and starlets from Germany and Hollywood, as well as articles about the latest movies that would be showing in the cinemas. It was coming up to Anna's birthday; it was the same date as Hedda's mother's, although they shared few characteristics.

"I'm going to be 13! A proper teenager! But I can't wait to be your age, you're properly grown-up," Anna said, leafing through the pages and folding down those that looked like they were worth returning to.

"My mother's going to be 46. That's definitely grown-up," Hedda said.

Poor Alice. She wondered whether her mother's birthday would be marked in the camp. Maybe one of the women had baked a cake, maybe they'd sing her a birthday song. She hoped her mother had received her handmade card, decorated with twisted flower garlands drawn across the card's front and back. Even with Anna's careful help, it had taken time to complete, and she hoped it had given Alice some pleasure.

The listings for the local cinemas were on the back pages. Despite the increasing restrictions, Jews were not yet banned from attending the cinema. Perhaps the reasoning was that no one would notice them in the dark, but more likely they just hadn't got round to adding this restriction to that list called "Jew Humiliation."

"Look! They're showing *Snow White* at the *Berliner Kino*. We could go for my birthday!"

Anna was running in dizzying circles waving the magazine high in the air. A glossy full-color article showed pictures from the film: there was Snow White, so pretty with her dark hair and shiny yellow skirt, with the dwarves sporting sweet faces and long white beards. This was a story that had come from Hedda's own land, Germany, and she felt proud that the Americans had chosen a Brothers Grimm tale to transform into this remarkable piece of cinema. It was a long film, over an hour, *Kino* said. The wait was almost unbearable!

The birthday trip was a welcome relief after the visits to the Consulate, the Refugee Center, and the dreadful offices of the Gestapo. Walking down Friedrichstrasse for the first time, she had marveled at the imposing buildings that lined the wide street. Here were housed the various departments of the party and the men and women who sat behind these grand entrances and shiny windows brought her out in a sweat. Like the buildings, the Gestapo officers were reducing her to the size of a mouse. What if they refused to see her? What if they arrested her once they knew her mother was in a camp? There had been so much to fear.

When she had found the right door, number 45, she stood on the spotless concrete steps for several minutes. She had just been about to walk away when the door opened and a woman dressed in a severe jacket and skirt asked Hedda what her business was and commanded her to follow. A long corridor stretched ahead of her and black-framed photographs formed a neat procession on the wallpapered walls. Uniformed men with rigid faces stared out. She assumed these were the important ones. Pictures of the Führer, shaking hands with party officials and foreign politicians, were displayed against gaudy gold leaf. Unlike in the posed portraits, Hitler was often smiling broadly, just like in the picture that hung over the desk at Hedda's old school. Herr Hitler surrounded by sweet-faced blond children.

Overseen by two men in police uniform, Hedda waited in a large room at the end of the corridor where others were already seated. A crystal chandelier hung from the ceiling and further black-framed faces of party members reminded the viewer, if they didn't already know, that the eyes of the Gestapo were everywhere. In one portrait an officer had a bony face full of strange protruding lumps. Another was fleshy and pig-like. Not a great advertisement for the party's perfect physical types, Hedda thought. The room echoed with silence and Hedda wondered about the others there, who were all men. They didn't appear to be Jewish, if dark hair and a certain nose shape was anything to go by, but she didn't look Jewish either.

A large clock ticked loudly. When Hedda had arrived, it had been 10:20 and it was exactly 3:20, her stomach rumbling loudly, when she finally followed a party official down another long corridor into a huge room. A single man sat in front of a giant eagle, the swastika within its claws, behind a large table. He was long nosed with thick glasses and wispy eyebrows above the heavy frames.

"Name?" he asked, not looking up.

"Hedda Israel."

"Age?"

"Eighteen."

"Reason for visit?"

"I am trying to leave the country with my mother."

Hedda noticed the yellow forms, completed on arrival, were stacked under his left hand so wondered why he questioned her. He had the information right there. Maybe he needed new glasses.

"What is it you want?"

"I understand I need papers from yourselves for visas if we are to travel."

Hedda was surprised to hear the confident voice that emerged; it didn't reflect the sheer terror she was feeling.

"Why isn't your mother with you today? And where is your father?"

He knew. It was on the paper in front of him. He just wanted her to say it.

"My father died last year. My mother is in Lichtenburg."

The man put down his pen, squaring it up with the top of the form, and looked directly at Hedda. Now she saw his ugly face – dull and gray skinned, with small squinting eyes, magnified by the glass.

"She's in a camp? So she's in protective custody?" He spoke sarcastically, knowing full well what the words meant.

"Yes." Hedda paused, not sure whether she should, or could, continue. She hadn't drunk anything since breakfast and her tongue was dry. Maybe this was how real fear felt.

"Well?" the man asked again.

Hedda licked her lips and cleared her throat. "I have been told that once I have a date of release for my mother, which the Gestapo can provide, then..." She wasn't sure whether to name the Jewish Refugee Committee or whether that would worsen his mood. Finally she said, "They can organize a work permit and visa, but they, that's the people helping me, can't do anything until I have the papers from yourselves, to show them the date."

The man had returned to his paperwork and didn't bother to look up. "This has been a wasted journey, young lady. We will not be able to authorize the release of your mother," he spoke the word as if it was a piece of chewy gristle in his mouth, "until we have a guarantee that she will be leaving the Motherland immediately afterwards. It is us who need to see the paperwork, not the other way round! Believe me, we are as keen as you are to see your mother's departure but we cannot risk your mother being released if there is any likelihood that she would remain to undertake further criminal activities."

"But she didn't–" Hedda started.

The man stood up. "Make a further appointment once you have the necessary paperwork. Not before. We do not enjoy our time being wasted."

Sunday was glorious. Bright afternoon sunshine lit up the lake in the park opposite the Kaleckis' apartment with sparkling spots of gold that leapt from the water's surface as the four walked side by side on their way to Anna's birthday treat. The flowerbeds overflowed with summer flowers: yellow and orange nasturtiums, tall stems of blue delphiniums and white lupins. This was truly a day when it felt good to be alive. It almost seemed a shame they would soon be in cinema darkness, but the excitement of what lay ahead was adequate compensation.

A queue had formed in front of the ticket booth and was already snaking round the block. Chattering children clutched their parents' hands, and even adults without children in tow showed similar enthusiasm. This was an event that all Berliners had been waiting for. Tickets were bought: "Three adults, and one child please, it's a birthday treat!"

It took several moments to adjust to the darkness of the wonderful auditorium and Anna reached out for Hedda's arm.

"I can't see a thing!" she whispered.

"Nor can I!" Hedda replied. She had never been to a cinema before, and it was taking her a while to adjust to this remarkable place, albeit one she could barely see. The floor tilted gently downwards and as she reached out her other hand, the one Anna wasn't squeezing tightly, she could feel the plush softness of the seats in which they would soon be sitting.

"Anna and Hedda! Follow us," said Borys and Hedda found herself shuffling to the right, past seated figures, until they found the four empty spaces where they would be spending the next hour and a half.

Once in their places, Anna asked, "How long before it starts?"

"I think there will be a newsreel first, and then the film," said Hanna.

Hedda had been wondering the same thing but hadn't wanted to ask for fear of appearing childish. She was glad Anna had posed the question and was surprised there was going to be even more entertainment.

At that moment, the huge curtains cranked back to reveal a giant white screen. How much red velvet had been needed to make those? she thought. Rolls and rolls and rolls. As the curtains came to a halt with a satisfying creak, the excited chattering of the audience dissolved and Hedda could hear the mechanical whirr of the projector from behind her. The anticipation was nearly over! The dimmed lights went out and the screen flickered into brilliant life.

There, in vast black letters several feet tall appeared the words: "*Der Führer begrüßt die Menschen im Berliner Stadion.*" [The Führer greets the people in the Berlin Stadium.] Loud rousing music filled every part of the cinema and Hedda waited nervously to see what followed. It was a black and white news film of Hitler at a giant rally in the stadium outside Berlin. Hundreds and hundreds of eagle and swastika flags flew from every flagpole. The music continued as the camera swept from left and right, capturing the magnificence of the occasion. Then, a large black car pulled into shot, and there was Herr Hitler, standing proud and waving to the thousands of people who were cheering and waving back at him.

The camera lingered endlessly on the faces, mainly of young children, younger than Anna, girls and boys shouting and laughing. His car passed deep ranks of supporters, hands flying back and forth in the air like mad window cleaners. Then he mounted a podium in the middle of the stadium and the camera panned around. In every seat, the people had magically spelt out the words *Gross Deutschland*, and raised their arms, an ocean of salutes, as they sang a patriotic song in total harmony. The film came to an end. The shortest of breaks followed, and finally the screen burst into color and the main feature began.

Had Hedda enjoyed *Snow White*? The Kaleckis walked slowly back through the park arm in arm with Anna, the sun still glittering on the lake and lighting up the leaves of the trees, although the shadows stretching across the path were now longer.

"Yes, it was delightful. The songs and the music were so lovely to hear. The colors were just so bright and, well, colorful! I loved it. Thank you."

Actually, Hedda had found her mind wandering frequently back to the images from the stadium whilst the jolly dwarves fussed over their new mistress. She wanted to raise the topic and couldn't understand why the Kaleckis weren't mentioning it. Surely they had been as amazed, as shocked, as frightened as she had?

Maybe they knew more than they were telling her. As she let the happy family walk a few paces ahead, she realized Borys and Hanna never discussed the government, Hitler and the Nazis, and what was happening to the Jews, not with her anyway. Why was it they had kept their jobs when others hadn't? Were they not who they said they were? She would sometimes hear them talking in Polish whispers and they always stopped their conversation when she entered the room. She was too frightened to ask. Apart from the yellow benches designated for Jews only, the ones that Anna would dare Hedda to sit on before sitting on them herself, giggling and joking, Berlin was a thriving city and felt normal. Anna had celebrated her birthday, the best ever, there was good kosher food on the table each day, Hedda shopped and was welcomed by the shopkeepers, the Kaleckis were still in work. Life went on. The film that accompanied the main feature was simply another German fairy tale, told by a master storyteller: Brother Hitler. The Wolf in the Forest.

11

SHATTERED

BERLIN AND EVERY LARGE TOWN IN
GERMANY

November 1938

It had been another bitterly cold day in Berlin with a vicious wind blowing and snow hanging in the gray sky. An ordinary day, apart from a letter. Hedda had last heard from her mother over five months ago and was beginning to worry that something dreadful had happened. In this letter Alice acknowledged Hedda's birthday card, even admiring the flower garlands, and described the current conditions in the camp. Hedda guessed her mother was painting a rosier picture than the reality, trying hard not to cause trouble that could jeopardize her release date.

Hedda had written back about her efforts to secure the correct paperwork, stating that they were nearly there in getting their visas and work permits from the British government. A total fabrication. The problem was in making arrangements for the two of them, getting guarantees of their good characters and work and accommodation for both. If it were just the young and employable Hedda it would have been sorted, the consulate would say, but it was much more complicated for Frau Alice Israel. And, she must know, there were people in England who objected to Jews coming across the Channel, the English newspapers describing the horrors of the country swamped by foreigners. Hedda thought the consulate took pleasure in telling her these stories to make her feel more grateful. Or maybe they just wanted to be honest.

She was now well into a routine of domestic duties and had carved out an enjoyable role as math and languages tutor, helping Anna with her studies. She had grown so fond of the young girl. She loved being part of this caring family, each of whom showed interest in the others' daily experiences, asking questions, enquiring about each other's feelings both good and bad. Consequently Hedda felt her own family's dysfunction even more deeply. She would dream that she was the older daughter, their firstborn, and Anna her darling younger sister. This fantasy provided comfort on darker days. She didn't think about her own sister, and although she assumed Edith was happy in Buenos Aires, it didn't really matter. They hadn't communicated since their father's funeral and Hedda wondered whether her sister would eventually evaporate completely from her thoughts and from her life. Not like her father, who came to her on a daily basis.

In her new family, she had learnt to prepare and cook proper Jewish dishes, challah bread twisted and braided, potato latkes, crispy but not greasy, and of course, the best chicken soup with fluffy matzo balls. Paul would have been proud of her. Her new cooking skills would stand her in good stead when she got to England, making her even more employable.

That wintry afternoon, when Anna arrived back from school, they spent a couple of hours on her mathematics. Trigonometry. Hedda had always enjoyed applying the precise rules and was surprised at how much she'd retained as they wrote out the problems that needed solving.

"Can I ask you something?" Anna said as they came to the end of the homework.

"Of course you can," Hedda replied.

"Is it difficult being on your own?"

"What do you mean?"

"On your own. Without your mother and father."

"But I'm not on my own, am I? I've got you and Hanna and Borys. You've made me feel so much a part of this family."

"But we're not your real family. Your sister. She's gone. Your father..." Anna didn't go on with completing that fact, "your mother is in the camp and can't look after you..."

"It's hard, but I'm lucky to be with you, in Berlin. Why, I'd never have seen such an exciting city if your family hadn't offered me work. *You're* my family. And hopefully I'll soon manage to get my mother out and then the two of us can start a whole new adventure in England. Although I'm not sure how she'll manage, not speaking any English. Goodness knows!"

"Will you write to us when you get there?" Anna had closed her math book and, without realizing, was gently stroking Hedda's forearm in a gesture that made Hedda's heart melt.

"I will. I hope we'll stay in touch forever and ever. I'll want to know all your career plans and your marriage plans – no hurry with that," Hedda said quickly and they both laughed. "I want to meet your delightful children when you have them and you will meet mine!"

"Your children will speak English!"

"Not if I come back to Germany. And your children will speak... What? Polish? German?"

"Oh, both! And Italian and French and of course English so they can talk with yours."

After supper and some chat about a difficult second year student of Borys', Hedda announced she was having an early night. This was really an excuse to get into bed and return to her new novel by an English writer called Walter Scott. Walter! About a dashing prince in love with two women, one of them Rebecca. A Jewess!

Hedda realized she must have fallen asleep with the book still open when she was woken by the sound of raised voices and doors opening and closing. It was around ten, she thought, the streetlamps still on and a deep orange glow in the sky beyond. There was a cloying smell of dust or ash or burning wood; a strange smell of things alight.

She pulled on a thick cardigan over her night dress and walked across the cold kitchen floor in the direction of the voices. They were speaking in Polish and as she got nearer, the pungent smell of bonfires was stronger. She put her ear to the door hoping to hear more. The Polish continued and though she could understand nothing, there was something about the speed and fear in their tone that suggested this was not their normal exchange of secret views. Hedda pushed at the door and the Kaleckis stopped talking. Anna ran to her, pulling Hedda towards the family group.

"We were just about to wake you," Hanna said. She sounded like she was trying to calm herself. "Have you seen what's happening? It's dreadful. The synagogue is on fire."

"I saw the sky! Is that why it's such a peculiar color? And the smell! Is the fire brigade there?" Hedda asked.

"We think there are some terrible things happening, more than we can see. My friends in Hamburg have called and they say there are people on the streets right now. They've been out all evening, smashing shop windows, throwing bricks, throwing stones. Apparently the police is doing nothing to stop it. We are scared."

Anna let go of Hedda. She cried and hugged her mother tightly. Through the window onto the park opposite, Hedda saw groups of figures waving sticks and wooden batons, running in all directions. Some were crossing the road and getting uncomfortably close to the apartment.

"Get away from the window! They know where we live. We need to move away from the front of the house."

They decided the safest place to take refuge was back in their own bedrooms, although Anna insisted she wasn't going to be parted from her mother and would spend the night in her parents' bed.

Despite everything, Hedda fell back into a fitful sleep, dreaming of shadowy figures chasing her through long corridors. When she finally woke, she immediately remembered the events of the night before and shot out of bed. She could feel the acrid taste of smoke every time she drew breath. As she walked through the apartment, there was an odd silence. She couldn't hear the Kaleckis; they must have overslept as a result of the night's disturbances, she thought. Anna wasn't in her own bed but she had made it clear that she would sleep between her mother and father.

Hedda approached their room and tapped quietly on the door. No one responded. She tapped again, this time a little harder and said: "Hanna? Anna? Borys?" Still no answer. She quietly turned the handle and pushed the door open. In front of her was a mad jumble of discarded clothes, skirts, trousers, jackets, along with open drawers and bottles of creams and lotions, undergarments, and jewelry. The bed was littered with photographs, papers, and Anna's exercise books, including the one containing her trigonometry homework. How could Hedda not have heard anything? How could she have slept through such a tornado of objects and people on the move?

The Kaleckis had gone. That was obvious. She left the bedroom and went into the living room, on the remote possibility that they were hiding there, the last place she had seen them together. It was remarkably undisturbed. On a small side table, Hedda spotted what looked like a hastily written note. She picked it up, terrified of what she was about to read. The handwriting was Hanna's and almost illegible in places.

Dear Hedda

We are so sorry not to say goodbye to you properly but know you will understand the reason we had to leave in such a hurry. We hope that as you read this we will be on our way back to Poland to stay with Borys' parents in Warsaw before returning to Poznań, our hometown. We plan to catch the early train that will take us as far as the German border, and then another into Poland. We didn't want to make things worse for you. You have so much on your plate right now and are getting much closer to sorting out the papers for your dear mother. If you want to stand half a chance of being successful, you need to stay in Berlin to deal with the authorities. Coming with us to Poland would have been a disaster for you and your mother, although, believe me, we did talk about it for a long time and Anna was very upset we had to leave you all alone. She wanted to wake you up but we thought it would just make everyone even sadder.

Last night will be a turning point for us all, and things will change.

By going back to Poland, we are far enough away to feel safe, but it's vital that you leave Germany as soon as possible, so redouble your efforts, dear Hedda.

Please feel free to remain in the apartment and help yourself to anything you want – we are not returning. The apartment is owned by the university so at some point they will want it back but until then – well, it's yours. We have left you some money in the kitchen drawer, so you won't be hungry immediately and I'm sure Herr Klinghoffer will provide you with some nice produce if you explain the situation. He has always been a dear friend to us, as you know.

Our address in Warsaw is 77 Teofila Lenartowicza. When you get to London with your mother, please write to us and let us know you are safe and well. Who knows? We may meet up in a couple of years. You can take us on a tour of London town. We would love to visit Buckingham Palace and we might even be able to take tea with the King!

With lots of love from

Anna, Hanna and Borys xxx

12

FINAL TOUCHES

BERLIN

November–December 1938

The mezuzah was lying at the bottom of the steps when Hedda left the apartment later that morning. Daubed on the door was a roughly painted yellow Star of David and the window glass was covered in fine cracks radiating out from a central point, as if a large rock gathered from an adjacent flowerbed had been thrown directly at the pane. Hedda knelt to pick up the broken wooden case, but its soiled appearance suggested something vile adorned it. She let it lie there.

A haze of black smoke lined the edges of the horizon, and as she walked down Olivaer Platz towards Kurfürstendamm, she saw large numbers of people gathered on the streets. There were men and women of all ages, children too, well buttoned-up, scarves wrapped around their mouths, though whether to keep out the cold or to prevent inhaling the acrid fumes was debatable. In the main street lay a glistening lake of broken glass across pavements and in the road, cars swerving to avoid punctures. Ugly jagged glass protruded from shop windows, giving an inviting if dangerous path to the goods within. Hedda watched a fur-coated

98

woman of older years climb through a shop selling expensive leather bags, her arms stuffed full of loot on departure. Further down she saw the same broken windows and doors scrawled with *Jude* and Stars of David. Large crowds enjoyed the spectacle of those who dared to thieve from the Jewish stores. Images of the Israels' shop, smashed and defiled, flooded her thoughts. Why had all this happened?

Morning turned to afternoon as she continued to wander the Berlin streets avoiding eye contact with those who threw bricks at glass fronts, drew yellow stars, stole and plundered. In front of a synagogue, one Hedda had passed on her Sunday walks exploring the city, stood a school-party, a teacher smiling as she pointed out the smoldering ruins of the roof to her young charges. There were pops and bangs as parts of the building sizzled and collapsed, and the children responded with cheers of delight.

When the afternoon light faded, she turned to walk home but of course the house would be empty. She was on her own. Crossing through the park opposite Olivaer Platz, she noticed that the yellow bench she and Anna had sat on so defiantly was marked and stained. She approached it carefully. It was covered in a thick brown substance that Hedda knew wasn't the soil from the empty flowerbed.

At the park's large metal gates, Hedda saw two figures, a small woman and a smaller child. The woman was bending down to the child who was clearly upset; Hedda could hear the girl's cries from a distance. The woman's scarf was pulled over her hair and it appeared she was trying to mask her face. When Hedda got closer she recognized Frau Roth, a woman she had been introduced to when she had accompanied the Kaleckis to the synagogue.

"Frau Roth? Lisa? Are you alright? What a terrible, terrible day this is." Hedda bent down and lightly touched the little girl's palm. Then she stood up to speak to the mother.

"They came today and took Samuel and David and Ivor! All of them!" she wailed. "They've all gone! I don't know where they are or what they were meant to have done. They just came and arrested them. Just like that, just like that..." Her voice trailed off, a glazed but desperate look in her eyes, the only part of her visible beneath the woolen scarf.

"Why did they take them?" Hedda asked, immediately realizing the mother was equally ignorant of the events of last night and today.

"I don't know, I don't know. They were holding papers. They said they were being arrested for crimes against the state. They left me with a piece of paper which I had to sign. I don't know what I'm going to do."

Lisa, the little girl, was still sobbing, long mucus trails sliding from her nose towards her mouth. Her mother pulled a dirty handkerchief from her coat pocket and wiped her daughter's face. "What about you? And the Kaleckis? Did they come for Borys?"

Borys! Of course. They were arresting the men, the Jewish men, and at that moment, Hedda realized the wisdom of the family's decision to escape from the hands of the Nazi captors. It was the right thing. But she was simultaneously filled with the horror of knowing she was completely on her own in this city where Jews were now being hunted down like vermin and her stomach flipped over.

"They went last night, Frau Roth. Back to Poland."

"What? They left you by yourself? How could they?" Frau Roth appeared to be outraged and Hedda jumped to their defense.

"They had to. They knew that if I'm going to get my mother out of the camp, she's in one, you see, I need to be in Berlin to sort the papers and visas."

Frau Roth's eyes narrowed still further as she understood her husband and sons were on their way to such a camp.

"But who knows what's going on?" Hedda said. But Frau Roth was no longer listening. She was staring vacantly ahead, her thoughts centered on the men, wondering when she would next see them. If she ever would.

During the following weeks, Hedda paid further visits to the Refugee Center and the consulate. Then she was summoned back to the offices of the Gestapo in Friedrichstrasse. They demanded to know why it was taking so long for the British to sort out her work permit. It was another horrible visit with the same long wait, the same uniformed officers, but this time considerably more threatening.

Back in October, she had been advised to write to anyone in England who might help in securing employment. She had contacted Betty, although she felt uncomfortable knowing the enormity of the request. Betty was occupied with her new job and a new boyfriend and sorting out work permits for a German Jewish girl was not going to be easy. Not surprisingly, Betty had not replied, and the Refugee Center had been pursuing other avenues of support. After that dreadful night, the queues at their offices had multiplied tenfold and everyone who could was trying to leave. Hedda resented the new applicants forming desperate lines down the streets, starting from the early hours of the morning: it wasn't fair. She had been trying since March, and now was at the back of the queue.

At times her loneliness threatened to engulf her. Since the meeting in the park with Frau Roth she had talked to no one apart from the Refugee Center employees. She hadn't even told Herr Klinghoffer at the grocery store. In her darkest moods, she would think of her father, images of his face clogged with damp earth lying in his grave. It made no sense. He was ashes. She would think of Walter and the springtime walks in the park, and she would think of his parents, his mother still working in the hospital mending children's broken bones. She would occasionally think of her sister, Edith, almost certainly sunning herself on some South American beach, and often of Anna and the Kaleckis and whether they had resumed university life in Poland. She thought of her mother in a community of supportive women, and she felt both envious and ashamed that she should consider her mother's circumstances preferable to her own.

At times she would allow herself the luxury of self-pity, and think about her prosperous childhood, surrounded by the best toys and fancy dresses and the doll's house with its own electricity, all gone. Now, here she was, abandoned in a strange city, eating one simple meal per day with the remaining money, wearing the same few clothes. Why her? She didn't deserve this. Then she would become angry with herself: there were many, many others in a much worse situation. I'm living in this beautiful apartment, she would think. And she would reassure herself with the knowledge that her non-Jewish appearance saved her from the worst insults and the street abuse that other Jewish Berliners were subject to. That thought would increase her guilt and make her feel ugly inside.

One December morning, ten days away from *Weihnachtsabend*, when all of Berlin was looking at its Christmas best, two large brown envelopes plopped onto the doormat of the apartment. Hedda was in the kitchen, trying to get some flavor and nourishment from scrawny chicken pieces and elderly vegetables, when she heard the delivery. Both envelopes were of a similar size, and both looked like official correspondence, certainly not the letter from Betty that she had hoped for. The first envelope was from the university. It read:

To Whom It May Concern

There has been an unavoidable delay in the request for the return of university-owned accommodation from the tenants... Here was a space in which someone had typed: *Herr Borys Kalecki and Frau Hanna Kalecki...* Here was another space into which someone had typed the address of the apartment.

The Property Department will be arriving at 9 a.m. on Wednesday December 14. Please ensure the property is vacant. There are three sets of keys that must be left. All furniture must remain in place as per the original inventory.

At the bottom was a scrawled signature in ink and then below it another handwritten sentence:

The second envelope contained three pieces of paper: one a letter, and the other two appearing to be Home Office visas. Hedda's hands trembled as she removed them from the envelope. Yes! The first paper she examined showed her name – Hedda Israel and her age – 17 – and below – "Work Permit Authorized" stamped in blue ink. It read: 'The British Home Office has approved a permit to enter the country to engage in employment as a domestic servant. A work guarantee from a future employer based in Upton Park, London, England is offered and signed. Accommodation is offered alongside the employment. She will be required to show an approved entrance visa and her German passport allowing her to travel.'

Hedda's hands shook with excitement and with nerves. Who was this employer? Was this something that Betty had organized and not told her?

She now turned to the other visa – presumably her mother's. On this she read Alice Israel – and her age – 46 – and below – "Work Permit Declined." It said there was a upper age limit of 45 years old for the issuing of work permits for domestic service, and the Home Office had no discretion in this matter. They would therefore be unable to grant Alice Israel a work permit and thus no entrance visa would be allowed at this stage. The covering letter provided some additional information about next steps and appeals and advised Hedda to make a further appointment with the Refugee Center to make the arrangements for her own departure.

Hedda returned to the kitchen and continued to chop the carrots and onions. She cried – onion tears, tears of relief and of despair. What now? How could she leave her mother in Germany? There was a job waiting for Hedda in London, in a place called Upton Park which sounded so green and rich and welcoming – Up Town in a Park. But there was no one to talk to, to share this momentous news with. Then she decided to call Walter. She still had his number from when they used to talk, and it was worth a try. Maybe there *was* someone who would understand.

She wiped her hands on a towel and pressed it against her eyes, drying her face thoroughly as if trying to pull herself together. She walked through to the small room off the kitchen that had been her bedroom and pulled open the drawer beside her old bed. There was a small black diary and at the back was a section for names, addresses and telephone numbers. Dabek. Walter. 063 8147.

The Kaleckis' phone had not yet been cut off and Hedda dialed quickly before she lost confidence, or the university cut the line. It rang and rang. There was no answer. Of course, his parents would be at work and Walter would be at school. Hedda had forgotten that for ordinary people, life went on as normal. Later that afternoon she tried again. It was likely that Walter would be home now; she presumed he was in his final year at school. The phone rang three times before a deep male voice answered, "The Dabeks. Hello, who is this, please?"

The relief, the sweet relief of hearing Walter's voice. "Walter, it's Hedda, Hedda Israel. I'm calling you from Berlin," she said, in a garbled rush.

There was a slight pause as if he were processing information from long ago. "Hedda! How are you? Are you safe? Is your mother out of the camp? My parents told me. How awful for you."

Without waiting for formalities, Hedda explained everything that had happened, the departure of the Kaleckis, the burning synagogues and the vandalized shops, the arrests and killings, and while he listened mostly quietly and patiently, Walter would occasionally interrupt with: "It happened here too, yes, we know of some arrests..."

Hedda asked him about their department store. It had been taken over by some Germans, he said, and was trading well, he thought. So not burnt down or desecrated. She explained about the many visits to the various offices in Berlin, the endless queuing and waiting. While in full flow, she heard a click on the phone line.

"Did you just hear something?" she asked Walter.

"Like what?" he asked.

"Is someone listening to us?"

"No," he replied.

Hedda described the visits she had made to the Gestapo, the long corridors, and how she felt like a prisoner every time she entered the building. She had had to sign various bits of paper to say she was now under the jurisdiction of the police and would only be allowed to leave "on their authority." She told him about her agonizing dilemma – that her mother was just one year too old for a work permit, but she, Hedda, had been granted a visa with guaranteed employment as soon as she arrived in London. What should she do? What *could* she do?

"Hedda, you must leave. You don't have a choice. If you stay, who knows what will happen? It will be you joining your mother, won't it? You'll both be trapped. No. Go. Once you're in England, there might be another chance. Someone might be able to help. You've got to go."

"How can I tell my mother? She'll be devastated."

"She'll understand."

"She won't. You don't know her. She will hate me. Forever and ever."

"Well then if she does, it doesn't matter anyway. You wouldn't want her around if she hated you."

"Oh, that's ridiculous. She's my mother."

"And..."

"And nothing. I'm her daughter. I have to look after her."

"Well, the best way you can do that is to leave as soon as possible and carry on looking after her from London. Honestly, you really don't have a choice."

He was right and the relief she felt in someone making the decision on her behalf was overwhelming. After some further conversation, mainly about the well-being of Walter's parents, Hedda thanked him repeatedly, said goodbye, and waited for him to put the receiver down. As she did, she heard the click again. Someone other than Walter was ringing off.

About ten minutes later the phone rang. It never rang, had not rung since the Kaleckis had left. She picked up the receiver and said in a whisper, "Hello?"

"Hedda Israel. This is the office of the Gestapo. You are required to attend tomorrow at nine o'clock. Please do not be late." A male voice spoke the words clearly and precisely.

Her face burned and her stomach heaved. The person at the other end of the phone rang off, a click indicating the call was over. She had been right. There had been someone listening to the conversation. This person would have heard about her frustration with the officers she had encountered, her anger about her mother's detention for no proper reason – they had heard everything. She felt drops of sweat soaking through her blouse. This fear was like nothing she had felt before, pure dread of what lay ahead for herself and for her mother.

She failed to sleep that night; the apartment was deathly cold, and snow fell on the streets outside, just in time for the Christmas festivities. By the morning, Hedda was in no doubt that she would be detained and sent to join her mother in Lichtenburg.

With typical efficiency, the snow had been cleared from the Gestapo steps and surrounding pavement as Hedda arrived, early for her appointment. She had packed a small case of items including a toothbrush, hairbrush, change of underwear, and a writing pad and two pens, fully expecting to be detained that morning. She waited in the usual waiting room, but this time for only a few minutes before she was called and ushered into the room in which she had sat so many times before. In front of her was a different officer; this man was huge, with shoulders like a bull. His cheeks sagged, and Hedda could hear his labored breathing as soon as she entered.

"Hedda Israel?" he barked. "You are currently making arrangements to leave?"

"Yes."

"And you have now secured a work permit for yourself to work in England?"

How did he know? She had only received confirmation of this yesterday.

"Yes."

"But your mother's permission to work has been refused, yes? She is too old?"

"Yes."

He stared at Hedda, his mouth opening and closing. "*Schade,*" he said. "What a shame."

"Yes," Hedda said.

"Without a work permit, we have no date as to when she might be eligible to leave the country and are unable to provide a date of release. But you are now free to leave. Your passport will be clearly marked and ready for collection in a few weeks. So Hedda Israel," he said, shuffling the papers in front of him, copies of the documents that she had received yesterday, "you may leave. But don't forget, the arms of the Gestapo stretch right around the world."

The man pushed back his chair as if to get up, and then thought better of it. "Complete the necessary documents on your way out."

Hedda got up, thanking him as she left the room. She wasn't being arrested unless there was someone waiting at the exit to place her in handcuffs and throw her in the back of a waiting van. On the pavement outside, taking care to avoid the patches of ice that were forming on top of last night's snow, Hedda knew she could finally look forward to a new life outside the hell that Germany had become. But one without her mother.

13

CROSSING BORDERS
BELGIUM

February 1939

From the grimy windows of the train, the fields sped by in continuous motion, a featureless mud brown, apart from small spots of ice where the winter sun had yet to penetrate. Even so, they were beautiful to Hedda. With every broken fence, and every furrow passed, she was further from the Berlin streets peopled with ugly faces, distanced from the ruined synagogues, no longer smoking but blackened and cold, the vandalized shops still decorated with scrawled yellow stars, and the daily humiliations of living life on the outside.

Since eviction, she had stayed in a small back room of the Klinghoffers' grocery shop. Their kindness had saved Hedda from wandering the streets and living out of a suitcase. When she returned from the Gestapo offices that day, she had gone to buy something for a meal. When Herr Klinghoffer asked why she looked so unhappy, Hedda allowed herself to break down in his shop in front of the other customers, sobbing until he shouted for Frau Klinghoffer to come down and hear Hedda's story. Although she wept, they were tears of relief and sadness equally. The

Klinghoffers did not hesitate and immediately offered her to stay with them, "nothing much, you understand," but a bed, a roof and meals to share with the family. They would rather she kept a low profile, and use the back entrance to the store for her own safety, but she could stay for as long it took to finalize the papers.

They were now passing through a small village and the family with whom she had shared the carriage for the last two hours were preparing to leave, packing up the last of their afternoon picnic, shaking out the crumbs from the children's laps onto the floor, and collecting their belongings. They had not spoken to Hedda since boarding at Cologne and yet again Hedda felt grateful if guilty that she looked so unlike The Jew portrayed in the newspapers and magazines – her light brown hair, upturned nose and blue-gray eyes presenting a safe Germanic picture. If the family had asked to see her passport, they would have *seen* her then: the ornate stamp of J across Hedda's name and date of birth, that single letter the clue to her identity.

The train was grinding noisily to a halt and Hedda realized they had reached the border. A large sign on the platform confirmed they were indeed at Aachen.

"Have a good onward journey, dear," said the mother to Hedda, the first and only words spoken to her. The young children shoved past, sticky hands using her knees as launch pads to propel themselves forward.

Once they had left, Hedda sat there wondering nervously what would happen next. She had crossed borders previously when they had holidayed in France, but that was in the family car during happier times; now she traveled on her own, on a train, and the National Socialists were in government. She had checked her documents over and over before boarding at Berlin, suitcase in one hand, handbag in the other, and had deliberately destroyed the letters from her mother, especially the last one received just a few days before she left. She was nervous enough without some government official reading that her mother was in a labor camp for women who had defied the state.

A peaked cap official walked down the corridor and pulled

open Hedda's carriage door. "Passport please, Fräulein," he commanded.

Hedda reached into her handbag and pulled it out, opening it up to the right page, the one marked with the J.

He looked her up and down. "Who'd have thought?" he said.

Hedda thought it best not to respond.

"And your exit permit?"

Hedda handed him the paper, stamped with the official party sign which he examined carefully. She stopped breathing.

He removed a small notebook from his upper pocket and scribbled something on the small pages, taking his time. Then, placing the notebook back in his coat and carefully replacing the pen lid to avoid ink stains, he looked closely at Hedda, to check if this *was* the girl in the passport and if the permit rightfully belonged to her. He cleared his throat, coughing loudly, and pulled out a handkerchief into which he spat. "Well, it looks like everything's in order," he said resentfully, before turning down the corridor to check other passengers.

Another official now stood in the doorway, this time a Belgian, also dressed in a customs uniform. "Passport, please?" he said in Flemish, the word sounding sufficiently like English for Hedda to understand.

She handed it over, and he flicked through it. "They want you lot out, don't they? Can't have been easy. Don't really get that Hitler bloke. Can't say that too loudly with the fellas on board. Dreadful. All the burning and stuff. Where are you heading? Let's see your ticket then."

Hedda removed it carefully from the compartment in her bag. It stated Berlin to Oostende, single fare.

He punched a hole in the side, then handed it back. "Best of luck. You'll be alright. Don't forget to get off at the end of the line; you don't want to fall asleep and find yourself on the train back to Aachen! Now that wouldn't be much fun, would it?" He laughed at his joke.

A group of four young men entered the carriage, chattering and laughing. Hedda moved closer to the window, trying to make herself as small as possible. They examined her up and down, said hello, and then returned to their conversations which Hedda was glad not to understand, the Flemish dialect so strong and guttural sounding.

After another half hour of border checks with various officials patrolling the corridors and shouting competitive commands to each other, the train whistled its pleasure of leaving Germany. She was out! She wished she could share this glorious feeling with a fellow passenger but the young men, clearly medical students from the anatomical textbooks they had pulled from their leather cases, were more interested in pointing out diagrams of female bodies and body parts. Instead, she removed two photographs she had rescued from Hanna's belongings. She hadn't taken much: a few winter clothes, a piece of jewelry, and some pictures. The first was of Anna, Hanna and Borys taken on Anna's birthday, the day of *Snow White*, the day the family knew things were changing. They looked happy nonetheless and the birthday cake with 13 candles had been delicious.

She had also taken a brooch, the one her mother wore on the day of her arrest, which she had decided to give to Anna as a 13th birthday present. It had been forgotten in the family's mad rush to leave. Hedda stroked it through the secret pocket in the handbag, where it was hidden in case she was searched by the officials. They would have liked to take a gold piece from a Jewish girl, that's for sure. It had six pointed edges in the shape of rose petals with a precious stone at the center, and it reminded Hedda of the sad story of *The Nightingale and the Rose*, in which the bird pierced his breast with a sharp thorn, turning a white rose red with the blood, for the sake of a love-sick youth. What a story! She would think only happy thoughts with this rose brooch, remembering her mother's selfless deed on that day and Anna's cheeky smile and ready laughter. The younger sister she never had.

The other photograph was of her family, Paul, Alice, Edith and herself taken in a Saarbrücken Foto Studio on Alice's 40th birthday.

Unlike the Kaleckis' birthday picture full of family fun, this was posed and stiff. Alice looked attractive, her face well made up and with a modern hair style, whilst Paul wore a well-cut suit to hide his increasing waist size. The girls showed off their new white frilled dresses, large ribbons decorating their hair. No one looked particularly happy, although they all smiled.

Hedda gently rubbed the face of her father as if he might pass through her finger and come alive to her touch. She thought of his collection of pipes, his beloved wireless, and his glasses perched on the end of his nose and wished he was with her now. He would be so proud of her efforts, arranging the emigration from Germany, away from the Führer. Paul had always known what was coming and had said so. Unlike Alice. Head in the sand, Alice. Glass half full, Alice. Every cloud has a silver lining, Alice.

Now Alice had sent Hedda a letter revealing her true colors, her real character, a letter which Hedda had watched catch fire and burn in the Klinghoffers' oven. The letter had arrived on the last day of January and was sent to a registered mailbox, the address of which Hedda had provided to the Gestapo once she had left the Kaleckis, not wanting to reveal her true location. It was dated January 5th, 1939, and Hedda was surprised by the length of time between writing and receiving; maybe Alice had thought twice before sending it given the letter's contents. It couldn't be due to the speed of the German postal service, which prided itself on next-day delivery anywhere in the country.

She had pulled the letter from the envelope, surprised that there were two pages instead of the usual one. She had wondered if there was more news.

Dear Hedda

I cannot put into words or express how I am feeling as I hold your last letter in my shaking hands. I am shocked, upset, and grief-stricken. I cry myself to sleep and, when I wake in the early hours of the morning, my tears start to fall. How could you do this to your dear mother? The mother who birthed you, fed you, raised you, and gave you everything your heart desired, the best life had to offer?

What have I done to deserve this undaughterly behavior? I am a victim here in this terrible place, and now I am even more a victim as you abandon me when I need you most.

How does this show gratitude? How does this show love? I think you must not love me to be able to leave me here. Is that the right thing to do?

It is not. First my husband leaves me on my own and now you.

I have spoken to others here and shown them your letter. They have used some terrible words to describe you, words I will not repeat. But they agree that no daughter would treat a mother in this fashion, unless the daughter is cruel and wicked.

You do not know or understand what it has been like for me here. You have no idea. My letters are read, and I am not allowed to say everything that I would like to say. But I will tell you that since my last letter, three women in my sleeping quarters have become ill and died. They were young and healthy. I am not well, and I think it may be me that follows them. I cough and cough and can hardly eat. There are no doctors and when the doctor does arrive, she says there is nothing wrong with me!

Why did you not do something when they told you my permit was declined? Why did you not challenge this? If the positions had been reversed, I would have fought for you. I would have told them, "No, that can't be right, you must give my daughter a permit." But you said nothing. You are a coward.

So what will happen now? You will forget me while you start your new life somewhere fancy in England. I hope you're happy. Think about your mother, wasting away when you are taking tea with your fancy new friends. You have locked me up and thrown away the key.

Your ever-loving mother, Alice

Although the letter was burnt and gone, the words and phrases were seared in her memory, and she felt the injustice as a physical pain deep in her stomach. How could her mother say such hurtful things? Her mother had no idea of what Hedda had experienced, day in and day out: the threatening conversations, the queuing, the waiting, the cold, the fear. Whilst she sat in some comfortable labor camp, surrounded by other women with no responsibilities, no paperwork to organize, Hedda spent every waking moment planning their future escape, however challenging that turned out to be.

Well, maybe her mother was right. Maybe, if she was un-daughterly, she would become an un-daughter. What was stopping her? Why should she bother to fight for her mother's freedom if her mother clearly despised her? For the first time, Hedda felt powerful. Her mother's future was firmly in the palm of her hand and if she closed that hand her mother was trapped, unable to escape, and if she opened her hand, her mother could walk free. The German officers were not Alice's prison guards. She was.

Close, open, close...

She would arrive in London, met by Sadie Simmons, her future employer, start work and get in touch with Betty: "Oh Hedda, how wonderful to meet you after all this time! We are going to have such fun together! But how is your mother?"

"My mother? Oh, she died in the camp. So sad. Pneumonia, they said. Tragic."

"Oh, that's terrible!"

"Yes, it is. But now, no time to lose. You must show me the sights of London, starting with Buckingham Palace. I've been waiting so long to meet the King of England."

Hedda played the imagined conversation in her mind, painting a vivid picture of her new life on foreign soil without her mother in tow; pleasurable thoughts, until the train's steady rolling and rumbling over the tracks lulled her into a dream-filled sleep.

"Wake up, young lady, wake up. This train terminates at Oostende. Everybody out."

It took several moments for Hedda to work out where she was

before gathering her belongings and stumbling onto the platform. It was dark, with a strong wind blowing, as she pulled on her gloves and walked out of the station in search of signs for the ferry to Dover.

It was about midnight when the huge ferry, crammed with cargo and drivers, pulled away from the port. Three loud toots signaled its departure, followed by the sound of chains clattering against the side of the ship. The wind had blown itself out since Hedda had stood on the dock watching the smaller boats tossing from side to side. It was a relief. She had never liked boat rides after a stormy trip on the North Sea, when she had felt sick for days after. She didn't want to arrive in England and immediately take to her bed.

On arriving at the ferry port, she had queued for a ticket. The Relief Organisation for German Jews had given her enough money to get herself across the Channel and buy a bus ticket into London, with a little left over for some food and drink. She had eaten a dry Belgian roll filled with some flabby cheese, all that was left at a miserable food counter next to the ticket booth. Another hurdle jumped – ticket bought and England in sight. Well, not yet. She had heard about the white cliffs of Dover, but they were still many miles away and anyway, it was dark with nothing to be seen but the black water ahead. Too tired to explore the boat, Hedda found herself a seat on the top part of the ship below the open deck, took out one of her two books, and was hoping to drift off to sleep for the duration of the journey. She was exhausted, traveling since the early morning, after an emotional goodbye to the Klinghoffers. She had said her unemotional goodbyes to the city too. It was not one she expected to return to.

Other passengers were dotted about, mainly working men in overalls and flat caps and thick black jackets. As she turned to the right page, a noisy group of two women and three men entered the deck from the opposite end and crossed to a small, raised platform. They proceeded to unpack a guitar, a set of two drums, and a trumpet. From what Hedda could see in the dim light, one of the men was blowing down the neck of the trumpet, whilst the other two were chatting with the women, who were adorning themselves with some Spanish looking headwear and changing into dance shoes. As she watched them, the taller woman caught her eye: she moved her head from side to side in such a way, tipping it back in obvious laughter, touching her hair with both hands, that Hedda felt a flip-flop in her chest, deep in her heart. She knew who it was. It was her sister, Edith, who had joined the dance troupe that had sailed to South America. This was unbelievable, incredible, too much of a coincidence, that here on this midnight crossing, miles from Buenos Aires, miles from home, she would find her older sister, about to perform for the exhausted passengers.

A working man in his fifties, smelling of tobacco and diesel, had sat down beside Hedda while she watched the preparations for the flamenco. She hadn't noticed him, so lost was she in watching Edith adjusting the mantilla. "Alright, love?" he asked.

Hedda didn't hear him.

"Alright, love? You look like you've seen a ghost," he continued.

Hedda turned to him. "*Das ist meine Schwester da drüben,*" she said.

"Sorry, love, nicht sprechen German," he said.

Hedda mustered her English. "That's my sister over there." She pointed at the tallest woman, now bending over and tying the laces of her shoes. "She's a dancer and a singer."

The working man howled with laughter. "Your sister? You been on the boozer tonight? Had too much of that Belgian beer? That's unlikely, I'd say. Doubt if they speak a word of the Hun. They're from Chorley, they are." He chuckled some more.

"Chorley?" Hedda repeated, a strange word which she hadn't come across before.

"Chorley, Lancashire. Chorley cakes? The Magpies? It's a place in England, not far from Manchester. Heard of that?"

Hedda had heard of it, and now understood that this Chorley was a place name.

"They've been doing the crossing for about five years now. It's a great act they put on. They tour the theaters in France. Built up quite a following. No more Spanish though than I'm an Arab," he explained.

Hedda watched as the guitarist picked up the instrument and started strumming it, followed by the trumpeter playing a pretty Spanish melody and the drummer keeping time on the two drums. The Chorley woman, who Hedda could now see was not Edith, began dancing to the music, twirling her hands in the air and clicking some castanets. The more she danced the less she resembled Hedda's sister. She was more elegant, more graceful. Had it been a trick of the light? Tiredness? Or a desperate, yearning wish to be in the company of her family, someone she had grown up with, who knew her name? The other woman got up and started singing a Spanish folk song with a remarkably good voice given the hour.

"What are you doing on the midnight crossing, love? All alone? You should be careful. I'm Fred, Fred Cooper," he said, reaching out a hand to shake hers.

"I'm Hedda, Hedda Israel," she replied, shaking his hand back.

"Ahh, you're one of those escapees, you are. Now I get it. There's been loads about you in the papers. Lots of people say you're coming over and taking the jobs and the houses. Me, I don't think that, love. The more the merrier, I say. Live and let live, that's my motto."

Hedda wasn't listening though. She was thinking about her sister. Edith would never have found herself on some freezing ferry on a dark night with only a small suitcase and handbag. The only image Hedda could bring into focus was of color and light, of bunting and flowers, sunshine and champagne, with Edith in the middle surrounded by young men and envious admirers. Edith would never have bathed Paul's pustular back or washed out the stained bandages, dug the beds in the cemetery when the ground was solid with winter frost, scrubbed the kitchen floors until they shone, queued and queued and queued in the pouring rain, and then queued again when the snow fell in hard clumps.

Edith wouldn't have done any of those things; but Hedda would. And she had. Hedda was not her sister. She did the right thing; she always had. She made the hard choices, guided by a strong sense of right and wrong even if that meant she would suffer. And at that moment, she knew that on the day after her arrival in England, she would be joining another queue somewhere in London, to secure the release of her mother from the camp at Lichtenburg. The fantasy of starting a new life without Alice had been a delight while it lasted, but that was what it was, a fantasy.

PHOTOS

Poster of Shop.jpg

Alice, Paul and Ruth on holiday

Edith, Alice, Paul and Ruth

Fun at the beach

Ruth in centre with London friends

Josef (Leon) Meller

Ruth and Josef

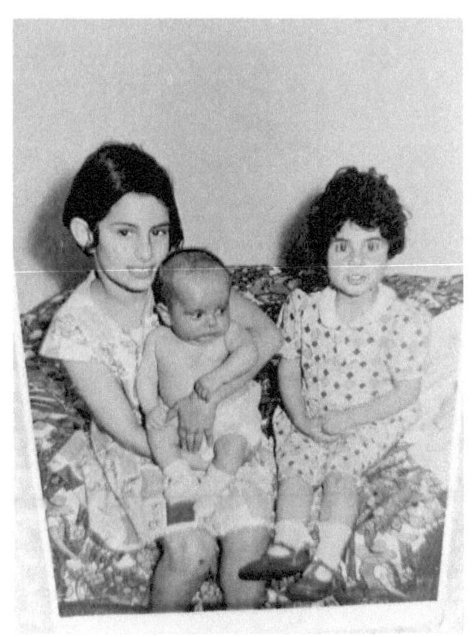

Claudia,Sonia and Rachel

Ruth, Rachel, Alice and Sonia

Sonia jumping for joy

PART II

14

STRANGER IN A STRANGE LAND

UPTON PARK, LONDON

February–July 1939

Hedda woke up, alerted by the rattling of the motor engine not far from where she drowsed, in and out of early morning sleep. Three hours before, the ferry had spilled her off into freezing fog and thick darkness at the port of Dover. She had found the coach station from where she would catch the first bus to Victoria to be met by Sadie Simmons, her future employer. A small group of travelers in thick coats carrying work bags and suitcases were beginning to board the Greenline. She reached into her pocket to feel for the ticket that would get her into London. Still there. She picked up her belongings and joined the line.

Hedda could see nothing from the window of the bus. She sat at the back, her head resting against the cold glass, and thought about the last 24 hours over land and sea, not quite believing she was out of Germany, out of reach of the Gestapo, the Nazis and the man himself, and on her way to the safety of a new family. To London. Big Ben, Buckingham Palace, the Tower. Just 19, Hedda thought she had grown ten years in the last year.

127

Morning had definitely broken by the time the bus pulled into Victoria Coach Station., She stumbled into the icy air along with the others, who strode off purposefully, knowing exactly where to go. Hedda stood fixed to the spot, looking around for someone who might be Sadie Simmons. Seeing no one who matched her description, she made her way away from the parked buses and towards what looked like a waiting area judging by the worn benches and seated figures.

"Hedda! Hedda? Is that you?"

A high-pitched voice shouted in her direction just as she reached an empty seat. "Hedda, wait! I'm Polly. Polly Simmons. I'm Sadie's daughter," the woman said breathlessly, still running towards Hedda. "You're coming to live with us. Mum couldn't leave the house this morning. She said to say sorry." She paused and waited. "You do speak English, don't you?"

Hedda's English seemed to have disappeared into the early morning gloom. This young rough-looking woman, with thick dark curls surrounding her yellowish skin, spoke in such a peculiar way that Hedda wondered if she was speaking some strange regional dialect like the Austrian country people she had encountered on family holidays. She realized she'd only ever heard English spoken by a German; even the man on the boat had tried out his broken German when he realized where she was from. This Polly spoke like a true Englander. It sounded funny and awful at the same time, like she suffered from a terrible cold.

"Hello," Hedda said to Polly who was towering over her, breathing deeply.

"Yes, it's me. Hedda. I... am... very... pleased to meet you," she replied slowly, trying out her English like a baby taking her first tentative steps.

"Pleased to meet you, too," Polly said, offering one of her huge hands for Hedda to shake. "Shall I take one of your cases?" she added. Not waiting for a reply, she picked one up and strode off.

Hedda followed, noticing brightly colored advertising posters and transport signs and people moving in every direction, down steps, up steps, forming queues at ticket windows, buying newspapers. Polly marched through them all, guiding Hedda to a moving staircase that led deep into the underground station. Victoria Station. District Line. The Upminster train.

With a loud shoosh of smoky noise, the train pulled away into a dark tunnel. People stood holding hanging straps, swaying with the train like seaweed. No one spoke. Standing men read large newspapers, whilst women sat on the rows of seats staring ahead, lost in thoughts. Every few minutes the train stopped, and some left whilst others entered. Hedda was relieved that she and Polly had seats beside the window where she could look out, although there was nothing to see in the black tunnels other than her own reflection. Hedda struggled to understand the strange vowels and words that the woman uttered but thankfully the noise of the train drowned out Polly's attempts to chat.

At Whitechapel, the train emerged from the tunnel and ran level with houses and gardens. A train that had become a tram, she thought, this was magic! Then it passed pocket-handkerchief gardens backing onto houses crammed together that reminded Hedda of the allotments she had seen in the suburbs of Saarbrücken when she was a child. Washing lines crossed scrubby patches of grass, and net curtains flapped in the breeze, masking small upper windows. The journey seemed to go on forever and she wondered where she was being taken – this must be further than London by now? She tried to decipher the strange station names proudly presented in clear lettering encased in round red circles: Stepney Green, Mile End, Bow Road, on and on, West Ham, Plaistow.

"We get off here," said Polly, as the train pulled into the place called Upton Park. They exited the station that looked more like a house, turned left and left again, and were soon walking beside a long terraced row of dirty brick buildings with front doors on the pavements.

"We're here. Welcome to your new home," Polly said as she knocked loudly on the door and an aproned woman opened it, smiling widely.

"You must be exhausted, love," said Sadie Simmons, the

matriarch. Sadie was a woman who'd had a tough life from the look of the sagging skin hanging from her cheeks and neck. Her eyes were surrounded by a thousand wrinkles and an overall veneer of slow decay.

She gave Hedda a plate of fried eggs with a slice of bread, and watched as the new arrival tore off small bits of the tasteless spongy loaf to dip in the yellow yolk. Sadie also spoke in those strangled vowels accompanied by a thudding nasal quality. Hedda wondered how she would ever manage more than basic exchanges.

"I am very happy to be here. Thank you."

"It's the least we can do to help. When we saw those adverts in the papers asking for people to give jobs to young girls to get you out, we didn't hesitate, we didn't. Not for a minute. We all thought that would be a good thing to do, didn't we? Got to look after our own."

Sadie had been joined by her two sons: Lenny, 12 years old, short, round and spot-covered, and Colin, 15 years old, taller, less round but spottier. Polly, the eldest of the family children, sat with them at the kitchen table as Hedda ate. The children all nodded in agreement with their mother. There was no Mr. Simmons; Hedda didn't ask, and Sadie didn't explain.

"And mum said, an extra pair of hands around the house, gotta be good," Lenny said.

His mother scowled at him.

"An extra mouth to feed, she said, didn't yer, mum?" added Colin. He stared at Hedda in that way an adolescent boy might do, horrified and curious at the same time. Hedda detected a smell of body odor coming from his direction and tried not to show her reaction.

"Shut up, boys," said Sadie. "We're delighted to have you here. We've got a nice little room for you off the back, and you can help in the shop and at the market. We make and sell children's clothes from the front room, so lots of comings and goings, lots of customers, lots of nice people. They'll like you, I know they will, and you'll like them. We know how to have a laugh. And Polly can't wait to show you around a bit more."

Poll nodded and Hedda believed her.

"The boys wrote down a list of the jobs for you to do. Thought it might be easier that way."

"Thank you. That will help," Hedda said. She wondered if washing their smelly clothes was top of that list. She had no idea what was involved in domestic service. She hadn't once considered what the staff in her old household had done. They drove Paul's beloved Mercedes and helped with the cooking, yes, but did they do all the washing as well? She supposed they must have done; there were no magical elves from the fairy tales to help.

"And it will be ten shillings a week for you to spend how you like, paid on a Friday, if that suits?"

"Cor, more than I get," Colin whispered under his breath and glared at Hedda.

Hedda remembered the rate specified in the Home Office paperwork was 15 shillings a week, the official amount set down for domestic workers coming into the country. She opened her mouth to say something and then thought better of it – she didn't want to appear ungrateful.

"So love, no time like the present. If you've finished your food," Sadie was already removing the plate and placing it beside the other dirty things, "you might as well get going. "I've got to get back. I've left Jean in charge as well as minding her own. Hope nothin's got nicked! Thought you could have a go at the bed sheets, they could do with a change. Those boys! The wash tub is out the back, use hot water from the kettle. We keep the scrubbing brush, soap, and board in the box beside the tub."

Polly followed her mother out and the two boys remained for a few seconds studying this new strange species before Colin shouted, "C'mon Lens. Better see what Uncle Dave's up to today." They ran out, leaving Hedda to the list and the washing.

The next day, following precise directions from Polly regarding which bus to catch, Hedda arrived at Bloomsbury House, High

Holborn, home of the German Jewish Aid Committee. It was Sunday – her one day off from domestic duties and a chance to get going with the main goal of securing employment for Alice. Hedda had slept blissfully, her first proper sleep in days, as much down to physical exhaustion as delightful relief.

She explained her mother's situation to the sympathetic officials who were located in similar grand offices to the Berlin Gestapo and who all spoke perfect German.

They issued her a booklet entitled "Helpful Information and Guidance for Every Refugee."

Despite the damp air, Hedda wanted to read the advice immediately and searched for somewhere to sit, eager to learn everything possible about her new home. The booklet was written in English and German, but Hedda covered up the latter and attempted the former, delighted she had forgotten less than she first thought. Sitting in Russell Square on a cold park bench, not painted yellow, she read:

Refrain from speaking German in public places; do not talk in a loud voice; do not read German newspapers in public; do not criticize government regulations; do not join any political organization and... spend your time immediately in learning the English language and its correct pronunciation.

She wondered how long it would be before she became attuned to the strange accents of Sadie and Polly, of Colin and Lenny, who spoke in ugly voices that hurt her ears. But not as much as the voice of the Führer, of course. His voice made her sweat and tremble.

Leaving Russell Square, she wandered in the opposite direction from where she had come, determined to make the most of her first day in London, England. The time was her own, hers to enjoy, she was free to do exactly what she chose to do.

The street she now found herself in led to an enormous gate flanked by tall iron railings, and she wondered if she had arrived at Buckingham Palace and would see the king. In front of her was a giant entrance fronted by wide steps, tall Greek columns that would have touched the sky if it weren't for the pediment of sculpted figures that sat on top of them. People of all ages were entering the building, families with children in tow, groups of smiling young people, and serious-looking individuals, so it couldn't be the palace. They wouldn't be allowing all those people in; she felt stupid for even thinking it.

She wished she had a companion with whom to share her impressions of this wondrous place. Maybe her father? Maybe Walter? She thought about him more often than she liked, remembering their kisses in the park, and wishing she had enjoyed them more. She must have been too young for that sort of thing. Now she would appreciate his tender embraces. Setting romantic thoughts aside she walked through the gate, up the steps and entered the British Museum.

There was too much to take in as she wandered through the galleries. Ancient artifacts from every continent and from every century were displayed in glass cabinets. She watched the visitors poring over the cases, discussing an object's history, its beauty, or trying to impress each other with knowledge and information. How could one museum hold so much treasure? She had never seen anything like this in Saarbrücken or Berlin. It would take more than a year to see all the items on show. She lingered over the small Egyptian figures, who were depicted baking bread, brewing beer, and rowing boats. They were beautifully carved, reflecting the daily life of the time, and she thought that if they made a figurine of her domestic chores, it would look rather similar, just with more clothes on!

Standing outside the huge museum doors, Hedda realized that she must eat something before she passed out with hunger. Where next? Impressing herself with her ability to negotiate the public transport system, she found a bright red bus that took her closer to the Thames. She had seen dreamy paintings of bridges that straddled light-reflecting water, painted at sunrise and at sunset, and she wanted to see this river for herself. It was a shade of muddy brown, all shapes and sizes of vessels moored and moving, but it was still recognizable as the Thames, not the Spree. It seemed relaxed and disorganized, unlike the Spree's clean efficiency.

She found a small tea shop at a place called the Aldwych and bought a mug of tea and a currant bun. As the booklet advised, she spoke English in a quiet voice. She thought to herself: I am here. I have arrived. I'm on my own but that does not matter. There is nothing I need to be afraid of. The men are not here. They don't know where I am. I am safe.

She was filled with a quiet joy, one she had not felt for many years, not since she was a child of eight playing at dressing up dolls with Edith by Lake Walchen on a warm summer's day. A blue sky streaked with puff-ball clouds, the sound of clicking crickets and drowsy bumble bees, her parents sitting in deckchairs chatting and laughing, the maid shaking out the red checkered rug ready for the picnic of rolls and meats, cakes and *Apfelsaft* and Mutti and Vati letting the children sip the too sweet white wine. The memory was glorious.

By half past four the sky was nearly dark. Hedda's mood had changed again and now she was feeling alone and scared. From Waterloo Bridge, she had watched the boats and the people drifting by, and had enjoyed her invisibility while observing the loving couples, arms intertwined, before the grind of a new working week. Now she felt sorry for herself. The joy had vanished, replaced by a sense of cold nervous dread. She was unsure how to find her way home. London was huge. Upton Park was a long way away. She knew no one. And no one knew her. Or cared.

Just after seven o'clock, Hedda knocked on the door of the Simmons' house in Queen's Road and Colin opened it. "We was wondering where you'd got to," he said as he closed the door behind her. "Mum was saying, I bet the poor girl's got herself lost, or something worse..." He sniggered.

Polly appeared from the small front room. There was a woman singing, "Sally, Sally" on the wireless; it sounded dreadful. Surely they weren't listening to that through choice?

"Blimey, Hedda. You gave us all a bit of a fright, you did. Mum's down the road with Jean right now. We've all had our supper.

There's some left out for you, just needs warming up on the stove. Did you find the place okay?"

"Yes, I did. I'm really very sorry that you all were..." Hedda paused, fishing in her mental English dictionary for the right word. "Vorried, sorry, worried, about me."

"Oh, that's alright, Heddi. Can I call you that? Heddi?"

"Heddi Teddy!" said Lenny, dressed in his pajamas, standing on the stairs eager not to miss out on the conversation.

"Oi! Get back to bed! You've got school tomorrow," said Polly, and Lenny scampered back upstairs, groaning at his big sister.

When Hedda entered the kitchen, she saw a saucepan on the stove, presumably with her portion of the evening stew. She also saw plates and forks, knives and bowls piled high. Her permit was did say, after all: Domestic Servant.

Four months later, Hedda's confidence had grown considerably despite the amount of work expected of her. She enjoyed helping at the Saturday market stalls, her ear adjusting to the English way of speaking and she'd even mastered some of the Cockney rhyming slang. Jean's husband often made up new rhymes to tease and trick her:

"Ere, Heddi, what do you think a Whatsall is, then? What's all the fuss? A London Bus!" and he would bend over chortling at his own wit.

Hedda helped sell the children's clothes and other items that came their way, sometimes silk stockings, sometimes bags and scarves, and her language improved as she felt herself becoming one of their community. This area was filled with Jews, most of whom were English by birth but whose parents had traveled from Eastern Europe, from Russia or Poland, or further.

What would her mother think of these ordinary folk? She would surely be looking down her nose at their uncultured ways, at their poor music choices. Gracie Fields? That dreadful singer on the wireless with her squeaky, scratchy voice singing popular songs? Alice would not approve, she thought.

Hedda enjoyed the banter and the chat with Sadie's customers who visited the house, and with the traders and the shoppers at the market. She allowed the younger men to flirt with her, receiving their compliments with a smile and giving kind words back. She didn't accept any invitations for a "day or night out," not wanting to be distracted from her visits to Bloomsbury House. In any case, she was too tired to consider anything other than an early turn-in each evening. The Simmons were a friendly family who knew how to laugh and how to enjoy themselves, but were they filthy! Dropped handkerchiefs studded with the boys' nose-pickings, dirty sheets and clothes covered in the grime and dirt of London living, resulted in endless washing. The saucepans and dishes were hers to deal with, even on her day off.

On a warm July day, sitting in the tiny backyard on a chair pulled from the house to enjoy the summer sunshine, Hedda was reading the *Daily Mirror*. It had few good words to report on Hitler and his increasing aggression, and Hedda formed the impression that people were finally waking up to his terrible ways. Despite the promise made to Mr. Chamberlain nearly a year ago, there was now serious talk of war. She needed to get her mother out. But even with thoughts of Alice stuck in the camp, Hedda managed to spot an item advertising a performance of *Aida* at Covent Garden. Her favorite! She loved the beautiful music, but most of all she adored the extravagant costumes and the scenes of Ancient Egyptian tombs and giant statues. She could take Polls with her and introduce her to beautiful singing, far from the grating Gracie.

That night, in darkness, Hedda left the house, walked up Commercial Road, and caught the night bus all the way to the Aldwych. From there she walked to Covent Garden Opera House where she joined the early morning queue already forming on the pavement for the release of day tickets. Fortunately, the warm day had turned into a warm night and Hedda enjoyed the anticipation of the doors being thrown open at seven o'clock to the opera-hungry men and women. She put her spare pullover carefully down on the pavement, leant against the wall and shut her eyes, bag tightly pressed against her lap.

A gentle shake on her shoulder pulled her out of sleep. "Two tickets for the Gods, please," Hedda said as she handed over two shillings to the woman in the ticket booth. Two tickets to see Aida with Polls that very evening.

The "Triumphal March" was triumphal, the brass instruments blasting out the military melody and when the chorus entered from all sides of the stage, Hedda thought she would swoon. The costumes and the layers of sound and rhythm were entrancing, and she was transported to an ancient land of hopeless love where she became the enslaved princess.

Polls had fallen fast asleep 20 minutes into the second act and when she woke, the cast were taking their bows. "Thank Gawd, that's all over," she said, but Hedda didn't mind.

Covent Garden. London. England. Hedda was falling in love with the city.

It was the end of July. Hedda returned from Bloomsbury House in a state of great happiness, mixed with fear and dread. Despite her age, an employer living in North London had offered her mother a position as a domestic servant, and a visa and work permit were being organized. Alice could be released from Ravensburg, her third camp, and would be sent to Saarbrücken to receive a sheaf of documents from the Nazi authorities: an exit permit, a certificate of good conduct, another document stating all taxes had been paid, and her passport stamped with a J. She would also collect her transit visa, her work permit and her entry documents sent by the English. Then she would travel to Dover and onto London and Hedda would meet her mother at Victoria Bus Station, just as she had been met by Polls. Like daughter, like mother.

Hedda hadn't seen her mother for two years. She had received three apologetic letters which tried to explain her mother's previous words, blaming the terrible camp conditions for making her say things she now so deeply regretted. She was covered in eczema but would make up for everything, she promised her darling Hedda, when they were reunited. Hedda felt such relief that her mother was finally free but dreaded what Alice's arrival would mean for her new life in London.

15

NEW FRIENDS
WEST END, LONDON

September 1939

Lyons Corner House on the corner of Tottenham Court Road was full to overflowing when Hedda arrived to meet Betty. It was another beautiful early afternoon and for weeks Hedda had been excited but nervous at the thought of meeting her special friend. They had spoken once or twice from one of those strange red phone boxes and Betty had described her appearance in great detail. "I'm five foot five inches, with blonde bobbed hair. It's growing now, I've decided I want it a little longer. I'm going to wear my favorite blue dress. Well, it's more a deep, dark blue than a blue blue..."

Inside, Hedda scanned the customers: there were ladies with short blonde bobs in yellow dresses and ladies with dark longer bobs in blue dresses but no one quite fitting Betty's description. Darting waitresses wearing starched caps and black dresses covered by white square aprons moved effortlessly amongst the tables. They carried trays with pots of tea, scones, and cream cakes and Hedda thought that this was the job she wanted, instead of the drudgery of the Simmons' housework.

"Yes, can I help you?" said the Nippy who stood close to the entrance behind a wooden podium.

Hedda noticed the line of pearl buttons in two neat rows that descended the front of her dress, and the stiff cap, embroidered with the letter L, worn so proudly. The letter L. The letter J. Hedda knew which one she would rather have.

"I'm meeting a friend here, but I can't see her anywhere," she said. She tried to speak as clearly and as English as she could, ensuring her "W"s were not "V"s. She hated the look that seemed to cross some faces when they realized she was German.

"We have two upper floors as well. Would you care to look up there?" the Nippy said with a friendly smile.

An upstairs. The place was huge. Hedda took the stairs to the next floor and heard light music drifting down, a violin, a piano, maybe a cello to accompany her upward journey. In front of her was another floor, full of crowded tables and efficient waitresses, and a group of dark-suited musicians sat on a raised podium. As Hedda searched for the blue dress and the blonde bob, she spotted a young woman standing up, clearly looking for someone. Hedda waved cautiously and the young woman waved back wildly, then twisted through the groups of diners until she reached her. She threw her arms around Hedda's neck and hugged her tightly.

"Hedda, my friend! At last! How are you? I can't believe that I'm finally meeting you! And you're meeting me!" She let out a yelp of pleasure and pulled Hedda back to the window table overlooking the street, where a handsome man got up, offering his hand to shake.

"Hedda, this is Anthony. Anthony, Hedda. This is just so exciting!"

Betty was gorgeous and she knew it. So much more lively in real life than her letters or even her telephone calls would suggest. She was a dynamo, a clockwork tin soldier, fully wound.

"Hello, Hedda," said Anthony.

He was incredibly good looking, like a film star, Hedda thought. Tall with a clear open face, regular features, and a sharp jaw. His hair was blond and flopped neatly over his forehead, ending just above piercing blue eyes. In Germany he would be heralded as a god.

"Sit down," said Betty. She signaled to a Nippy who bounded across the room in double quick time. Who could refuse this bubbly princess? "We would recommend a pot of tea and the fruit cake is delicious! Does that sound acceptable? Not too much damage to the waistline, either!"

Hedda nodded.

"A fresh pot of tea for three, please. Oh no, make that a pot for four. Viktor! Over here!" shouted Betty as she spotted a dark-haired, bespectacled young man at the top of the stairs.

The new man approached the table and Anthony stood again, shaking Viktor's hand and indicating a spare chair.

"Hedda, you need some introductions. I'm just too rude. It's all too exciting!" said Betty, not sure whether to stand or to sit. "This handsome man is Tony really, and he and I are 'special friends.'" She managed a wink at both Anthony and Hedda simultaneously. "Tony's a work friend of Peter and he should be here too. And this other handsome man is Viktor but he can speak for himself, obviously." Betty threw a wide smile at Viktor who was settling into the seat and studying the menu.

Hedda noticed Betty had perfect dimples as she smiled. She could be a film star!

"I was saying to Tony, wouldn't it be wonderful for you and Viktor to meet. You will find you have lots in common."

Viktor was fiddling with some heavy horn-rimmed glasses, not seeming to hear Betty's words.

"Viktor?"

The glass rubbing continued.

"Viktor!" she said with a little more teacherly command, "tell Hedda a bit about yourself."

Viktor's face screwed into an awkward expression.

"You know what I'm talking about. Don't be dense, darling. About why you're here, not here in the tea house, here in London."

He cleared his throat nervously and addressed no one in particular. "Well, I'm not sure what I'm meant to say or what you need to know. I'm from Vienna. Obviously a Jew. I've been over here for nearly a year and a half, thanks to Anthony who supported my work application. I'm one of the lucky ones... It's taking an age to sort out my employment. For some reason known only to the English, neither my Austrian education nor my medical training qualifies me to work in the English hospitals, so it's all taking rather a while. In fact, it seems there's a real push to stop us Austrians from taking English doctors' jobs. Did you see that recent stuff from the Medical Practitioners' Union, Tony?"

"I'm not with them on that, typical small-mindedness and protectionism. Fancy calling for strike action," Anthony said.

Hedda had no idea what they were talking about but was loving the contrast between these cultured people, who seemed so assured and grown-up, and the stall holders and street traders of Upton Park. Another world.

"We're Enemy Aliens, aren't we? Can't say it's a title that I enjoy," Viktor said, looking uncomfortable.

Betty was already impatient with the conversation's descent into politics. "Oh, stop complaining. You know it doesn't actually mean anything. It's just two silly words. Anyway, we look after you," she said. "Hedda will think you are a total grump and want to leave." She threw another of those dimpled smiles at Hedda. "He *can* be cheery, you know, he must have eaten something disagreeable last night."

Hedda wasn't really listening to Viktor's words, so taken by Betty's confidence in chatting with these men.

"It's been frustrating, we know," Anthony said, reaching across the table and taking Betty's hand in a show of support. "The thing is, Viktor's an incredibly talented doctor and it's such a shame that he can't practice yet. We're both in the same game, cardiology."

Hedda looked puzzled at the unfamiliar word.

"We look after people's hearts, except when they're broken of course."

Hedda noticed Anthony squeeze Betty's hand tighter and felt a small stab of envy.

"The hospital could jolly well do with Viktor's services."

"Tony works as a physician at King's College Hospital in Camberwell. I met him through Peter. The big brother. Must have been about six months ago." Betty tried to feign a casual indifference, but Hedda could tell Betty knew exactly when it was. "Peter's been working at the hospital for ages now. Well, at the Maudsley Hospital where he deals with the mentally ill. He's really late. Typical." With a sweet smile, Betty removed her hand from Anthony's and poured the tea recently delivered.

"And you?" said Viktor to Hedda in an effort to show a little more civility than he had so far. "How long have you been here? You're from Germany, aren't you? Your accent is a bit of a giveaway."

Hedda rather liked Viktor's direct approach.

"Betty said that your mother is here?" he continued.

Hedda could see Betty throw a look at Anthony that said: "They're finally getting on."

"Yes. My mother came over just a month ago. She was offered a job in a place called Colindale, but it was too far and she only managed it for about three weeks. She can't speak a word of English and hated the work, so she's moved to a women's hostel in King's Cross. She's not doing anything right now. I haven't seen her since that first meeting. I haven't really had the time off." From Viktor's direct gaze he appeared to be listening attentively, so Hedda continued: "And your family? Have they managed to get out?"

Viktor shook his head and cleared his throat. "They're still in Vienna – my younger brother and both my parents. They haven't given up though. They're trying to get to Palestine."

"Oh. I do hope they will. I've got an older sister, but she emigrated to Buenos Aires nearly two years ago. She did the right thing."

"I have two uncles who are in Dachau right now. They went there after the burnings and destruction. I don't know any more." Viktor looked down at his cup of tea, his thoughts on the events in November when his family members were arrested and hauled away to the camp.

"You two!" Betty said, oblivious to the grim subject matter under discussion. "I knew you'd get on. Didn't I say so, Tony?"

With Viktor's attention lost in images of beatings and broken glass, Hedda allowed herself to keep her gaze on him. She thought she rather liked him despite his gloomy conversation. He was interesting, brooding; she liked his dark, intelligent eyes, his distinctive nose, the stubble that covered his cheeks and jaw and the way his hair needed a jolly good haircut. She felt a sense of home and, for the first time since Walter, she started to imagine handholding and the sharing of intimacies.

"If my brother isn't here soon, then I say we should eat his slice of Battenberg," said Betty.

"Here's the old boy now," said Anthony as Peter crossed the room, newspaper tucked under his arm and flopped down in the empty chair saved for him.

"I am so sorry, everyone," he said, reaching across to Anthony, Viktor and Hedda in turn, shaking all hands, then getting up and planting a brotherly kiss on Betty's cheek. "I was just about to set off when the hospital called; a patient needed some urgent attention, and I just couldn't let her down. Poor girl. Suffers with delusions and is having a particularly bad time right now."

"We forgive you darling, as we always do," said Betty. "And you finally get to meet Hedda after all this time." Betty turned to Hedda. "I talk about you ceaselessly. We all think you've been so brave."

Peter turned his full attention to Hedda. Like Tony, he was another potential recruit for the perfect specimen – lean, tall, with an angular face that seemed to jut out in all directions. He smiled with a small mouth surrounded by pale freckled skin and had a marvelous display of bright red hair.

"Hello," he said. "Betty certainly has spoken a great deal about you. And about the difficulties you've faced with your mother. It sounds like you've worked very hard. You're a brave girl. Anyway, well done! You're here now. Who knows what's going to happen next? Mr Hitler certainly has ambitions to take on the world," he continued, pulling out a newspaper and making space on the table, already cluttered with teacups and half-eaten scones. "It says here," he said, reaching into a jacket pocket for his reading glasses, "that the Soviet Union's gone into Poland; the poor Poles are getting it from all sides, that's for sure."

The faces of Hanna, Borys and Anna jumped into Hedda's mind. Their swift escape back to Poland, straight into the arms of the enemy. She saw Anna, her head bent over her trigonometry textbook and arm in arm with her dear parents as they strolled through the park back from the cinema that day, and she remembered how she had longed to become a full member of their happy family.

"Don't know what took the British so long to declare war. It was obvious once he'd gone into Czechoslovakia that he wasn't going to stop," said Viktor.

"Now, now. One doesn't go into war lightly. It's a serious business. Not that I think we had any choice in the matter. But we'll get this sorted within the year, you'll see. It might take us Brits a while to come to a decision, but once we do, well, we don't mess around," Tony said.

"I wish I had your faith," mumbled Viktor.

Hedda hoped Tony was right.

The music had stopped and the musicians walked amongst the customers, pausing at tables to make inconsequential conversation and collecting requests for further melodies. Sunshine streamed through the windows, dust motes dancing in the rays, prompting Betty to say: "Let's enjoy this beautiful day while we can. Hedda, this is *your* special day. Where would you like to go next?"

They walked along Great Russell Street under a peerless sky, despite the month suggesting cooler days. Peter took the lead followed by Tony and Betty arm in arm, and Viktor and Hedda brought up the rear. On a day like this, who would think the country was at war? It all seemed so far away. Thank goodness Britain was surrounded by water, Hedda thought. And now here she was in the company of new friends on her way to the British Museum at her request and everyone's approval. The foreign girl had selected an institution which they took for granted but, that first Sunday in London, had overwhelmed her. The statues and obelisks, the antiquities and broken stone carvings: too much to see, too much to understand. Now she would view them with the eyes of a Londoner, and it would be altogether a different experience.

As they walked, Viktor and Hedda chatted quietly in German. Both had read the booklet issued to them on arrival. Viktor's accent was unmistakably Viennese, a fact probably lost on Betty and Tony and Peter, in the same way that Hedda wouldn't be able to distinguish a Scotsman from an Irishman. They talked about that November night and the aftermath, sharing the horrors of the burning synagogues, the men paraded through the streets for onlookers to scream vile abuse at, others beaten, arrested, rounded up, and sent to unspeakable places. They spoke of the stampede to leave and how hard that had been, with the endless papers, the handing over of their property, and the humiliating *Reichsfluchtsteuer*, the tax paid to the Nazis to exit the countries that would otherwise murder them. The chat was easy and with every step Hedda felt more comfortable; she liked the way he phrased his sentences as if choosing the precise word, and the way he turned his head to check Hedda's reactions. She felt that stirring deep inside.

That first day in London, she had watched enviously as young people thronged through the museum's doors eager to soak up the past and now here she was, a member of this noisy happy group. If she looked hard enough, she wondered if she could spot that other Hedda amongst the visitors, standing there watching her new self.

Vast heads of Egyptian pharaohs stared straight ahead as they walked through the Great Hall. How did those heads ever arrive in one piece all the way from the deserts where they had stood for thousands of years? Like her and Viktor they were immigrants. But maybe not eager ones, she thought; no time to say goodbye to the ghost kings and queens deep in the sand-carved underground, uprooted from their homes and thrust into awkward positions to be gawked at by foreigners.

"We must show you the mummies. See how they compare to your mummy," giggled Betty, who had joined Viktor and Hedda gazing at the Rosetta Stone, trying to make sense of the typewritten information on the sign that looked more ancient than the stone itself.

They climbed the stairs at the end of the gallery and entered a smaller hall filled with perfectly preserved Egyptian artifacts, wooden boats and model houses, carved fishermen, and pots and bowls. There at the end were the mummy cases, painted in blues, pinks, and greens and covered in magic eyes and hieroglyphs. How had these people achieved all this beauty and craftsmanship so long ago?

"Those Egyptians knew a thing or two about the art of preservation."

It was Peter's clear English tones, not Viktor's Viennese accent. In the museum, she had seen Peter and Tony chatting away, probably work-talk, so was surprised to find him standing right beside her.

"*Ja, Ich glaube du hast recht,*" [I think you're right] said Hedda, lost in her Egyptian reverie.

"*Die Ägypter waren sehr intelligente, ausgezeichnete Ärzte,*" [The Egyptians were very intelligent, excellent doctors] replied Peter.

Hedda turned to him, amazed. "You speak German?" she asked. "And really well!"

"Thank you, but certainly not well. Is '*ausgezeichnete*' the right word? It's certainly a bit of a mouthful to say." He laughed.

She noticed the smile before the laugh, his whole face crinkling into competing lines. "It is," she said, and they walked slowly along the neatly arranged mummy cases, plucked from their graves and now waiting for the approval of their visitors. She felt she should speak again as he had made the effort to engage her in conversation.

"How do you speak German so well?" she asked him.

"That's very kind of you to say," he said as they paused in front of a particularly ornate gilded mask on a wooden coffin. "I took it as an additional subject during my medical studies. The fields of psychology and psychiatry are peppered with eminent Austrians and Germans. Of course, the most famous chap of all is your

Sigmund Freud. Or Viktor's, I should say. It's useful to know some German and to be able to read essays in the original language. Of course, my understanding is completely basic and when I say read, I'm talking about the essay title and the author's name. I don't get much beyond that."

He laughed again. Hedda formed the impression that Peter must be *ausgezeichnet* with his patients and remembered the kindness of Walter's doctor mother. She imagined his patients immediately improving under his warm and gentle care. How could they be depressed with him around?

"Look, for some reason this golden pharaoh puts me in mind of a particularly delicious glass of something. Strange how the brain makes connections, don't you think? Time for us all to partake of a late afternoon tipple. What do you say?"

Hedda nodded yes, she agreed. It seemed like a magical suggestion. He walked towards the others who were studying a row of canopic jars and discussing which organs went were.

"The liver and the heart," said Betty.

"Not the heart," said Tony. "As a cardiologist, I think I know better! Never argue with a heart doctor," he said, grabbing her round the middle and planting a delightful kiss straight on her lips.

Hedda felt herself redden and was glad when Peter spoke up: "Chaps, I think it's about time we took our new friend to one of our wonderful drinking houses. I say the Museum Tavern, nice and close by and where another of your compatriots used to drink."

Hedda looked puzzled.

"He's talking about Karl Marx," Viktor said. "We're not the first Enemy Aliens in the country, that's for sure."

Hedda was delighted by the dark interior of the saloon bar where she now sat, clutching a glass of sweet cider, even better than her childhood *Apfelsaft*. She'd tried a few watery beers on a Saturday night with Sadie and Polly, but this was much nicer. Wooden panels and stained-glass windows surrounded her and a beautiful fireplace, obviously not yet lit on this warm day, nestled in one corner. An endlessly long and shiny counter covered in mats and glasses completed the scene of English conviviality.

The friends sat at a small table on wooden chairs and a worn leather banquette and conversation flowed, from the doctors' demanding work to Betty's Chelsea employment, to war and the preparations now taking place in London. Children were leaving for safe homes away from German bombs, and they were all relieved not to be the ones waving goodbye to darling offspring. Peter and Tony were on to their second double whiskeys, which smelt horrible to Hedda's untutored nose. Viktor was sticking with a pale ale, and as the second glass of sweet cider took effect, Hedda grew more confident in joining in the chat.

"My job is not very nice," she said, the conversation having turned back to work.

"Can't be much fun, having to clean up other people's mess, that's for sure," Betty said.

"They're really not very clean. And they leave everything for me to do. When I get home this evening, all their dirty dishes will be waiting for me. They wouldn't think to wash them up themselves. It's like I'm their servant..." Hedda realized the ridiculousness of her last statement. "Well, I *am* their servant, aren't I. That's all I'm allowed to do. My permit says domestic servant."

"Poor Hedda," said Betty.

"At least you *can* work," said Viktor.

Hedda chose to ignore his last comment. "I'm not sure about the older boy. When I was in his bedroom that smells terrible, like of stinky French cheese..." She stopped and they all laughed. "Anyway, I was trying to change the bedding, and he brushed past me with his hand and..." She stopped, embarrassed by the memory of the incident.

"And what? We're all intrigued," said Tony.

"His hand touched my behind, and I'm sure it wasn't an accident!" Hedda took a large gulp of her drink.

"You should be flattered that you are attracting the attentions of a younger man," said Peter.

"Peter! I'm so sorry. My brother says the most silly things. I wouldn't take it too seriously. The poor boy has probably never taken a girl out and you *are* very pretty."

"He wasn't going for her pretty face," roared Peter.

"That's enough!" Betty meant it.

"Have you thought about finding another job?" Viktor asked, as embarrassed by Peter's ribaldry as Betty was.

"No, not really. I've not really been looking."

Viktor took out the crumpled newspaper he had been carrying around all day, the *Jewish Chronicle*, and turned to the small ads. His finger traced a slow line down the small box advertisements requesting domestic help. "Here. What about this one?" His finger stayed put on three lines of text below the "Situations Vacant" header: *Responsible Person wanted for Household where Wife is Unwell; all Household Duties, including care of Daughter of 8 years old.*"

"Well, what do you think?" asked Peter. Everyone was looking at Hedda expectantly.

"Oh, I don't know…"

"You don't want another cheeky pinch on the rear end from your child admirer, do you?" Peter added. "Look. No time like the present. There's a phone box just outside. Let's give it a go."

Before she could say no, Peter stood up, draining the last of the whiskey, grabbed the paper at the same time, and was maneuvering Hedda outside.

"Read out the number," he said and when a man's voice answered, he inserted some coins into the phone slots and said to the voice on the end of the line: "I've got a young lady here who is very interested in the role you advertised in the Jewish Chronicle."

Hedda heard a tinny male voice at the other end of the line saying the job was still available.

"I can vouch for her and I'm a doctor friend. She's standing beside me. Would you like to speak to her?" Without waiting, Peter thrust the phone at Hedda who spoke into the mouthpiece. "Hello?" she said quietly.

The man, Herman, explained that his wife, only 36 years old, was in a wheelchair crippled with arthritis. He worked in a sausage factory in Aldgate, and they had just bought a house in Kenton that needed a bit of work doing to it. Hedda had no idea where that was. Close to Upton Park? Near Chelsea? Not far from Camberwell? The job was hers if she wanted it. The pay would be 17 shillings and sixpence a week.

While the man was talking, Peter watched Hedda, trying to read her response. From her nods, coupled with her small smiles, he decided the job must be suitable. "Tell him you'll take it," he said.

Noticing Peter had already taken out a small notebook and pen, she said: "Please may I hand you back to my friend?" and returned the phone to him. Lodging the handpiece under his chin, he scribbled down a few words and numbers and Hedda, slightly squiffy from the sweet cider, had a new job.

***

She walked in through the front door of the Simmons' and, as expected, there was a pile of unwashed crockery and cutlery stacked up beside the sink. She took off her coat, placed it on the back of one of the kitchen chairs, and started to boil some water. Music was coming from the front room and Hedda could hear loud chatter and laughter.

"Hedda! You're home! How was your day? What was Betty like? Tell us all!" Sadie said, appearing in the doorway.

Hedda continued to scrape the plates, stacking them ready for a wash. "Yes. Good. It was a wonderful day. Thank you."

"Oh, what a treat. So pleased for you. Anyway, I wanted to tell you, it's going to be busy next week. The Curtis family have put in a large order for winter trousers. I think they want to get themselves sorted before the weather starts to take a turn, so I'll need you on the sewing machine first thing tomorrow. Your sewing's really improved!"

And it had, Hedda thought. Now she could sew in straight lines and zigzags, she could attach buttons and press studs, she was able to stitch and unstitch. All for ten shillings a week. Hedda picked up the last of the pans and sunk it into the depths of the soapy water. Then without looking up she said: "Sadie, I've been offered a job." The pan was taking all her attention.

"You what?" Sadie said, her heavy frame shifting into the kitchen from the doorway.

Hedda scrubbed at the pan with renewed determination. "I've been offered another job, working for a man in a new part of London. His wife is crippled so she can't help with housework." Her voice was quiet but she knew Sadie had heard her. She waited for her employer's response. Nothing.

"I've accepted it," she said. She pulled her soapy hands out of the sink and looked round. There was Sadie leaning on the table, her face tomato-red with anger.

"Is that what you were really up to today? Going behind our backs like we were nobodies! You ungrateful cow!" Sadie shouted. "After all we've done for you. If it wasn't for us, you'd still be in Germany. We got you out, don't you forget that!" She was towering over Hedda, breathing her sour breath. Her shouting had alerted the rest of the family, and Polly, Lennie, and Colin ran in to see what the fuss was about. They were used to their mother flying off the handle so just to be safe they remained at a distance.

"I know. I am sorry. I can stay for as long as you think best. Help you with the Curtis order?" Hedda hadn't felt quite so scared since the day the Gestapo listened to her telephone call with Walter.

"Oh no. Forget that. You're not welcome. You're not bloody welcome. You can leave tomorrow. Ungrateful German cow." Sadie turned and flounced out, trailed by the children.

When they were safely back in the front room, she carried on with her work. She poured more boiling water into the kitchen sink, picked up the bar of soap, and dipped the remaining greasy plates into the water. This would be the very last of the Simmons dishes she would wash with the caked-on grease and congealed egg, left to harden over the course of the day.

Tomorrow. A fresh start. A new opportunity. She remembered she hadn't even looked at the paper with the man's name and address, stuffed in her coat pocket since the telephone call. Where did he say he lived? She dried off her hands and pulled out the scribbled note.

Gayton Road. Kenton. Harrow. Middlesex. Then: *Mr. Herman Abrahams c/o Stern Sausages. Aldgate High Street.* And then: *Dear Hedda, It was lovely to meet you today. I hope you thought so too. If you would like to, shall we meet again? My telephone number is CAM 3671. It would be simply "ausgezeichnet" – or excellent – as we say in England.*

Yours, Peter Carter

16

CONFINED SPACES
NORTH LONDON

October 1940

It had been over a year since Britain had declared war on Germany, and for all that time Alice Israel had been living as the oldest resident of Collier Street Women's Hostel behind King's Cross station. Her room, like all the others, was small and shabby. She shared a bathroom and toilet with five other refugees, ranging in age from 22 to 48.

Despite the many months spent in the camps, Alice's face was remarkably unlined. She could pass for five years younger and she knew it. She was popular with the girls in the hostel; she enjoyed a joke and a laugh and didn't take herself too seriously. She liked a drink when a bottle of something delicious came the girls' way and was a decent cook, able to prepare the occasional meal for the residents on the limited wartime rations. She added flavor to the most tasteless ingredients through judicious use of herbs and spices which she managed to procure – from where, who knew?

Alice didn't do much during the day. She still spoke next to no English and gave up her domestic service position almost as soon as she had started; it wasn't for her, she said, much to Hedda's annoyance. She received a small monthly payment for basics from the Jewish Aid Committee, which Hedda would top up on the occasional weekend, meeting her mother beside the canal behind the station. Visits had been restricted by the daily air raids and blackouts, and Hedda wasn't sad about that. Alice took shelter in the fetid, filthy underground while overhead German bombers destroyed buildings, and killed husbands, wives, and even tiny children returning to London after evacuation disasters.

In contrast, Hedda's year had been considerably more eventful. She had been hiding in the Anderson shelter at the back of the garden in Harrow. Bombs had been falling night after night after night. She dreaded the darkness and couldn't sleep, rushing to take cover when the sirens sounded, returning to bed at the sound of the all-clear.

Lillian, Herman's wife, had to remain inside the house, crawling on bruised hands and knees from her heavy wheelchair to nestle beneath the shelter of the floral tablecloth. Herman stayed with her.

Their daughter, Dorothy, would clutch Hedda's hand tightly as they scrambled through brambles into the inky darkness with not even a candle or torch lighting their way. Inside the shelter, Dorothy would put her head in Hedda's lap and Hedda would ceremoniously cover them both with the stale-smelling blanket. A dusty bulb hung from the corrugated-iron ceiling and if the sound of the planes faded, they would dare to switch it on. Then Hedda would recount the stories from her childhood: *Ashputtel,* the German Cinderella whose ugly sisters cut off their heels and toes to fit into the glass slipper, or the story of *Struwwelpeter* who never cut his hair or nails and was doomed to remain unloved. Better to be terrified by these horror stories than the real events happening above them in the black skies over Wembley.

When they returned to the house, Lillian would often be wet, too long under the table to hold it, and her clothes would have to be removed and changed. But despite the fear and the cold and the discomfort, Hedda enjoyed her hide-outs, alone with little Dorothy who reminded her of dear sweet Anna Kalecki. She loved Dorothy's total trust in her, the warm cuddles in the shelter, her young skin close to Hedda's, and she imagined herself as the mother to this little girl whom she would nurture to adulthood and beyond.

She hoped and prayed that Anna and Hanna and Borys were safe away from the worst ravages of the war, but in her heart she knew they were rotting in a camp somewhere or worse.

Surviving the raids and keeping house for Herman was hard. The work was backbreaking. Cleaning, cooking, caring for Lillian, shopping, washing, drying, on and on. But she was paid more than the published rate and had a full day and a half off at the weekend, and when she returned from seeing Peter, there were no dirty dishes waiting on the kitchen counter.

Peter. Peter, her grown-up lover: she had fallen in love with him and he with her. She loved every part of him, his tight chest and broad shoulders, his thatch of red hair which never sat straight on his angular face, his freckles, his small, neat, smiling mouth that nearly broke her heart, his deep and uncensored laughter, his voice, so clear and confident but yet so tender. And his love for her. Isn't that what increases desire? Her desire to know him and his desire to know everything there was to know about her. Hedda. 20 years old. Never been desired. Until now. And their physical love was joyous, all teenage anxieties and awkwardness removed, replaced by total uncensored absorption in the discovery of what her body and mind could do.

———

On a damp, early autumn day, sitting on their usual bench beside the canal, Hedda had finally mustered the courage to tell her mother about Peter, her handsome red-headed Englishman.

"So, how are you?" Hedda said.

They were sitting shoulder to shoulder, partly to avoid the damp from penetrating, partly to enforce the mother-daughter bond. They spoke in German despite official advice. Hedda's increased confidence in understanding the strange London vowels and her ability to speak the native tongue meant these days she felt more comfortable with English; she even used the occasional strange turns of speech – pull your socks up! – a particular favorite. German was reserved for her mother and for her lover when practicing his language skills.

"I'm doing well," Alice responded.

A thermos of strong, sweet coffee was perched between them, and Hedda wondered where her mother found the beans when so much was in short supply. But the coffee tasted good and Hedda was grateful.

"But the air raids are dreadful, truly dreadful!" Alice carried on. "Thank goodness the entrance to the Underground is so close. We often go down, even before the siren sounds, to get a decent bit of platform. I've got used to the awful smell and there's a good atmosphere. People are very kind and sometimes we sing."

Hedda was glad her mother didn't complain; she had taken shelter there only once and could hardly breathe for the stench and the heat.

"The girls are good. There is Christine from a small town not far from Saarbrücken. Do you know, she thinks she once visited our shop when she was a little girl! And Margot – she's from Munich and has seen so much, terrible things – we tell her to keep her mouth shut, we don't want to be reminded, and there's a new girl called Elizabeth. She manages to bring in occasional bottles of beer. She's very popular, I'm sure you can imagine."

Alice's positivity impressed Hedda. She had bounced back from her months of incarceration with barely an emotional scar.

"And you? What's your news? How is the family?"

"They're well, although I can't say we enjoy the raids. It's very scary and only last week two houses were completely destroyed two roads away. We knew the family – they had a girl Dorothy's age but she was away in Kent. She's an orphan now. Her father was killed earlier this year. These bombs – these Germans."

There was a thoughtful silence and a stray black and white cat appeared from the bushes padding slowly towards the water. Three Canada geese made an emergency landing, flapping their wings and honking loudly. A pair of ducks swam further down the canal.

Hedda took a breath. "I have some news. Some good news and some not so good news."

Alice parked her cup of coffee and looked at Hedda.

"Well, the not so good news is that the area that I'm living in has become 'Protected.'"

"What does this mean?"

"It means that I can't live there anymore. You and I, we're considered Enemy Aliens, aren't we, and Wembley is now a Protected Area. They're putting war factories there, so I'll have to leave and get a new job. At least I'm not being interned."

"That's dreadful. You liked the job so much and it was good money. I'm so sorry."

"Well, don't be. I've already sorted things."

"You have?"

"Herman helped. My work permit has been altered. I'm now a machinist. Fancy. I'm going to sew uniforms and parachutes for the fliers. I'll be working in a factory closer to you, so that's really good, and the work will be easier than working for the Abrahams. I will miss Dorothy hugely, she's such a sweet thing, and I know she will miss me. But the pay is better."

Alice looked even more interested. "How much, my darling?"

"Thirty shillings a week, and more for piece work," Hedda replied. "I wondered, once I've been there a few weeks, whether I could see if there was work for you, too?"

Alice looked appalled at this suggestion. "I don't know about that. My hands aren't what they were."

Alice held them out in front of her, but Hedda was unable to spot a tremble or a wobble. She didn't pursue the topic. Her mother should be working and contributing to the war effort, not relying on the good intentions and actions of others. She should show more gratitude. Not for the first time, Hedda was reminded of her mother's selfish approach to life.

"When does the new job start?"

"Tomorrow! I didn't want to tell you until it was all sorted but now it is, there's my news!"

Mother and daughter sat on the bench watching the wildfowl

tail-end into the gray water, black feathers pointing north, and thought about new beginnings. Hedda hoped her mother was pleased by the change in her daughter's circumstances.

"I have some other news too."

"You do?"

"Yes. Let's walk and talk. I'm getting chilly."

They strolled alongside the canal and through the back streets of King's Cross back to Alice's lodgings. As they passed others on the path, their conversation stopped, not wishing a word of German to be heard by those out braving the Sunday morning drizzle.

"I've met someone. We really like each other. I met him nearly a year ago. He's the brother of my pen friend, Betty."

Hedda couldn't read her mother's response, the walk and the fine mist masking the women's faces from each other.

"Why didn't you tell me before? That's good news, yes? Is he Jewish?"

"No. Does that matter?"

"No, no! Of course not. And what does he do?" Alice asked, clearly excited by her daughter's romantic news, irrespective of his non-Semitic birth.

"He's a doctor. A psychiatrist. He's very clever. Since the war started, he's been working at a hospital not far from here and also for the army in a specialist section. He's not allowed to say anything about that, though."

"I'm very happy for you."

Hedda felt a warm thrill of pleasure at her mother's response.

"Of course, all I want is for you to be happy. That's what all mothers want for their daughters: for you to meet a nice man, have food on the table, have a family, and..."

"And what?"

"Look after your mother in her old age?" Alice said, looking straight ahead, smiling.

"Of course, I will! Don't I look after you now?"

"You do. You're a good girl."

Arriving back at Collier Street, Alice fished for the entrance key to the hostel. They walked up the three flights of stairs to the third floor, no golden-gated lift here, and Hedda noticed her mother's discomfort, a slowness in each step. Maybe it was her legs not her hands that were the health issue. Inside the room, Alice eased herself onto the bed, relieved to take the weight off her feet. She removed her coat and headscarf.

"Will you stay a bit longer?"

Hedda studied the room, no bigger than a police cell, a bed, a table and chair, the tiniest of wardrobes – only room for one. "I won't, Mutti. I need to get going." As she approached to give the customary goodbye kiss, she noticed an envelope on the bedside table with an address written in distinctive German handwriting.

"Who's this letter from?"

"Ah! I forgot to tell you. I heard from Edith."

Alice stretched over, picked it up and started to remove the contents. Typical. Important news Alice had completely failed to share with Hedda.

"Mother! What does it say?"

"Well, she's no longer with him. He turned out to be a no-good waste-of-time. After all that! At least he managed to get them out. But from the sound of it, he drank all the theater profits and had a wandering eye, it seems. Thank God she didn't marry him. But..." Alice paused dramatically, as if it were her on the stage in the spotlight. "She has a new man, who sounds magnificent. He operates a shipping company. Moving goods along the coast up to Brazil, cruising past Uruguay and Paraguay. Another world, Hedda! And she is so happy. He has a beautiful house close to the port, with servants and gardens and she has become the mother to his young daughter. His wife died only last year."

Her mother beamed with delight at the glamorous life Edith was living, imagining herself surrounded by luxuries, waited upon by staff.

"And of course, the Argentine stays out of the war. And that's a good thing for Edith and her husband and child. But for us, back here without their support, maybe they're cowards. Oh, what do I know? We must live every day as if it were our last, don't you think?"

Hedda nodded her head, still reeling from the South American news. She partly envied her sister, always the lucky one, pursuing the lights and the music and the money and, well, why not? Hedda wouldn't mind sipping South American cocktails overlooking the busy port, watching the deep red sun lowering into a warm sea, without the nightly dread of bombs dropping overhead. But then, she wouldn't have met Peter, would she? Peter or port life? There was no contest.

"You are right and I must be off. Wish me luck for tomorrow when the new job starts." She planted a kiss on Alice's right cheek. "Usual arrangements? See you in three weeks?"

Peter's living quarters that she now shared with him were not far from Mill Hill East Underground station, a short bus ride to his place of work. He could have stayed within the new hospital grounds, The Maudsley now relocated from Camberwell to an evacuated school in leafy north London, but when the offer of a house share with two other doctors became available, he chose that.

It had worked out well. Within three months of their first meeting, Hedda had moved into his digs at his invitation. "You are sure, Peter, really?"

She had waited for him outside Lyons Tea House that first time, sick with nerves, wondering what possessed him to ask her out, terrified she would disappoint. She lacked both the stunning good looks of his sister, as well as Betty's confident and charming personality. She had worn the same dress as previously and hoped he wouldn't notice. She had pinned her mother's brooch to her coat lapel and put on a dark-green beret and matching gloves.

On arrival, running straight from a shift at the Maudsley Hospital, he looked genuinely pleased to see her and took her by the arm.

"I hope you don't mind," he said, and suggested they walk to Trafalgar Square. He pointed out the closed National Gallery, pictures moved to a place of safety, and then down to the river. He was entirely fair in his conversation, neither bombarding her with questions, nor expecting her to ask him too many, but sharing information in equal measure. He told her that he had been intrigued to see who this German pen friend was, and that he hadn't expected someone so unassuming.

"What does unassuming mean?" Hedda asked as they walked past the Houses of Parliament and Westminster Abbey.

"It means you're not boastful about what you've managed to accomplish, you're modest, thoughtful. It's a good quality. It's shows you think about others," Peter explained.

"I'm not sure why I would *want* to boast? It's not like I had a choice; I had to do what I had to do. You would have done the same for your family," Hedda said.

"I would. That's true. But I would have also been declaring triumphantly from every rooftop – mission accomplished! Yah Boo Sucks to you too, Herr Hitler!"

They had crossed Westminster Bridge and Peter had called out to the passing barges below. Hedda was both embarrassed by his confident demonstration and impressed by his fearlessness. On the other side of the river, they walked to the Imperial War Museum and Peter explained it used to be a hospital treating his sort of patients – those considered suffering with madness or mental illness. Hedda said she couldn't imagine ever having the time to feel mentally unwell and Peter laughed.

"It's true though," she said, "I've always been so busy that by the time I get into bed I fall asleep immediately and then it's back to work again!"

"You have a straightforward approach to life," Peter said. "I like that. Not many people I meet do." He placed one arm on Hedda's shoulder, and with the other gently touched the lapel of the coat. "Such a pretty brooch," he said. "Where does it come from?"

"It was my mother's," Hedda answered, "but I gave it to the daughter of the family I stayed with in Berlin. The ones that left overnight. Anna left it behind, they were in such a hurry, so I took it back. Kept it hidden when I traveled. I'm sure the guards would have loved to confiscate a golden brooch. Do you like it?"

"I do, it's charming. Like you are." He bent his head towards her and she didn't move away. He placed his lips on hers and gently kissed them. The feeling thrilled her. She kissed him back, entirely lost in the moment and when they parted, he said: "Maybe, if you would like, we might continue getting to know one other. If you don't think I'm too old and wrinkled?"

"Really? Are you sure?" Hedda answered. What would this talented doctor want with her when there were so many pretty, sophisticated, intelligent English girls to choose from? It made no sense.

"I wouldn't ask if I didn't mean it. But we are both busy, and there's a war on. How about, if you would like, we use our time well and be our true selves and hide nothing? I haven't been close to anyone for a few years now. I'm free, if you would like that?"

"Yes," she whispered from the new world she had entered and they kissed again.

On the way back, hand in hand, they had discussed the practical arrangements of their next meeting – Sundays being the only real option in between medical and cleaning duties. They waited at Hedda's bus stop and when the bus arrived, he watched as she climbed aboard and found a seat, never taking his eyes off her until the bus pulled away towards Wembley.

They spent their limited free time together, starting in Peter's flat overlooking Camberwell High Street, occasionally walking the streets of London, and sometimes on a double date with Betty and Anthony. Betty adored their relationship from the very start, constantly congratulating herself for bringing them together: "It's like a fairy tale and I'm the Fairy Godmother!"

With no time to waste, they had quickly become lovers, sharing facts and feelings, childhood memories and adolescent anxieties. They spoke in English when outside, but often in German when inside and on their own, Peter keen to improve his German, not that he needed to. He was practically fluent. But it was something that Hedda could give him, a small token, in exchange for the gifts he gave to her. Gifts of tender words, loving looks, deep physical pleasure, and the knowledge of being loved – absolutely. The sense of disbelief that he was in love with her had dissolved during the first three months they were together. She stopped asking for reassurances after he lost his temper one morning. Although he rarely angered, Hedda saw her repeated requests were hurtful. Why couldn't she just accept his love? Did she think he was a liar? Was he not to be trusted?

<hr>

Returning from the visit to her mother, Hedda let herself in the front door, ran up the stairs, two at a time, pushed open the door to their bedroom, and flung herself on top of him where he was propped up on the covers reading a medical book.

"I told her! I told her! And she was really happy. She liked the sound of you. She wants to meet you!" Hedda pulled off her coat and shoes and tossed them to the floor. She grabbed the book from his hands, threw it down, and removed his reading glasses, showering him with kisses on his eyes and nose and mouth.

"Enough of this, my darling girl," he said, and grabbed Hedda's wrist, pulling her onto him.

"So, what else did you tell her about me?" he asked afterwards. They lay in bed, Hedda's head resting on Peter's right arm.

"I told her how well made you are, and how good you are in bed, but sadly, tragically, unfortunately, you aren't circumcised..."

"You didn't, did you?" Peter looked horrified.

"Oh Peter, you're worse than me. I'm sure your patients pull the wool over your eyes all the time." Hedda was delighted to have slipped in another of those strange expressions.

"And she really wants to meet me?"

"She does. Do you know, I don't think I ever told her your name. I described you, told her all about your work."

"Really?"

"Not everything, obviously, but about your interest in trauma, and what makes people do what they do. I didn't describe any individuals."

"I should hope not!"

"She seemed really impressed."

Peter got up and started to dress. It was late afternoon, already dark outside, and he was starving. "Dear girl, we need to eat. Get some clothes on. I simply cannot concentrate until something sits in my stomach. Hunger has rudely taken over."

Down in the kitchen, Peter cut some chunky slices from a large white loaf, which Hedda spread with margarine and jam. Not much of a nutritious meal, but the raspberry jam was sweet and the bread was still fresh. Later on, they would cook up a meal with the other residents, one of whom entered as they sat enjoying their afternoon tea. He was a middle-aged man who had clearly lived a solo life, judging by his ill-fitting clothes and down-at-heel appearance. Hedda noticed the worn patches on his cardigan and the way his trousers hung and wondered what advice her mother would give him.

"Eric, my dear chap, good to see you on this delightful afternoon. Back from your walk?" said Peter, stuffing the last piece of crust into his mouth.

"Peter. Hedda. Nice to see you, my dear. Yes, a decent walk, when all's said and done. Good to see there's been no more bomb damage since I was last out. We're expecting further raids this evening though. I spoke to our neighbors over the road for the very first time and the mother told me that her son had sadly passed away during the evacuation from France. It sounded like he came under heavy bombardment while trying to board. Tragic."

Hedda tried not to picture the dead man but an image of Walter lying on the beach, eyes staring blindly upwards, entered her head.

Eric went on. "The woods were pleasant, a gentle enough afternoon. And I thought about things."

Peter took this as an invitation to enquire. "Anything in particular?"

"I was thinking about how we might increase our understanding of what makes up the mind of those prepared to do dreadful acts. The individual criminal of course, we can study in their prison cells – we prod them and poke them as to their childhoods, their exposure to abuse, the absence, or not, of love, their education, their linguistic abilities, their economic circumstances, their socialization, their peers, and so on and so forth. We can begin to join the dots to understand an individual's propensity for violent acts or deviant actions. We can hypothesize on the individual's mental state, their neuroses and thought processing. With this information, we start to explore the relationship between hereditary and cultural influences."

"And where is this taking you?" Peter asked.

Hedda carried the plates to the kitchen sink and returned to tidy up the table. The conversation was work related, and one in which she felt she could make no useful contribution, so she would rather busy herself with the domestic duties that came so easily. She turned on the kitchen tap.

"Where this is taking me is to a deep well of ignorance, my dear chap, a shocking realization of how little we know about what makes man do what he does. Take your work. There you are studying your patients, hoping to understand their mental aberrations in order to rid them of their anguish and pain, but you are working in the dark! You treat the very surface but fail to treat the depths beneath. For instance..."

Hedda was listening as she rinsed the plates, wondering where Eric's thoughts were taking him next.

"For instance, take the German mind. The Nazi minds. And then consider the ordinary 'man in the street,' the millions of those that have blindly followed their leaders into war, who have embraced every aspect of the Nazi machine. What is it that makes a whole nation behave in this manner? And the Nazis. Were they born to commit evil? What makes a Nazi mind? What constitutes the mind of the pretty German girl who sees thousands of innocent people rounded up, taken away, and nonetheless throws adoring baskets of flowers at their captors?"

Hedda turned off the tap and faced the two men still seated at the table. Eric noticed her attention and turned his focus on her.

"And you, Hedda? What is your mind like? Do you have a 'German' mind, too? You were born there, raised there. You have German parents, a German schooling. I imagine you ate German food, listened to Beethoven and Wagner and read Goethe and Schiller. What makes you any different to that little German girl, cheering on her heroes?"

Hedda felt her face flush and her body tingle. How could he say this to her? Peter crossed to Hedda and placed a protective arm around her.

"You go too far. Hedda is no more German than you or I." Peter knew his fellow doctor was provocative, but this was too much; he could feel her body shaking and understood her anger.

"I'm Jewish!" she screamed.

"I know you are, on paper," continued Eric, unresponsive to the distress in her voice and her blotched neck and face. "But is your identity that of a Jew? Or that of a German? Peter has mentioned you don't follow the religion. You certainly aren't kosher."

"What's that got to do with anything?" Hedda said. She shrugged off Peter's comforting arm and walked towards Eric. "I'm both. How can I say, I'm German, I'm Jewish? I shouldn't have to choose!"

"That is exactly my point, dear girl, you must share some of the mentality of the German, then. And what is it that makes up the collective German mind?" Eric remained oblivious to the emotions in the room.

"I'm nothing like the Germans! You don't know what you're talking about! You have no idea what it's been like and no right to talk like this! You weren't there when I was thrown out of school, when my family lost our shop, when I was scared of who I was. When they were marching through the streets, when they were rounding up the Jewish men, night after night, when my mother was seized and sent to the labor camp. We didn't know if we'd ever see her again." She paused. No one filled the space. "You talk so coldly."

"It's alright," said Peter, reaching out to her.

"No, it's not alright," she said, shaking him off.

Finally Eric seemed to acknowledge the distress and pain that filled the kitchen like a suffocating smog. "I'm sorry, dear girl, I seem to have upset you," he said. "I apologize for my insensitivity. Others have told me of this failing. You say I speak coldly. But I try to speak as a dispassionate scientist. A psychiatrist. An enquirer after knowledge. I ask questions. I study the human brain and in my small way, try to understand what makes man do what he does. If we can understand our motivations and our urges, and how the world in which we live impacts our minds and our actions, then, maybe, maybe, we can start to eradicate violence and hatred and, dare I say it, evil. I apologize again. I meant no harm."

Eric slowly approached Hedda and held out his hand in an offer of peace. She took it. "I confess, I have no real idea of what you've been through. And we have no idea of the current suffering of those left behind. This war is essential. As is the work that your darling Peter is doing right now to cure sick minds and make people well again. He's lucky to have met you, and you to have met him. And to tell you the truth, never having been in love myself, I'm just a tiny bit envious."

Hedda's hand remained in Eric's and Peter joined them. The handholding shifted into a tender hug of three and Hedda's distress turned to calm, her new life amongst these men filled with the safety and security that England provided, despite the German bombs falling night after night.

17

UNDERWEAR AND PARACHUTES

NORTH LONDON

October 1940–July 1941

The factory floor hummed with a sound like a thousand swarming bees as Hedda stood in the outdoor corridor with the other girls, ready to be met by Mr. Hardcastle, the foreman.

Mr. Krivitsky, the factory's owner, had briefly introduced himself, greeting each of the girls with a trembling hand. In a softly spoken, accented voice he told them to wait for the factory tour that would be led by Mr. Hardcastle, the real boss of the place, who was a much better man to run the factory floor. But, he continued, he felt proud of all his ladies, and he wanted them to know that. His twin brother and he had set up the business over 20 years when they came from Ukraine and their business always welcomed immigrants. His dear brother was no longer with them, but he carried on the family business in his memory.

Hedda stood there, smartly dressed, keen to make a good impression on her first day of work and felt delighted to be welcomed in this manner. She looked around at the others and wondered who they were and what had brought them there. Better not ask any questions; she wouldn't want to stand out.

"This is my first job, it is. I'm wetting myself!" said a sweet-faced girl who looked no older than a child and was happy to get some conversation going.

"I've never done anything like this before," said another. "But anything that helps our men. And I couldn't get a job in an office."

At that moment a door opened from a small side room and a middle-aged man appeared, dressed in dull brown overalls pulled tight over his round stomach. He was clutching a clipboard to his chest. He looked around at the girls and smiled. "Girls, girls, girls. Lovely to have you here. What a great-looking bunch you are!" He removed a pencil from behind his ear to take a register. A couple of the girls giggled. "Register time. Just like being back at school," he said.

Mr. Krivitsky placed a paternal hand upon his shoulder and removed himself from the roll call.

"Nancy Bowman?" the man called, louder than needed.

"Here," a voice from the back responded.

"Sarah Clark?"

"Hello."

"Vera D'Arblay? Oh, there's a posh one!"

The girl who was Sarah chuckled appreciatively.

The strong Cockney voice of the small sweet-faced girl replied, "That's me, sir."

"Hedda Israel."

"Yes, here." Hedda was relieved her name was on the list and she definitely had the job.

"You're one of our overseas visitors, aren't you? Welcome. We employ a lot of you ladies as Mr. K. probably told you. He had an identical twin, you know, though he was six inches taller. No! Just a joke! One of my many." He paused to see how his banter was going down; the girls were paying attention but it looked like the joke was lost on them. "Hope you've settled in okay, Miss Israel?"

"Yes, thank you. I've been here for nearly two years."

"You're practically one of us!" He turned to the last girl on his list. "Ingrid Katz?"

"*Ja, das bin Ich,*" a quiet voice peeped from a tall woman, probably a good five years older than Hedda. Ingrid kept her head down to evade notice.

"*Wir sprechen* only English here, darling," said the man. "Good. All present and correct." He looked up from the clipboard, tucked it under his arm and smiled. "So, my name is Mr. Hardcastle, 'Sir' to you, only joking, and I look after all the lovely ladies. I've been here many years, so what I don't know, just ain't worth a bean." He laughed. "It will be me who gives you your work each day, and it's me who decides what work you're best suited to, so I'll be keeping an eye on you all and that's always a pleasure." He winked at no one in particular. "Well? What are we waiting for? Let's get going."

Inside, the factory floor was alive with noise: whirring wheels, clattering metal and the buzz of people at work. As Hedda scanned the room she saw women of all ages seated at individual stations, hands moving swiftly between the various parts of the sewing machine, guiding the fabrics through the plate, adjusting the cotton reels, and turning and snipping the completed pieces from the connecting threads. Large bolts of sludge-colored material stood lined up like eager recruits in the far corner, mainly to be turned into inconspicuous uniforms. As the group followed the foreman up and down the rows, Hedda noticed the many different operations. She could see that some were working on the trickier parts of the garment such as buttonholes, pockets, and pouches, whilst others worked on large fabric pieces which looked far too big to be part of any military men's outerwear.

When they'd walked the length of the floor, Mr. Hardcastle indicated they were to leave by a door at the back that led to the staff canteen.

"It's easier to talk out here," he said when they were all assembled around him in a neat semi-circle. Hedda's ears buzzed, and she could feel an ache in her left temple.

"So, what do you think? Were you impressed? Never a dull moment, that's for sure. Any questions?"

"Mr. Hardcastle? I've not really done this before," said the Posh One. "Do we get any training?"

"Good question. It's Vera, isn't it?" He winked and she blushed.

"Memory like an elephant, me. And call me Ray. I'm a simple man at heart. We like to start all our girls on the easy pieces. They'll already be cut for you and your job will be to attach them together using a simple overlock stitch. Don't worry, you'll get training, we wouldn't let you loose on our precious Singers before you know how to use them."

Vera looked relieved.

"Then, when you're confident and I think you're ready for something a bit trickier, I'll progress you, and that means a little bit more money in your pay packet at the end of the week. The perks of piece work, so to speak. Anyone got much experience?"

Hedda decided it was best to keep quiet about her skills. She didn't want the girls to think she was bragging.

"No? Well, everyone starts at the bottom anyway and works their way up. All's fair in love and war, as they say."

Ingrid, the German speaker, appeared baffled by most of Ray's words and Hedda vowed to help her if there was a spare moment.

"What sort of items are made here?" asked Nancy, a sensible seeming woman, more suited to teaching a class of mathematics students than sitting at a sewing machine.

"Another good question, my dear."

No wink for Nancy. And obviously not that good at remembering names, Hedda thought.

"We were making all types of ladies' undergarments before the business got turned over for war work. Girdles, knickers, brassieres, slips, and we were just about to move our production of silk stockings to using the new nylon when the new orders came in. It's not easy to sew this nylon, it has a sticky feel, and we need to learn its fiddly ways to avoid waste. Every piece sewn incorrectly costs us money and then we have to charge more and that means less money for the war effort. Right now we're on a huge order for the Royal Airforce." He executed a mock salute. "Everything you can possibly imagine. We're making their undergarments, overgarments, and the nylon parachutes that go in their backpacks. When our brave boys are bailing out over France, you can bet your life that one of our girls has sewn up his uniform and that he's drifting down safely thanks to you. You're essential to the war effort. Don't you forget it!"

Vera cheered in response to Ray's rousing speech and waved an imaginary flag in the air. The others smiled and Hedda whispered to Ingrid: "*Es wird gut* [it's going to be fine]." She couldn't decide what sort of man Ray Hardcastle actually was but was prepared to give him the benefit of the doubt. His heart was probably in the right place and he clearly liked to crack a joke, though she was less keen on his sideways looks at Sarah and Vera and would make it clear she had a very fierce boyfriend if he ever decided to come too close.

A couple of months later and well into the routine of KV employment, Hedda sat in the staff canteen with Valerie, her good friend, over a lunch of bland meat pie and some overboiled potatoes. She missed food with flavor, but the canteen meals were remarkably cheap and Hedda and Peter could both eat at work so as not to have to worry about cooking in the evening.

She enjoyed the factory camaraderie, the warmth inside the noisy building contrasting with the first falling of wet snow outside. During her days she thought occasionally about her mother and frequently about her lover. The girls she started with had made their own friends and even Ingrid had taken up with two other refugees from the same part of Austria. Hedda had met Valerie on her third day of work and instantly loved her sunny smile and her positive outlook. They had shared many stories and Valerie knew all about Peter; in return Hedda had heard about Valerie's man troubles. Her current boyfriend worked away from London, in an important army position.

"Where do you think he is now?" Hedda asked, mashing the soft potato with the edge of her fork and adding it to a piece of pie.

"I have absolutely no idea. I don't even know if he'll be allowed home for Christmas. I doubt it. So, Christmas with Mother and Father and Timothy beckons," Valerie answered.

Hedda realized she should probably spend Christmas with her mother and wondered whether Peter would wish to spend it with his family. Maybe he would be required at the hospital that day?

"How are you getting on with persuading your mother to take the job?" asked Valerie.

"She's still reluctant because of her English but I think she's coming round to the idea, especially having a little extra money. And I've told her there are others from Germany and Austria."

"Why don't you have another word with Ray?"

"Do you think I should?

"I do. He won't say no, that's for sure. They need all hands on deck."

"We're not on a boat!" Hedda laughed.

The lunch time siren sounded, accompanied by the scraping of many chairs and multiple groans.

"Back to work. Anchors aweigh!" Valerie said as they returned to their stations.

That afternoon, Ray was conducting his usual patrols up and down the lines, leaning in over his favorites, his arm casually draped over a shoulder, his cheek close to theirs. Hedda had worked out he was harmless and that the ladies seemed to enjoy his jokes and banter. Valerie and Hedda worked in the same section reserved for the more skilled seamstresses and were relieved his attentions mainly focused on those still working on the basics, including the large nylon parachute pieces which required long lines of careful stitching but nothing more intricate. This new wonder fabric was apparently a huge improvement on the old silk canopies: the Air Force couldn't get enough of them. As the needles whirred up and down the giant nylon lengths, the pale pieces billowed like the clouds through which they would eventually descend. The off-cuts lay on the factory floor until the Running Girls collected them, along with refilling bobbins and spools and answering workers' requests. There would be no wastage. Everything not used was recycled.

When Ray entered the advanced section, Hedda stopped sewing and raised her hand.

"Hello, young Hedda, what can I do for you, this blazing afternoon?"

Hedda could see the snow settling on the window and smiled at his gentle humor. "You know I mentioned my mother a while ago now," she said.

"Yes. Living in King's Cross? Am I right?"

"You are, you are."

"Memory like an elephant, me."

"Could I talk to you about a possible job for her?" She tilted her head to one side like a sweet sparrow.

"Of course you can, my darling. What? Now? Follow me into my humble abode."

She sat in Ray's small office close to the factory entrance, in front of a worn-looking desk. The last time she had sat in front of a desk this untidy was her final meeting with Frau Theiner, her old school principal in Saarbrücken. How long ago that seemed. Another lifetime. Ray's desk was covered in sewing reels and fabric swatches, broken parts of old sewing machines and catalogs, and she wondered whether he ever used his desk for anything other than ad-hoc storage. The kind face of her old principal appeared before her. Where was she now? Hopefully somewhere safe from harm. What if she were in England, in London, in North London, and they were to bump into each other one day? How wonderful that would be. Hedda hoped Frau Theiner hadn't been recruited into working for the Party but feared that many good Germans had no choice in the matter.

"So, my dear. Your mother?" He cleared a small space amongst the clutter and placed his elbows there, propping up his saggy chin with his fists. "Remind me. Her age? Her experience? When would she be free to start?"

Hedda stated that her mother was 48 and used to run a large department store specializing in ladieswear, so knew about fashion and how clothes were put together. She wasn't actually a seamstress but would learn quickly and was keen to take up employment and contribute to the war effort. This last statement wasn't true, but

Hedda was keen to present Alice in a favorable light. She would be free to start immediately.

"I'm not sure we'll be taking on anyone this side of Christmas, but certainly in January if not before," Ray said.

"That's good," Hedda replied and looked pleased.

"So my dear, you obviously want this job for your mother." He paused. "What's it worth?"

"Excuse me?" The smile dissolved on Hedda's face.

He looked steadily at Hedda, who waited. He repeated himself slowly: "What's it worth?"

Hedda now realized his intentions and was annoyed at her own naivety. Was now the time to mention her fearsome lover? "I think my mother should start on the same pay we all did, 20 shillings, plus piece work rates?" She smiled at him and risked a wink. They both knew what had just passed between them.

"Of course, nothing less. Just fooling with you." He picked up a small pocket calendar from the mess on his desk. "Tell her to show herself on Monday December 30, half past eight sharp. If she's as pretty as you, I look forward to meeting her."

Hedda spent Christmas Eve with Alice, exchanging small gifts of lavender soap and some packets of tea and biscuits. On Christmas Day they walked from Collier Street into Holborn and Hedda pointed out the offices of the Jewish Refugee Committee. Alice hugged her daughter and thanked her for sorting out her release and Hedda said she was so happy that her mother was safe and well in England. The bombs had temporarily stopped dropping on London but they both agreed that the German bombing of Manchester so close to Christmas was cruel and heartless. Those Nazis had no regard for human life.

Two days before the last calendar page was torn off and the year turned to 1941, Hedda's mother started work at KV Clothing. She worked steadily through the cold winter months in the basic section on the factory floor, sewing the large nylon pieces that made up the parachute canopies. Despite her poor English, Alice settled in quickly and was well liked. She would sit in the canteen laughing with workers from Germany, Austria, and Poland as well as some of the English girls, Sometimes Hedda envied her mother's popularity but was nonetheless pleased that Alice was finally contributing to the war effort and putting her time to good use.

<hr>

It was a late spring morning, and Hedda and Peter had been arguing for the past hour. Despite the warm day, there was a chill in their bedroom.

"I don't understand why you're making this so difficult, darling," said Peter. He was standing beside the open window, smoking one of the many cigarettes he managed to get through each day. "Really, it won't be for long. I promise."

"I know you say that now, but once you and your doctor friends get there, none of you will want to leave. That's what you're like."

"But this is such an incredible opportunity. Something like this never happens. We'll be able to increase our understanding like never before."

"So let the others go. There's Eric. And Richard. And what about the team from the other hospital – the Tavistock? There's already enough doctors. You won't be missed." Hedda had risen from the bed where she'd been slumped for the past ten minutes and was pacing the room, carefully steering clear of Peter's tobacco smoke.

"The point is that we each come from our own specialist angle. We'll be using different approaches to understand how he thinks, how his mind works. There'll be round the clock observation and analysis of his subconscious through his dreams. Fascinating! And the more of us go, the quicker our work will be completed and then I'll be home again, you'll see."

Hedda was exhausted by the debate.

"Honestly my darling, I promise you. A fortnight and I'll be home again."

"I know. And you've made up your mind, anyway. You can be really stubborn when you want to be," she said and approached him at the window. "I never want to get in the way of your work, but I just can't bear a day without seeing you, that's all. I won't cope."

Peter stubbed out the cigarette on the windowsill rather too firmly, and when he turned his face was twisted and annoyed. She hadn't seen him like that before. She'd seen him cross with others, especially when he was tired from treating too many patients but not with her. She instinctively backed away.

"Please Hedda – grow up!" he snapped and lit another cigarette, screwing the empty packet into a ball.

"Peter!" She felt herself trembling. This was a new side to him. "You said we should be honest. Say how we feel!" she replied. She returned to the bed and covered her face to avoid him seeing her upset.

"Can't you see how melodramatic you're being?"

"I don't know what that means. Go and do this important work then, Doctor Carter, I really don't care!" She rolled towards the wall. She heard him walk over, cigarette smoke wafting towards her. His hand reached out to her, but she pretended not to notice and shifted further away.

"Look darling, you know I love you. I don't want to be apart either."

Hedda grunted at his feeble attempt to make amends.

"You must understand this really is an opportunity like no other and you're an intelligent woman who should see that. If we can study his mind, then we're better placed to defeat these damn Nazis and avoid further casualties. This is the Deputy Führer after all. There are big things happening right now and we must put our own needs aside."

Hedda winced at the condescending reprimand. "You think I'm being selfish, don't you? That's what you're saying.!"

"Not at all!"

"Everyone leaves me. First my sister, then my mother, then my father, and now you!" Hedda was shocked at her own words, almost the same as those Alice had written in that dreadful letter. She was becoming her own mother and she didn't like it.

"That's ridiculous. You're one of the least selfish people I've ever known. You always think of others. You always do the right thing. You? Selfish? Never!”

Hedda rolled back over and wiped her face. She pushed Peter aside and walked across to the table where the newspaper lay, describing Rudolf Hess’ parachute landing in Scotland and his capture by the British authorities. No one could believe the man’s daringness and his stupidity. Flying into the country on a peace mission! The whole world imagined Hitler’s anger at his idiotic deputy.

“So what happens now?” she said, flicking through the pages, well over a week old. The argument had blown itself out and they needed to discuss next steps.

“My understanding is he’s about to be moved to somewhere in the south of England. That’s all I know, honestly. And I wouldn’t be allowed to say where it was, even if I did know. Once he’s settled, the team will move in and start work. No date yet, but I think it might be next week.”

“And what would happen if you did say no? I know you’re not going to, and I don’t want you to, but...?”

Peter walked across the room back to Hedda and pulled her towards him. “It would be professional suicide. And I’m not prepared to commit that. I’ve got too much to lose. I’m looking at spending the rest of my life with you, and I’d rather do that alive than dead!”

At that moment, Hedda adored him again. His commitment to his work, to his patients, and to her. He would be back in no time.

The July heat on the factory floor was suffocating. It was one of those days when nothing was going right. Hedda had made several careless sewing mistakes on her uniforms, having to discard large items into the basket beside her and start again. She hated the waste and the time lost, as well as the money not earned. She had been moved to the more complex part of the production process, assembling pieces and working on the fiddly parachute backpacks.

She needed to concentrate fully but couldn't prevent her thoughts turning to Peter, what he was doing and why it was taking so long. They had spoken on the phone and he'd been home twice to visit since leaving. He was not allowed to say too much but she'd managed to wheedle some information out of him: apparently Rudolf Hess was a hypochondriac and thought everyone was out to poison his food. The medical team had decided he was extremely unstable. He told one doctor that Jews had psychic powers and could control others through their thoughts! Hedda said she would give it a go but didn't expect much success. She wondered what these doctors were really seeking. To further their own medical theories, to progress in their careers? How could they possibly understand what it was like to be characterized as a disease-carrying rat, as sub-human? Surely one didn't need a doctor's qualification to say the Nazis were just plain evil.

That lunchtime, Hedda was chatting with Valerie over a boiled egg salad served with the usual tasteless bread. Val's boyfriend had proposed on his last visit back home, and they were discussing wedding plans and whether to ask Ray if they could conjure up a wedding outfit using the work sewing machines and any off-cuts. Outside of working hours, of course.

"I think he might agree," said Valerie. "He's a romantic at heart is our Raymond."

As Hedda considered Valerie's judgment of Ray's personality, she noticed her mother enter the canteen and sit down with two German friends. Having staked her place, Alice was about to get up again to collect some food when Ray appeared and started chatting with the three of them. They seemed to joke and laugh, and she wondered what he was saying that her mother could understand. Maybe her mother's English was better than she made out? She watched him place an arm around Alice as he so often did, lean in, and whisper something into her ear. Alice turned to look at him, smiling and nodding. Then he leaned in for a second time, whispered something else, and allowed his arm to run slowly down her back. When he left, the three women chatted a little longer before Alice remembered she'd not yet eaten and rose too.

"Did you see all that?" Hedda asked.

"No. What?"

"Ray. With my mother. He said something to her. I think he might be after her in some way. I don't think it's purely romantic, either. Should I say something?"

"No! It's none of your business what your mum gets up to. Why shouldn't she have a little fun?" Valerie smiled and Hedda looked appalled. "Yes, I know we don't want to ever think of our parents in that way, but they have needs too, you know."

Hedda reluctantly agreed. "My mother and Raymond Hardcastle. Horrible. My day has just gone from bad to worse!"

At the sound of the factory whistle, the women stopped what they were doing, tidied their work stations, said their cheerios, and made their way out. In the glorious summer sunshine, there were no coats to pick up and most of the women kept their handbags with them on the floor, against regulation. Valerie had made a rapid exit, keen to see Thomas before his departure the following morning, so Hedda left on her own. She decided to take the exit at the back, wanting a longer walk via the canal to enjoy the day and clear her head. She stopped short when she saw two figures, a man and a woman, in the shadow of the open factory doors that lead to the back yard.

Her mother was holding two large brown packages tied with string. She placed them in her bag, not her usual one, but the carpet bag she had brought over when she first arrived from Germany. Hedda couldn't see either of their faces in the shadows cast by the late afternoon sunlight, but watched as they shook hands. Alice then walked across the yard to the factory gates, whilst Ray strode back into the building, whistling. Hedda made sure she wasn't seen, waited a few more minutes to ensure Alice was well away, and then moved on. Whether she would be able to clear her head after what she'd just witnessed, she was no longer sure.

18

TIDINGS OF GREAT JOY
DECEMBER 1941

The daily air raids had finally ended, thanks to the talented young fliers of the Royal Air Force. Hedda often thought about the heroic young men, their short lives ended prematurely to save those on the ground. She thought of their mothers and their lovers and screwed up her face when she imagined the mangled corpses and the women caressing their lifeless bodies. Best not to think too far ahead and enjoy each day while you can: eat, drink, make love, as any day may be your last on this precarious planet. Hedda was no believer in life after death. She loved the one she had, sharing her heart and soul with her dearest, Peter Carter.

Alice only knew of her daughter's relationship from the occasional updates over tea in the canteen, so it was a relief when the time had come for mother and lover to meet. They agreed that a public house not far from the hostel, close to the towpath and full of pre-Christmas cheer, would be pleasant.

The White Star overlooked the canal and was used by all sorts: romancing couples, and local workers, English and foreign, from the many war work factories that filled this area of North London. It was one of those wonderful places where drinkers could feel both left alone and welcomed simultaneously. A couple of previous attempts for her mother and Peter to meet had been unsuccessful.

There was always a reason: fear of the siren sounding to announce an air raid, or firebombs exploding at the end of the street. Now that the bombing was over and Peter was finished with the Nazi deputy, a date was set.

Despite the rain falling from heavy clouds, the canal still had a particular beauty and the full moon, making occasional appearances, illuminated the dark water. Hedda and Peter stood there for a moment, a large umbrella held above their heads, watching the fragmented reflection.

When they entered, the pub wasn't yet full. They had sensibly arranged to meet Alice early and find a table away from the door, away from the draughts and away from what might be an awkward conversation. Hedda hoped not. She hoped Alice would behave herself, and Peter would forgive her mother's sometimes strange thoughts and ideas. He knew how stubborn Alice could be and had heard about the letters she had written from the camps.

They found a snug place to sit and Peter bought the drinks. Hedda had taken a particular liking to sweet cider ever since their first meeting in Bloomsbury. He returned with his whiskey and Hedda's half pint.

"She's bound to like you, how could she not?" Hedda said. She was watching the door intently.

"I completely agree, darling, there's nothing about me that she couldn't like – I'm handsome, I'm smart, I'm a successful doctor, I'm..."

"And what else?" Hedda knew he was about to say something foolish.

"I'm a glorious and delightful redhead!" he said, ruffling the thatch of hair.

"Well, that's not the reason I love you," Hedda said, "I love you because..."

"Yes?"

"Because you cook the best scrambled eggs ever!"

"Hmm... I'm not sure that's why the young Juliet fell for her Romeo," he said, and at that moment Alice appeared in the doorway, scanning the tables in search of her daughter and the boyfriend.

"Mother, over here," Hedda shouted, getting up to meet her.

Alice was already removing her headscarf. They met in the middle, exchanging kisses, Alice fighting with the wet umbrella.

Peter stood up and offered both hands to Alice as she approached the table, the umbrella finally closed and a puddle now forming on the floor. "Hello Alice," he said holding her wet hand in his, "I'm Peter Carter, but I'm sure you know that already. It's a delight to finally meet you. Hedda has told me so much."

"Hello, hello." She looked flustered and fussed with her handbag, trying to retrieve some important item that turned out to be a large handkerchief with which to dab the rain from her face.

"Yes, hello Peter," she said and sat down, stuffing scarf and handkerchief back in her bag, and clicking it shut. "My English is not so good, I'm sorry. Hedda has probably told you. Her dear mother does not speak well."

"You are speaking fine, I think."

"That is very kind of you, but I speak in German, mainly, when I'm not at work, and at work, we must not speak as we must work!" She laughed at the joke and relaxed.

Peter went to the bar and bought a cider as she requested to have the same thing as her daughter.

"Do you like him?" Hedda asked as soon as he was out of earshot.

"He seems very nice. *Er ist ein schöner Mann.*"

"Speak English, mother."

"He is handsome. And what *wunderbar* hair! So *rot!*"

"English!"

"I like his red hair."

Peter returned with her drink and Alice delicately sipped from the glass, swiftly followed by a larger one. He settled back in his seat, facing mother and daughter. He saw the same round faces, upturned noses, and wide brows, but Hedda had youth on her side as well as a greater honesty and openness written within her features.

"How do you find London life? " he asked Alice. He had lit the first of many cigarettes and there was already a fug developing in the corner of the pub. "Not much fun in the last months, I think we'd all agree, with the bombs and the raids? At least that's all over now, thank goodness. But terrible things are happening abroad. Dreadful news coming out of Russia."

"I don't like to think of it," Alice said.

"They say they are killing thousands of Jews over there," said Hedda.

Alice nodded, sighed, and accepted the cigarette Peter offered her. Hedda was surprised. She had no idea her mother had taken up the habit.

"Terrible, just terrible," Alice continued through her first puff. "Hedda and I feel very grateful to the British authorities for their kindness. What would have happened to us otherwise? We have luck."

"Certainly, we are hearing some terrible things," Peter responded.

He knew more than the newspapers printed, information that had leaked through to British intelligence. Specialist police squads were rounding up thousands of Jews, innocent women, children, and babies alongside the men, taking them into the forest, forcing them to undress and dig their own graves before lining them up and shooting them dead. The doctors discussed the dreadful details with Hess, observed his reactions, and listened to his thoughts and opinions. Did he condone this? Was this right? How could he justify this? Peter was glad that neither woman knew the full extent of the Nazi horrors.

"There is talk of unspeakable things taking place in Russia. I'm very happy that Hedda is safe here in London, and delighted she managed to get you out, just in time," Peter said.

"I know, I know. She is a very good daughter to her silly mother," Alice said, draining her glass. "I have a lot to say thank you for." Alice pulled her daughter towards her and kissed her noisily on her cheek. "She is a good girl."

Hedda was enjoying the evening despite her initial worries.

Even her mother's new indulgence in cigarettes was not spoiling the event. Alice and Peter were getting on like a house on fire. The conversation had turned its back on the war to the safer topic of Alice's lodgings, and the pub had gradually filled with pre-Christmas revelers keen for a good night out. With the end to the bombings, people were determined to enjoy themselves and not hold back. Loud chatter, laughter, whoops, and shouts filled the air, along with an ever-thickening pall of cigarette smoke, through which appeared a small flat-capped man, cradling a large cloth bag to his chest..

"You're a smoker, mate," he said to Peter, who had just stubbed out another cigarette in the overflowing ashtray. And your lady friend?" he went on, noticing Alice's red lip-sticked stub. "You might be interested in some Players?" The man pulled out several packets from the bag. "Or I've got some Craven A, if you prefer?" With a neat movement like a magician with a pack of cards, he swapped the cigarette packets. "I've even got some Capstan Navy Cut. Now they're particularly hard to get hold of at the moment. I can give you a good price if you take five packets."

Through the fug, Hedda noticed a woman, presumably his partner, making a similar offer to another group of drinkers. She watched the money change hands and the woman move to the next table.

"Thank you so much, but I won't this evening. Another time, maybe?" said Peter and the man cleared the table and moved off, safe in the knowledge that other customers would certainly purchase at those knockdown prices. London was a city of smokers and most of them seemed to be here in the White Star.

"I think his offer is good?" Alice said, as the man left. "And you smoke and I do, just on special occasions like tonight, so why do you not buy?"

"I don't really know. I suppose because it's wrong. It's a kind of stealing."

"But he pays money for the cigarettes?" Alice said, "He sells them with a little extra for himself? We had a shop in Germany where we made 'extra' until it ended."

"That's called profit and it was business," Hedda said, annoyed that her mother didn't understand.

"Yes, Hedda has told me," Peter responded. "I'm sorry. And, you're right. Maybe the cigarettes were properly acquired. But probably not. He's probably breaking the law and therefore I shouldn't be encouraging it, especially not in my role. It wouldn't look good to my employers."

Hedda and Alice shook their heads in agreement and sat for a moment, contemplating Peter's words.

"But I think everyone is doing such things?" Alice then said. "I think there are some people who have more money and can buy 'extra'? The girls at work talk about it. How they know someone who got tasty meat or extra eggs or good butter. I think the whole world is, how did you say, 'breaking the law'?"

"I don't think that makes it right though," said Hedda, embarrassed by her mother continuing to press the point. "I don't think we should do bad things just because others do."

"But these are difficult times."

Hedda wondered why her mother appeared to condone black market trading. If she were in Nazi Germany she would be arrested immediately. Why did she never learn?

"Well, I for one would like another drink, what say you ladies?" said Peter, hoping to change the subject. He picked up all three empty glasses and made his way to the bar, now crowded with damp-elbowed drinkers, propping it up. He squeezed in beside two smoking men, in animated conversation.

"Well, you can only take so much, that's what I think. They think they can get away with anything. They think they run the country," said one.

"After this war is over, England will be owned by them. Dirty Jews. That's what they plan," said the second.

"The place is swarming with them."

"Greedy they are, greedy."

The first man stopped talking to order two more pints and Peter took his chance to challenge their views:

"Excuse me, but I couldn't help hearing what you were saying.

There is no reason to criticize the Jews. It's Hitler and the Nazis and Mussolini and the Fascists you should be directing your anger towards. The Jews are being killed in their thousands in Europe."

The second man sniggered and said something under his breath.

"Don't you understand, mate?" said the first man. "We let them come over here, alright, I get it, Mr. Churchill was doing a good thing to begin with, but there's loads of them now, loads, and they take over. They take our jobs, they take our houses and they like their money, don't they. They like collecting it, but they don't like paying proper."

"That's just not true," Peter said, knowing this was an argument he wouldn't win. He looked over at Hedda and Alice who were deep in conversation and thankfully oblivious. "Most aren't even allowed to work right now, so how can they be taking your jobs? They've all been interned, haven't they?"

"Yeah, and best they stay that way too. Pity the Isle of Man. It's probably sinking from the weight of them all!"

The second man laughed at the idea, then, turning his head to scan the pub, said: "Oh I get it. Is the younger one your girlfriend? Her over there? With the old lady? I've got a feeling, Joe. Got a feeling..." He tapped his nose.

"Yeah. Got it now. I thought I heard a '*Sieg Heil*' coming from that direction."

Both broke out in vulgar laughter and raised their arms in mock salute.

"Don't you dare!" Peter roared, and grabbed their arms, smashing them down on the counter. "Don't you dare!" he said again, so loud that Hedda and Alice heard him.

Maybe realizing they'd gone too far – after all, The White Star welcomed all comers, not like the Raleigh Arms down the road – the men decided to take the discussion no further. It was Christmas, the season of good cheer. They picked up their glasses and drank down the full pints, placing the empties on the counter with a satisfying thud. "And a Happy Christmas to you too, mate," Joe shouted as, collars up and hands in pockets, the two men sloped off into the pouring rain, the full moon now completely obscured by thick black clouds.

<hr>

Another Christmas event, this time a festive dance with Betty and Valerie at the Royal Opera House. The last time Hedda had been in Covent Garden was when she'd queued overnight, hoping that Polls would enjoy the gorgeous music as much as she did. Not so, but it had still been a delight to have a companion to share it with. Now she was meeting Betty "Up West," the first time they had met in person since the bombings over a year ago. She was excited to see her friend again, and be back in the Opera House.

In the large auditorium, couples shifted and swayed back and forth to the musicians on the stage, previously occupied by the pharaohs and slaves of Aida. A smell of cheap perfume mixed with warm bodies filled the air and the dim-colored lights twinkled to add to the Christmas feel.

The women sat together chatting, occasionally lifting their heads to scan the scene. There was just too much to catch up on, and dancing must wait until they had exchanged their news. Not that they hadn't been asked for a dance. All three were pretty and attracted the eyes of the solo men who approached them frequently, particularly Betty with her blonde bob and bright red lips. No rationing on lipstick, Mr. Churchill had said, we must keep up the morale of our men. All three wore dresses that flattered their figures and made sure their eyes were bold with shadow and liner, and their lips were pillarbox bright.

"So, sister-in-law, well you practically *are*, how are you finding my big brother?" asked Betty excitedly. Hedda sat between them both, and Betty was clutching her hand in anticipation of the news and gossip. "Is he driving you to distraction with his lateness? Is he still slurping his soup like he used to? Do tell."

"He's a delight, an absolute delight. I love him so much." Betty squealed with pleasure. "He does leave the kitchen in a dreadful mess though, and smokes far too much. But apart from that, he's the perfect gentleman and I couldn't be happier, honestly."

"Oh, my little German darling! That's just the best Christmas news, ever," Betty said, squeezing Hedda's hand, then leant across her and said to Valerie: "Have you met him? He's no looker, my brother!"

"I've not, but I feel like I have," Valerie replied. "Hedda never stops talking about him. And she's shown me a photograph. I think he looks lovely, especially his hair."

"It's the Irish in him, we think, or Mother hasn't been entirely truthful with us."

They smiled at Betty's naughtiness.

"Writing those letters when we were just children. Who would have thought it would end up like this? Wedding bells for you, my darling!"

"Hold on, we've certainly not got that far. They're more important matters for Peter to focus on," said Hedda who, even in the dim light of the dance hall, was blushing violently.

"But you're practically married now, darling, living in terrible sin. Don't think I disapprove. We can't hang around forever, can we?"

Valerie looked uncomfortable. She was waiting for the return of her fellow, living at home with her parents and younger brother before she embarked on anything more serious.

"And how about you?" Betty asked, apparently reading Valerie's thoughts. "Do you have someone?"

"I do. He's an officer in the army, stationed in Italy, so we don't get huge amounts of time together."

"But they're getting married," Hedda intervened. "You've set a date, haven't you?"

Valerie positively glowed.

"Oh that's wonderful, darling, I love a good..."

A uniformed wide-shouldered man was suddenly standing in front of Betty.

"I wonder if you might take the next dance with me?" he said.

She nodded eagerly, and standing up, threw a quick wink at her two friends before taking his hand and walking onto the floor.

"She's so much fun, isn't she?" Hedda said.

They watched as the soldier swung Betty around the dance floor to the sounds of "In the Mood," the trumpet blasting out the feel-good melody.

"She is, she is," said Valerie.

In truth, she found Betty rather overwhelming: someone to take in short bursts to prevent exhaustion, but Valerie could see how devoted Hedda was to Betty, and Betty to Hedda. They were practically sisters, after all.

When Betty returned out of breath, promising her partner another dance later on, conversation resumed. The band was playing an up-tempo medley of Christmas tunes and the atmosphere was becoming increasingly lively. "And how did my brother get on with the 'Meet the Mother' meeting? I hope he didn't say anything embarrassing or reveal any naughty secrets?"

"No!" Hedda replied. "As usual he was the perfect gentleman and at the end of the evening, he walked Mother to her lodgings. She was actually rather tipsy so I'm glad he did, otherwise she might have ended up in the canal."

They laughed.

"He was perfect and she really liked him. But enough about me, what about you and Tony?"

"Fine. But he's working such long hours at the hospital we hardly see anything of each other. It seems that everybody's tickers are failing dreadfully right now, so there's a never-ending list of patients to see. But all's fine."

There was something about the repeated "fines" and the over-enthusiastic smiles that made Hedda think that everything was *not* fine but, just as before, there was a young man standing in front of them, this time reaching out his hand to Hedda. He was tall and blonde and quite good looking, and Hedda immediately thought of Walter. She wondered how Walter was and what he was doing. She wondered whether he was fighting in the army on the German side. She wondered if he was alive. She hoped so.

Hedda took the man's hand, and without any words spoken, they walked to the middle of the floor as the music started up again. The band still played Christmas melodies but now the tempo had changed; it was slower, sweeter, more sentimental. The young man drew Hedda towards him to match the music, his right arm carefully placed in the small of her back, his left arm extended to hold her right hand.

"Hello," he said above the band, "my name is George. And you are?"

"Hedda. Pleased to meet you," Hedda said, feeling the contrast between their physical closeness and these formal introductions to be absurd.

George led her into a slow waltz which Hedda struggled to follow; she'd never really danced before. He pulled her closer to guide her more easily and allowed his hand to run up her back as if counting each vertebra.

"Let me lead you; you'll be fine," he said, and his hand pressed hard against the top of her back, forcing her chest to rest against his. "That's right, just relax and let me do the work."

Hedda felt anything but relaxed. She wondered how long the musicians would keep repeating "Jingle Bells." On and on it went, first the violin taking the melody, then the trumpets, before seamlessly flowing into another popular Christmas tune. George had taken a step closer to her, so that not only their chests touched, but Hedda could feel his warm breath all over her face. Not the familiar tobacco breath she loved, but the breath of a stranger, someone who was now pressing his groin hard into her pelvis, far too close. The band played "Silent Night," *Heilige Nacht*, a song that Hedda knew so well from childhood, memories of Christmas trees and carols at midnight.

"This is my very favorite carol," she said, pulling away from his tight grip. "Thank you so much for the dance. It was lovely," she squeaked and almost ran to her friends without looking back. No more dances for her this evening, she decided. That hadn't been nice.

"You're back a bit early," said Betty, "the song's still playing.

Nothing wrong, I hope?" She turned from Valerie and noticed Hedda's downturned mouth and troubled eyes. "Are you alright, darling? Did something happen?"

"I think he was getting a little, how do you say it, fresh?" Hedda said timidly.

Betty tried not to laugh. "Oh Hedda, you absolute sweetheart. They all try it on on the dance floor especially at this time of year. It's like a Christmas gift from us to them. You mustn't think anything of it."

"You did well to stop dancing when you did," said Valerie.

"I won't tell Peter, I promise," Betty joked.

"But I didn't do anything, Betty!" Hedda was shocked that Betty could joke when surely she could see how upset she was.

"I'm sorry, I didn't mean anything. You're a good girl. Look, I'm going for another dance. I'm going to find that gorgeous specimen I was dancing with before. Won't be long." She swept off into the mass of dancers.

"Are you alright?" asked Valerie.

Through the dim lighting they could just see Betty in the arms of someone, though whether it was the "gorgeous specimen" or someone new was hard to tell.

"She's quite a character. Quite different from Peter, I think? Don't misunderstand me, I think Betty's very nice, but she's very sure about things, don't you think?"

"She seems different," Hedda replied. "I can't put my finger on it, but I think something's happened."

"Like what?"

"I don't know. And I don't like to ask."

"Shall I? It might be easier coming from me?" said Valerie and whilst Hedda thought about that, the music came to a stop and Betty reappeared.

"He was gorgeous! Oh girls! I'm having such a wonderful evening!" Betty plopped down and wiped her face. She looked at them both. "What have you two been talking about? You look so guilty! I think you've been gossiping about me?"

"No!" Hedda feigned outrage.

"We were just wondering about you and your boyfriend," said Valerie.

"And do you really think this is your business?" There was an edge to Betty which Hedda had not heard before.

"I'm concerned about you. That's all," Hedda piped up.

Betty stood up. She raised one hand as if taking an oath and then folded her arms across her waist. "Guilty as charged. You are absolutely right. Got it. Tony's left me."

Hedda jumped up and said, "That's awful. Why didn't you say?"

"Well, if you really want to know, it was mutual, we both decided it was for the best. He'd had a bit of a fling with a pretty little nurse in the hospital."

"She can't be nearly as gorgeous and funny and clever as you," said Hedda.

"Actually, there's a bit more," said Betty. "I had a bit of a thing as well, before he started. Not for long, you understand. But he was away and I was lonely and, well, these things happen." She looked miserable and slumped back down.

Whilst Hedda was not impressed with her friend's behavior, she thought Tony could have forgiven her.

"And there were more."

Hedda felt sick. "How many more?"

"One more, two more, ten more?" Valerie said.

"What do you take me for?" Betty snapped. "There were two others if you really want to know, but so short. They meant nothing. But he still ended it when he found out."

"Do you blame him?" asked Hedda, "He must have been so hurt."

"Of course I don't blame him, I've been an absolute pig. But life's hard right now and we don't know what's round the corner. Maybe it was meant to be. I've been in contact with Viktor. Do you remember him, Hedda?"

Hedda nodded her head. She hadn't thought about him for months and felt uncomfortable. A fellow Jew, a fellow refugee, a fellow enemy alien. She wondered how he was and where he was.

"I do remember, yes. How is he?"

"Not good. He's stuck on the Isle of Man and it's humiliating and degrading. Being classified as an enemy. He's a doctor, for God's sake. He writes me letters. I write him letters. I think we rather like each other," she said coyly.

Hedda remembered Viktor and how she felt about him the day they met. She had liked him too. For a short moment, she felt a pang of jealousy. He was far more suited to Hedda and they had so much more in common. It wasn't right that Betty should be liking Viktor in this way, almost certainly leading him on to break his heart. She considered warning her off, then thought better of it.

"Oh Betty, what a mess. But I do love you, you know," said Hedda.

"And I love you too, my sweet darling Heddi."

In front of the women stood another man in uniform, eagerness written all over his round face. "Would any of you lovely ladies care for the next dance?" he asked, proffering his hand in their general direction.

"It would be my absolute pleasure," Betty said without hesitation. "Tidings of comfort and joy to all men, that's what I say, darlings." She stood up, wiped her hands on the skirt of her dress and allowed herself to be led onto the dance floor. "What an interesting Christmas this is turning out to be," she said to no one in particular.

19

DIFFICULT DECISIONS

SUMMER 1943

The war dragged on and on. By summer 1943, 18 months after that eventful Christmas, Germany was beginning to lose its fight with the Soviets, but not before an entire village of civilians from Belarus were burnt alive. The Allied Forces had defeated the Italians and Germans in desert battles, and Joseph Goebbels, Germany's Minister of Propaganda, had declared a "Total War." Back at home, fights broke out between Black American soldiers and British police in the North of England, and Aberdeen was badly bombed.

Viktor had been released from his Isle of Man internment camp and was back in a South London operating theater, cutting open chests, revealing engorged hearts and faulty vessels. With minute strokes and incisions, he restored his patients' chance of life. Several steps on from their exchange of letters, he and Betty met whenever possible and made love when time and space allowed. She had fallen for this talented dark Jew with his strange Viennese accent and bleak outlook.

Rudolf Hess breathed in the good Welsh air of Abergavenny, where he enjoyed the relative luxury of his own hospital room. Despite the many psychiatrists sent to study his every thought and deed, no conclusions were drawn, and following his amateur attempt to kill himself by jumping from his prison balcony, it was decided that a mental facility would best meet his needs.

In North London, Peter sat with yet another battle-scarred officer, listening to the soldier's recollections of mutilated bodies and severed limbs. He sometimes wondered whether the act of retelling worsened the nightmares these men suffered each night. Trauma. There was no cure.

Meanwhile, the average man and woman continued to display their usual stoicism, stepping over mounds of broken buildings to deliver milk, avoiding giant potholes in the road to sit in stuffy offices or stand in suffocating factories producing ever more armaments and munitions, while mourning their dead and dying. And others, enjoying the freedoms granted by a police force whose eyes were focused on the war effort, indulged in a little black-market profiteering: cigarettes, meat, alcohol and of course – ladies' stockings.

And now, look up. If the factory roof were removed, Hedda and Alice, Valerie and Raymond, Mr. Krivitsky and all the other girls would see a glorious blue English sky, streaked with just the faintest of cirrus clouds. Over in North Africa, they would watch parachutes float gently down against an azure backdrop, their descent controlled by light-as-a-feather steering lines, thermals occasionally wafting them sideways and upwards before the softest of landings on the yellow sands of Tunis. They would slap each other on the back and say: "We sewed those silks. We secured those seams."

Also attached securely to the factory floor of KV Clothing were the heavy sewing machines that turned and whirred ever faster to keep up with the endless orders. 70 new workers had been brought in to meet demand. Production was devoted exclusively to the manufacture of canopies, ropes, cords, and netting to keep out the mosquitoes in the tropical jungles, using the latest technological nylon fabric sent from factories across the Atlantic. Women worked around the clock in 12-hour shifts, machines squeezed closer to each other, making the runners' lives more precarious as they knocked against treadles and tabletops, their thighs increasingly dark with bruises. Threads and bobbins spun like crazy carousels and the noise was deafening. Whilst the employees were always encouraged not to talk on the factory floor, conversation was now impossible. They were trusted to take their toilet breaks when "nature called" and the ladies would often congregate there, for an extra break or a chance for an exchange of news.

Ray continued to be firm but fair and made sure everyone was acknowledged for their efforts. Sometimes at the end of the week, he allowed them to knock off a little early, or there was a bit extra in their pay packets, or he brought in a crate of light ale and left it in the canteen with a note saying, "Help yourselves, you deserve it!"

He had no favorites but sometimes Hedda felt he was especially nice to her; not in a funny way but in a kind, fatherly way. Because of their sewing skills, Ray had moved Hedda and Valerie to supervise the newest employees' section, which was close to the offices of Ray and Mr. Krivitsky, and where Alice worked. Mother and daughter's paths rarely crossed but with this move, Hedda was able to see her mother bent over her machine and sandwiched between two new ladies.

At midday, an hour before the lunchtime whistle, Hedda was finding it difficult to concentrate. She had rushed out without breakfast, having slept through the alarm and Peter on night shifts not there to shake her awake. She looked up to check the time and her eye was caught by her mother. She couldn't quite make it out but Alice appeared to be turning round, bending over and unbuttoning the top of her overalls. Hedda continued to watch as her mother carefully slid several of the off-cut pieces into her clothing, pushing them down to below her waist, making room for more. Then she buttoned herself up, stood up and stretched, and left the floor in the direction of the canteen and the toilets. What was it Hedda had just seen? The workers were clearly instructed to leave all fabric pieces and dropped cotton reels on the floor for the runners, saving time and ensuring efficient working practices.

Trying to go unnoticed, Hedda left her base and walked towards the large doors. She stopped when she saw Alice emerge from the locker room. She watched her mother enter the toilets, carrying her usual large bag, and, feeling like a spy, hung back before quietly following her in. Only one of the cubicles was locked when she entered.

"Mutti? Mutti?" Hedda said in a sharp whisper. "Are you there?" She heard her mother flushing the chain, a zip opening, and some muffled rustling. Alice appeared, red in the face, her eyes looking anywhere but at Hedda.

"Hello, my darling, we don't often see each other at work, do we? Funny! We both needed to use the facilities at the same time!" Alice spoke in German and Hedda allowed her. No one else was around and this way, her mother couldn't hide behind language barriers. She spoke in German too.

"What are you doing?"

"What do you mean, my darling? I'm using the toilet!"

"I saw you put something in your overalls!"

Alice was silent for only a moment. "Yes, I did, but there's nothing wrong with that! Those pieces would have gone to waste otherwise. They're just thrown away. Mr. Churchill tells us all to 'Make do and Mend', so that's what I'm doing. Sensible, I think."

"What on earth do you mean? What are you making and mending? Are you taking them home?"

"No!" Alice sounded outraged. "Of course not. They're reused. It's for a good cause."

Two English women had entered the toilets and Hedda stopped her German talk, pretending to be deep in personal conversation with her mother. She smiled at the two, waited for them to wash their hands and leave, and then resumed:

"Please tell me what's going on." She tried to take the anger from her voice, speaking softly and slowly.

Alice sighed. "I give the pieces to Ray. They are turned into ladies' nylon stockings."

Hedda let out a loud groan.

"We're not harming anyone. Everyone gains. Mr. Churchill says we ladies must look our best, yes? Don't the posters tell us, 'Beauty as Duty'? We're all so desperate for stockings and this way we can make our ladies happy. It's not a bad thing to do."

Hedda couldn't believe her mother. "Stop talking about Churchill! it's nothing to do with him! And what do you mean, our ladies? They're not *your* ladies. You have no right to do this. It's bad. It's really bad!" Her mother's stupidity had made her so angry that she was shouting far too loudly.

Alice let out a childish groan. She had become the young girl reprimanded by her teacher and played the part well. She hung her head low and her knees sagged.

"It's completely against the law. It's criminal. You know that? Of course you do!" Hedda leant against a basin, unable to look at the pathetic sight her mother had become. "Is that it then? You supply the fabric. You give it to Ray. Or is there more than that?" Her voice was under control again. She couldn't risk others walking in and hearing even if they were speaking in German; there were other German speakers in the factory.

Her mother looked up briefly but said nothing.

"Oh my God! There is more, isn't there. I can tell by your face! I feel sick!"

Alice reached out to take hold of Hedda's hand but she pulled away.

"Tell me. Tell me the rest."

"There's a place where Ray dyes the nylon and then turns it into the stockings. I take the stockings from Ray and there are some ladies who buy them from me to sell them on. It's quite simple, almost like the old days when we were selling women's fashions."

"It's nothing like the old days," said Hedda. "Who are these ladies?"

"Just friends I've made. They're very nice, very respectable. You mustn't be so upset with your mother, Hedda. Everyone is at it."

"*I'm* not at it." Hedda spat out the last two words. "You will stop – now."

Alice whined in her most sickening voice, attempting a last appeal by playing the innocent infant.

"And if you don't, I promise I'll go to Mr. Krivitsky and tell him everything!" Hedda was practically screaming again.

"That's a terrible thing to say. You wouldn't really do that to your mother?"

"I'll give you till Friday. If you haven't told Ray by then, I'll go to the police."

"The police? You make me very sad."

"No, you make *me* sad. I can't believe it." She burst into choking tears. "After everything we've been through, you would do this? It's such a...." Hedda was lost for words, then found the perfect one, "such a betrayal!"

***

Hedda waited till Friday. She made sure she saw her mother as little as possible and told no one, not even Peter. Fortunately he was still on occasional nights, and she was often asleep when he crawled into bed. She was glad as he would almost certainly know that something was wrong. This way he never needed to know. She was so ashamed. He would decide there was something fundamentally wrong with her family. She had never quite rid herself of the nagging doubt that in the end, he wouldn't be comfortable settling for a Jew. Their children would be Jewish and would he, a true-blooded Englishman, really want that for his offspring? They'd never talked about it.

It was easy to keep the secret from Valerie, who was increasingly preoccupied with her upcoming wedding at Marylebone Registry Office, which had been delayed from June to October. Poor Valerie was terrified he wouldn't make it back in time and she would be waiting on the steps for a groom that never arrived.

Friday lunchtime rolled around and the canteen filled with hungry diners, who ate, drank, talked, and stretched out their aching limbs. The day was hot and the canteen smelt of sweat and human labor. Dresses and overalls were sticky and the women dabbed their faces with whatever they could grab, including the smallest off-cuts. Hedda and her mother had packed their own sandwiches and settled down in the furthest corner. Other women shared the table so they spoke in quiet voices, partly in German, partly in English.

"Did you speak to Ray?" Hedda asked as softly as she could.

"I did. It's all sorted. I've told him I'm not doing it anymore."

"Really?" Hedda thought it sounded too easy after her mother's fiery defense at the beginning of the week.

Alice nodded her head.

"And what did he say? Was he alright about that?"

Alice took a bite of her sandwich and chewed for a few moments. "First of all, no. He was not happy, not happy at all. But when I explained how upset you were and the things you said, then he understood. You are a very valued worker, Ray thinks the world of you."

"I don't care what Ray thinks. Does he understand that he must stop too?"

"Of course. He gave me his word." Alice took another bite of her sandwich.

"And that I'd go to the police?"

"Yes, I said that."

"So that's it, then?"

"Yes, my darling. I hated seeing you so angry with your poor mother who loves you dearly. You have done so much for me." Alice took the last bite of the sandwich, removed a small cotton hanky from her overall pocket, and wiped her mouth. "This handkerchief came all the way from Germany, so is rightfully mine. Look. it even has 'AI' embroidered in the corner."

Hedda was flooded with relief despite her mother's cheap jibe. It had been an awful week of worry, with no one to confide in. And now it was over. Finished.

———

The muggy summer had turned into a warm autumn. Mr. Krivitsky, with a beaming Ray Hardcastle standing beside him, announced a day off for everyone. All production targets had been met, exceeded even. They all deserved a full day's paid holiday for their hard work and sunny faces. A spontaneous cheer went up with a couple of the ladies running over and planting a big kiss on his elderly cheeks, turning them bright red.

Monday, September 20 was a beauty, with a gentle breeze in the air. It was the sort of day when strangers in the street greet each other with friendly smiles and good wishes. On a day like this, no one would think the country was deep in a world war, with thousands dying every day. Hedda had long wanted to hear the string quartet which played in the National Gallery to exhausted London workers. Always too far to travel during her lunchtime, today she planned to take her mother there for a surprise treat, picking her up unannounced from the hostel, and then taking the Northern line to Charing Cross where they could walk to the concert, arm in conciliatory arm. Why – they could even have lunch together in Lyons Corner House; that would add still further to a day of forgiveness, her mother's own special day of Atonement.

She arrived at Collier Street shortly after 11 o'clock and rang the bell. A young woman in her nightie opened the door. Her nose was streaming and she looked as if she would be better off tucked up in bed with a hot drink.

"Oh hello. I'm not feeling too well, that's why I'm at home." Lizzie wiped her nose on her sleeve. "Are you here to see your mother? I think she just popped out, about ten minutes ago."

"Do you know where she's gone?"

"Sorry, I just saw the back of her and heard the door slam. Do you want to go up and wait? We keep spare keys in the kitchen." Lizzie shuffled down the corridor and returned holding the key to Alice's room. "Here we go. Can you let yourself in? I'm going back to bed."

Hedda climbed the stairs and stood in front of the door to her mother's room. She hoped she wouldn't be gone for long. She had wanted to surprise Alice, never thinking she might be out. She would wait half an hour but if Alice was not back by then she would leave and enjoy the concert by herself.

She turned the key in the lock and pushed open the door. It was such a small room that she saw the packages immediately, laid out neatly on Alice's bed, completely covering the pink eiderdown. Each large package was made up of several thinner ones, tied together with string. Tucked underneath the knot that secured them was a small label. Hedda approached the bed slowly as if it housed an unexploded bomb and read the distinctive German handwriting on each: Vera, Carol, Mary L, Mildred, Mary G, Sarah, Hannah, Virginia, Ruth, Alice. She reached out her hand to pick up the nearest, the one labeled Ruth. She slipped the string off and carefully prized open the paper until she could see a gossamer-thin piece of black nylon. She placed Ruth's package back on the bed, did a quick count of the names, then turned and quietly left the hostel. Lizzie would be back in bed and Hedda's mother would probably never know her daughter had paid her a surprise visit.

What next? Everything her mother had told her was a lie. And the scale of it! Each package contained about ten pairs of stockings, and there were ten packets. This was no small-time enterprise between Alice and Ray. This was organized crime.

Hedda had no idea what to do next. She walked along Collier Street, past King's Cross station and down Euston Road. She continued south, the sun still shining, until she found herself back in Russell Square where she had sat on her second day in England, trying to secure her mother's release from the Nazi camp. She watched the pigeons pecking the dry ground, squabbling over territory. The occasional robin landed close, turning his head in the hope a few crumbs might be dropped his way. Two squirrels scampered down the tree in a mad game of tag, with the chaser never quite catching the chased. She was envious of their easy lives; she could hardly bear the decision she now faced.

She had *said* to her that she would go to the police. She had *told* her that. Alice knew that if she didn't stop with the profiteering, Hedda would have no choice but to tell the authorities. She couldn't have made it clearer. Obviously her mother just didn't care! Here they both were, thanks to the generosity and kindness of the British government and this was how her mother repaid them? She was a criminal. No better than all the others selling stuff from under shop counters, selling on ration tokens, peddling goods that had "fallen off the back of a lorry." She would tell Peter everything that evening. He would know what to do.

———

She was waiting for him downstairs on his return from the hospital, increasingly impatient with yet another of his over-long shifts. Surely he was senior enough to have the occasional evening off? When he entered the kitchen, he looked exhausted with dark circles under his eyes, suggesting he hadn't eaten yet again. Probably the last thing he wanted to do was to discuss Hedda's news. For a moment, she thought she might abandon the whole thing, but knew that was impossible. Even if she said nothing, he would only need to take one look at her to decide something was wrong.

He had taken off his jacket and was searching the larder for the bottle of whiskey recently bought by Eric for the household. All the doctors enjoyed a drink or two after their shifts.

"Hello little darling, how was the concert?" he said as he poured himself a large glass and went over to the tap to add a couple of drops of water. He had explained that it brought out the flavor when she had questioned whether he was doing it to make it go further.

"Did your mother enjoy herself?"

Always so thoughtful and attentive. He didn't think to recount his day of horror but went straight to enquiring about hers.

"We didn't go."

"Oh darling, why not? You were so looking forward to it. Did you manage Lyons?"

She shook her head.

"Have you eaten anything today? You're looking pale." Peter returned to the larder in search of something more nourishing than a whiskey.

"Can we go upstairs? I've got something to tell you."

"Darling girl! What on earth is wrong? Tell me now. I'm worried."

Hedda had already left the kitchen, so Peter followed, glass in one hand and bottle in the other.

She sank down onto the bed. "It's alright, it's not about me or you. It's about Mother."

"Is she unwell? Is that why you didn't make the concert?."

"Please let me speak. And don't say anything until I'm finished."

He took a large swig of his drink, already refilled to the top, then pulled the chair away from the table to be closer to her. She looked him straight in the face and described everything that had happened: the first sighting, the ultimatum, the promise of reform, Alice's lies, and finally the discovery of the packages stacked and labeled on her mother's bed.

"What shall I do? I don't know what to do."

Peter had been listening in his usual attentive way. He finished the drink and then, in a firm voice unfamiliar to Hedda, he said, "I can't possibly advise you. It's not for me to make such a decision. This is your mother we're talking about here. You have to decide what's for the best." He looked at his empty glass, poured another drink, then lit a cigarette.

"That's not fair! You know about people much more than I do. You're a psychiatrist – you know what people think – even my mother! Please, help me." She paused. Nothing. "What would *you* do?" She tried her hardest to keep the desperation out of her voice.

"I honestly have no idea what to advise you. How can I know? I don't remember studying the aberrant behaviors of the black marketeers while at Oxford. And I'm tired. I love you dearly, but I have no capacity to know what on earth you should do."

"Yes, I can see that," she said.

"Don't begrudge me a drink," he said. "At this moment it's completely medicinal. Anyway, what I would do is irrelevant." He waved the nearly empty glass in the air, adding visual emphasis to the word.

"Irrelevant? If it was *your* mother, then what would you do?"

"But it isn't. It makes me smile even thinking of Bethan engaging in such activities. The closest she ever got to thieving was when she removed some tired carnations from the chapel and placed them on a lonely grave. Your mother is breaking the law. If truth be told, I'm surprised, possibly even a bit shocked. She's an enterprising woman, isn't she? What took place in Germany, well, it's all beginning to make rather a lot of sense. She's what we might call a taker of risks, an explorer, an adventurer. She doesn't quite appreciate the consequences of her actions like the rest of us."

He drained the last drops and waited for Hedda to respond. She didn't.

"Look, darling, she's *your* mother. Flesh and blood and all that. How are you going to feel if you get her into trouble? It won't be nice for her or you. And you will have to live with that."

"You're saying I should keep my mouth shut, aren't you?" She spoke each word slowly, considering the implications.

"I'm not saying anything of the sort." He was becoming irritated, a familiar state when he'd had too much to drink. "Because on the other hand, if you don't say anything, then you're going to have to live with your mother's crime. And my God, you'll find that difficult. Because you, Hedda, you are a 'good girl.'"

Hedda hated his tone, mocking and unkind.

"From what you say, it's not just Alice, but Ray, a solid working-class man that you're going to grass up. All a bit of a mess, really."

Peter placed the empty glass on the windowsill and lit another cigarette from the one he'd just finished. He leaned out of the window, trying to breathe in the fresh night air.

"Stop being so horrid. I beg you, just tell me what to do!"

He turned from the window and placed both hands on her shoulders. "I can't, and I won't. Whatever I say, whatever advice I give you, you'd end up blaming me. It would cause bad feelings."

Hedda sobbed quietly. She had wanted him to wave a wand and solve her problems, and he was stubbornly and drunkenly refusing to do so.

"Darling. I'm madly tired, and now? Now I'm going to go to bed. I've got another early start. Here's my advice: sleep on it. In the morning, either go to the police with what you know or forget about it forever and pretend you never saw anything. Dream sweet dreams."

He swayed his way towards the bed and Hedda watched him flop down before she left the room. For the first time, she was unable to be in the same space as her lover. She would go for an evening walk and decide next steps.

Even though Peter's whiskey-induced restlessness had kept her awake for much of the night, she had eventually managed a light sleep. When she woke, he had already left. On the table beside the empty bottle and glass was a folded piece of paper. Hedda had only once received a written note from him, that evening when he had asked whether they might meet again. She doubted this would provide the same delightful pleasure. Barely legible, it must have been written in haste, but its meaning was clear.

Darling Heddi

I'm sorry. I wasn't very helpful or sympathetic last night, was I? I didn't give you the answers you wanted. In my defense, I'm tired right now and I hear some dreadful things which probably turns me into a grumpy bear. I don't like to tell you all that I hear from the men who've come back from the fighting. They've seen horrors and now I see their horrors, but I don't want my darling Heddi to see them. It wouldn't be fair.

Anyway, you wanted my advice so here goes: be a sensible grown-up girl and stick with what your head and heart have decided. I realized I was only properly grown-up when I stopped relying on others to take the difficult decisions, at about your age too. And if you still can't decide, then toss a coin, a large round penny will do the trick. Heads you tell, tails you don't.

I love you. Peter

She folded the note, then tore it into several pieces which she placed in her handbag. It wasn't what she wanted. It was a sort of apology, and she did understand his work was hard but she didn't like his patronizing lecture on age. She had always thought it might become an issue. She fished out a penny coin from her purse, placed it on her thumb and finger and flicked it in the air. It landed on the carpet just beside the bed. Good. That was her decision. And the coin had agreed with her even if Peter couldn't and wouldn't.

She left early and caught the tube, getting off one stop before her usual one. In front of her was a worn looking door with a blue light above it. She climbed the three steps and entered the police station. There were several men and women queuing at the desk. When it was her turn, a pleasant-looking police sergeant said, "Good morning young lady. And what can I do for you?"

Without hesitation she answered him. "Yes. Thank you. Good morning. I would like to report someone for breaking the law. My mother."

20

IN THE INTERESTS OF JUSTICE
NOVEMBER 1943

Marylebone Magistrates Court, on the corner of Seymour Place and Marylebone Road was a busy, bustling building from the moment it opened at 9 o'clock in the morning until late evening, when the heavy doors slammed shut and the keys turned in the lock. Everyone, rapists and murderers, petty thieves and forgers, robbers and violent individuals, first appeared here before being filtered to their next ports of call; a further day at Marylebone, or off to star at the Old Bailey, or remanded and sent straight to the cells below, and from there onto Pentonville or Holloway or the Scrubs.

In the dock stood a motley crew: eight women and one man, some dressed in their very best clothing, some wearing the first items that came to hand on this cold, wet morning. The women identified themselves to the crowded courtroom: Carol Andrews, Hannah Borek, Vera Cohen, Mary Galloway, Alice Israel, Mary Leonard, Sarah Miller, and Mildred Smith. Virginia Roberts was rather unwell, so she was a non-appearance, and Ruth O'Malley was nowhere to be found. Some said she'd managed to get on a boat back to Ireland. And the one man? Raymond Hardcastle, of course.

In the public gallery were friends and relations of the offenders.

Mildred, a part time prostitute, lived a chaotic life and there was no one to cheer her on. Mary Galloway's husband wouldn't take the time off work, and Sarah, Vera and Mary Leonard's husbands were either dead or fighting overseas. Carol's mother had turned up with a neighbor, ashamed and angry at her daughter's criminal activities, "led on by the Jew no doubt," whilst Hannah's eldest son, a skinny boy of about 16, sobbed noisily as his humiliated mother stood before him, her head hanging down.

And Alice? Who stood there for her? It was her younger daughter, Hedda, watching from the public gallery, sitting apart from the rest. The daughter who was responsible for today's events. That day, when she had boldly entered the police station, so certain of her morals, was the day that Alice and Ray and the other ladies, all trying to make an extra bob or two, maybe one less trick to turn for Mildred, maybe a treat for Vera's children, were condemned to become common criminals. Hedda had heard the whispers of "Dirty f'ing Jew" between Mrs. Andrews and her companion. She understood their feelings, their rage and shame equally justified. She tried to keep her eyes low to avoid catching their attention.

The court was in session and the charges read out: between January 1941 and September 1943, they knowingly and unlawfully sold stolen goods of a value unknown. The legal clerk read the second charge directed solely at Ray and Alice: "you are additionally charged that, between December 1940 and September 1943, you unlawfully stole fabric from KV Clothing from which you manufactured nylon stockings on another's machinery. Machinery not owned by yourselves. You handled stolen goods and organized others to sell stolen items."

Having put the charges, each of the sorry-looking individuals was asked to enter a plea: "Guilty," they each replied. Some spoke in loud clear voices, Mildred shouting her response, used to appearing before the magistrates for soliciting.

Vera and Hannah whispered their words, forcing the Justice to say in a booming voice, "Speak up, ladies. No need to be shy." When it came to Alice, beautifully dressed in a well-tailored matching jacket and skirt, every hair in place, her reply was so strongly accented that someone in the public gallery shouted out: "German traitor!"

The Prosecution for the Crown presented the facts of the case, describing how Hardcastle and Israel were at one point manufacturing over 60 pairs of black nylon stockings a week, using off-cuts from the nylon rolls imported from America. This expensive nylon was for the sole purpose of industrial use, military production including parachute canopies and other vital pieces of equipment such as tow ropes and netting.

"This has been a highly efficient, one might say, military operation, with Hardcastle and Israel working together for over two years, building their sales team. All the women involved have profited from the unlawful manufacture of the nylon stockings; they have bought the stock from Israel, and then sold the items on to their own customers. While clearly Hardcastle and Israel are culpable of greater criminality, it must be said that all the women knew the stockings were stolen, and had no regard for this fact, seeking simply to profit from stolen goods. I ask you to consider severe sentences for all who stand before you today, sentences that reflect the enormity of their criminality – stealing and profiting from our military efforts."

A lowly solicitor appointed by the court stood up to provide a basic defense – to find anything that might make the bench look more kindly on the criminals. He started by pointing out they all had pleaded guilty at the first opportunity, thus saving the court time and money. Then he went through each of them by turn. Along with Mildred, both the Marys had previous convictions for petty thieving, though Sarah, Carol, and Hannah had never been in trouble before. They were terrified that they might be sent down and unable to provide for their families and he hoped the court would take this into consideration.

Next the solicitor turned to Ray. This was difficult. What could be said in mitigation of a man who had been running a highly profitable racket from his place of work, abusing Mr. Krivitsky's trust over several years? The poor man had to dig deep into his legal briefcase. He cleared his throat.

"However misguided his actions were, Ray Hardcastle believed that he was doing a service to both the women who sold the stockings, providing them with a bit of extra spending money at the end of each week, as well as their grateful customers, who were delighted to purchase beautiful stockings at a decent price. It is fair to say that if those ladies with considerable spare cash in their pockets did not exist, then a thriving black market across this country and especially in the capital would also not exist." He paused and looked around the courtroom. There was total silence.

"We all know the urgings of this government to the women of Britain, to look their best to keep up the morale of our brave fighters and, mistaken as it may seem, Ray Hardcastle was supporting this effort." He smiled at the bench who did not smile back. "Factory production did not suffer in any way; in fact, under Mr. Hardcastle's excellent stewardship, production targets were always met or exceeded. We ask this court to take all these factors into account when determining Mr. Hardcastle's sentence."

"Thank you, Mr. Lewis. And your final defendant?" the Presiding Justice of the Peace asked.

"Thank you, your Worship. This is Mrs. Israel. She arrived in this country in 1940. I don't need to point out to you that this lady was escaping the worst persecution of the Nazi Party. This country has pursued a supportive policy of allowing persons of Jewish descent to take refuge here. She has been most grateful and although she doesn't speak much English, she has settled in, worked hard, and made the best of it, despite the many difficulties she has faced. Might it help your Worship, for a Good Character reference to be made?"

The Presiding Justice, a balding red-faced man turned to the other two Justices, seeking their opinions. They conferred for the shortest time, heads bent together, then separated. The request was granted. The clerk scuttled out and a minute later was followed back in by a tall man, who was asked to remove his hat and take the oath.

"Your name?"

"Peter Carter."

"Your occupation?"

Peter answered quietly but clearly.

The defense lawyer stepped forward and took over. The clerk resumed her position, pen in hand to capture every word.

"Mr. Carter, would you tell the court how you know the defendant, Alice Israel, and for how long?"

Peter spoke clearly and addressed the bench as requested. "I've known *about* Mrs. Israel since September 1939, when I first met her daughter, Hedda Israel. Her daughter had been living in London since February of the same year, trying to organize her mother's release from a German concentration camp."

Peter looked up to the public gallery and saw the face of his lover. He tried to remain stony but couldn't help but offer her the smallest of smiles, at which she smiled back, immediately attracting the attention of the others. They glared and pointed at her behind their hands and Hedda looked at her feet again.

"It is fair to say I only met Mrs. Israel in December 1941. My work has been extremely busy and very demanding and of course Mrs. Israel has also worked long hours for the war effort."

"For her own efforts, more like," shouted Carol's mother. "Dirty immigrant."

The clerk glared and shushed simultaneously.

"And what impression did you make of her?"

"I thought she had experienced considerable stress before arriving in this country. She had been imprisoned in three different concentration camps, and conditions were unpleasant. Her husband had died unexpectedly while she was locked up, and when her daughter secured employment in this country in 1939, I'm aware the mother became extremely depressed, One might say she despaired. She lost hope and assumed that she would die alone in the Nazi camp without ever seeing her daughter again."

"You are a psychiatrist, Mr. Carter?"

"Yes, as stated."

"And you have experience of patients suffering stress, I believe."

"Yes, a considerable amount of my work is focused upon patients who have experienced challenging conditions, and whose decision-making becomes impaired as a result. They struggle in day-to-day activities, can make impulsive choices, and may find it more difficult to weigh up the rights and wrongs of their actions."

"How might this apply to Mrs. Israel?"

"It's possible she may not have appreciated the criminality of what she was undertaking. She may have been more open to persuasion. A vulnerable woman. A foreigner in a strange country. This, coupled with her poor language skills and her gratitude to her boss Mr. Hardcastle, may have resulted in poor decision-making."

"Anything else you would like to say, Mr. Carter?"

"Not really. Only that I believe Alice Israel to be a woman of good character whose daughter has worked extremely hard since she arrived in the country. First in domestic service, then in factory work for the war effort. She would be distraught if her mother were to be sent back into a prison environment."

"Thank you, Mr. Carter. You can stand down."

Peter looked again at the public gallery and saw Hedda silently sobbing, her head sunk low in her hands. She didn't see him pick up his coat and hat and leave the room. She didn't see him exit the courthouse, walk the short distance to the underground station and board the train back to Mill Hill Hospital. Patients to see.

The bench returned. They had been discussing the offenders for nearly an hour and were now ready to deliver the sentences. The gallery was deathly quiet. The Presiding Justice smoothed down his head with one hand and arranged the papers in front of him. He looked up. The two other Justices stared steadily ahead at those in the dock.

"We have listened very carefully to the facts of the case. We have taken into account the individual circumstances of each of those involved, including their previous levels of offending, their good character and the consequences for their families."

The Justice took the "Receivers of Stolen Goods" one by one, outlining fines they would pay, and in the case of Mildred, Sarah and Vera, a fortnight each behind bars. They looked relieved; the fines would almost certainly not get paid, and in the chaos of wartime justice, no one would chase them up. A fortnight was manageable and not something unfamiliar. They would be out in no time.

"We then come to the two defendants, charged and convicted of the additional offenses. Mr. Ray Hardcastle and Mrs. Alice Israel. Both showed a blatant disregard for the vital work they were employed to undertake; both abused the trust of the owner of KV Clothing, Mr. A. Krivitsky who has built his business steadily over the last 35 years, transferring production from civilian clothing to military equipment as soon as requested by the British government. Both Hardcastle and Israel had every intention of carrying on their criminality as long as they could, developing their business empire, and it was only thanks to the quick thinking of Mrs. Israel's daughter that this evil was stopped for good."

There was an audible gasp from somewhere in the courtroom. So it was the daughter who betrayed her mother, who grassed up Vera, and Carol, Mary Leonard, and Mildred, Mary Galloway, Sarah and Hannah; it was the daughter who thought she was better than all of them. Those Jews – they were all the same, deep down.

"Whilst we heard the helpful testimony from Mr. Carter and we sympathize with the experience of Mrs. Israel's time in prison camps in Germany, this does not excuse her actions. Both offenders believed they were simply above the law of the land and had no regard for the impact of their actions on others. I don't have to remind you we are engaged in another Great War, and whilst we are proud of the combined efforts of our loyal and brave men alongside the Allied Forces, we still have a very long way to go before we defeat the evils of Hitler and those who fight alongside him. What you two have done undermines and makes a mockery of those who put their lives at risk for you and for others, every day. You betray them."

The Justice stopped and cleared his throat, ready for the final onslaught. He picked up his pen, holding it high to point at Alice. "Mrs. Israel. This country gave you safe refuge. It didn't have to. This country trusted you. You abused that trust. You held that trust in contempt. And you, of all people, with everything you have been through, should have known better. You should have shown your gratitude every day through hard work and good behavior. Unlike the loathsome country you have come from, this is a fair and just country. And that means good behavior is rewarded and bad behavior is punished."

He put the pen down and folded his hands in front of him. "Ray Hardcastle and Alice Israel. You will each receive a custodial sentence of 24 months. It will be up to the prison authorities as to whether, depending on your attitudes and behavior, this can be reduced by any length, but this bench recommends you each serve a minimum of 12 months. At the end of your sentence, under the Aliens Restriction Act of 1919, this country has the right to deport you back to your home country. If we are still at war at that time, the deportation decision will be delayed until peace is declared. That will be all."

There was a moment when the court was completely silent, and then noise erupted from every corner. Mildred was singing, "Roll out the barrel, we'll 'ave a barrel of fun!"

"Follow me, Ladies and Gentlemen, you are now under the loving care of His Majesty's Prison", said a prison officer as they descended to the cells below. Laughter, shouts and cries echoed in the gallery, and the general chatter of the court resumed.

Hedda hung back, watching the court reshape itself, keen to avoid any accidental meetings in the waiting area outside. Just before her descent, Alice had turned to Hedda in the public gallery and waved at her daughter, placing her hand on her heart and blowing her a kiss, and in that moment Hedda wished she could turn back time. She had made a terrible mistake. Her mother was now back behind bars and Hedda was no better than the Nazi officers. Her mother's last image of her daughter was of her scowling face.

"Please leave the courtroom, Madam," said the clerk, noticing that Hedda was not moving.

Mr. Krivitsky had thoughtfully given Hedda the whole day off, but she had no idea what to do or where to go. She thought of calling Betty, but Betty would be at work and probably not allowed to take a call in working hours. Valerie was at her sewing machine, and Peter? She had thought Peter might wait and that they would find a nice quiet place for a spot of lunch, but he was at the hospital. Helping others. Others more important than Hedda right now. The only place to while away the remaining hours was the British Museum, but that had been bombed and was closed. Then she remembered the London Library in St James Square. Standing outside the open doors of the courthouse, she examined the dark skies but decided against her umbrella. She would take her time, stroll down Bond Street and Piccadilly, and think her thoughts. Thoughts she wished belonged to someone else.

21

HAPPY EVER AFTER?

NOVEMBER 1943–DECEMBER 1944

Since the court date the previous week, Hedda and Peter had tiptoed around each other, a horrible veneer of politeness coating their limited conversation. He had worked additional shifts at the hospital, spending longer than he should with each patient, listening to vivid nightmares filled with death and dying. These were men who struggled to understand why they remained living when the man two inches away had been blown to pieces. They were men who couldn't sleep and, when they did, wished to be awake.

The day after the hearing, Hedda had caught a late train home, lingering in the small café visited by factory workers. She had cradled her cup of tea and flicked through a newspaper, keeping her head down to avoid chatter. But everyone was eager for gossip and news to take their minds off the endless war.

"Is that what you wanted? Did you think your mum would be put away for so long? Do you know where she is? Are you going to visit her? You're a heroine. Your mum is a nasty piece of work, deserves everything she got."

Hedda was less concerned about their opinions of Ray; Mr. Krivitsky had thanked Hedda repeatedly, even offering her "a small token of his appreciation," which she had declined. Taking money

219

as a reward for sending her mother to prison would feel uncomfortable to say the least. But she understood he wanted to give her *something,* and accepted an additional day of holiday. The authorities told her that Mrs. Israel was in Holloway Prison and settling in well. Hedda would be allowed a visit in a month or so, just before Christmas.

A week on and it was Sunday, a late autumn sun highlighting the bare branches of the trees in the North London gardens and parks. Hedda and Peter sat with Eric and Lionel, the latest resident of the house confined to bachelorhood, making conversation over the breakfast table, the subject of war always present. Newspapers lay open on the table next to cups of coffee and pieces of toast.

"Dreadful news, dreadful. Poor defenseless animals. 4,000 of them," said Lionel, referring to an article that described the weeklong bombing of Berlin. The zoo hadn't escaped the Allied Forces' air raids and as Lionel talked, the *Snow White* cinema with its luxurious red velvet seats flickered into Hedda's mind. It was probably rubble now. They had destroyed the Opera House. She wondered whether the Kaleckis' apartment still stood.

"I think I'll spend the day in town," said Eric. "There's absolutely nothing we can do dwelling on the lost souls of elephants and giraffes. Do you fancy it?"

Lionel thought it was a splendid idea, which meant Peter and Hedda would have the run of the place, the whole day to themselves. No excuses not to talk.

Peter was the first to break the awkward silence. "I think we should talk," he said. "There hasn't been much opportunity this week."

"I would like that. This last week has been awful," she said. "I hate this dreadful atmosphere. It makes me feel very sad."

The woods at this time of year were carpeted in a thick layer of gold, red and orange leaves just waiting to be tossed and kicked. If nothing else, they could breathe in the fresh air and clear their heads of the mess inside. Peter took Hedda's hand once they'd entered the woods and they followed the path that led to the stream. It had deep sides and flowed speedily, white flecks over stones, following days and days of rainfall. They stopped and watched the light play on the water.

"So, how are you?" he asked.

It was a start but she hated his formality. She pulled her hand away. "What a funny question!" Where to next? She'd batted away his opening move.

He persisted. "But I don't think you are fine, are you? Why *would* you be fine? You seem unhappy."

"Gosh! You don't have to be a psychiatrist to have noticed that! And I'm not one of your patients!" she said sharply. Clearly the anger she'd been feeling over the last week was waiting to come out, and here it was, frothing and foaming like the surface of the stream. "Sorry," she said, "but I can't bear you treating me like I'm a specimen to be examined. We're not in the hospital now."

"I'm sorry, my darling." He put his arm around her. "I didn't intend that."

She paused, then said, "I think I did the wrong thing. I've been thinking about it all week. It's been going round and round in my head. I should never have gone to the police. I got so many people into trouble. Those poor women." It was easier speaking like this, tracing the water's edge, looking at the tree shadows straddling the path, not looking directly at him. "I wish I could go back in time."

"You did what you felt was right at the time. You thought about it, weighed it up, and came to your decision. That was what we'd discussed."

Hedda didn't remember much "weighing up." She couldn't even remember entering the police station that morning; it was all such a blur.

"Now it's all over, what *would* you have done? If it *had been* a member of your family?"

"We've been over this before. It's not for me to say," he answered, an awful dead response.

"Why not?" Hedda's voice was rising, frustration building. "Why can't you be honest with me and just tell me? You must have known what could happen. Why didn't you tell me? When I asked for help, why didn't you? You just told me to grow up. You should have told me to leave things alone and I would have done."

"Don't you understand? It had to be your decision to make. You had to take responsibility for that decision, no one else." A rising blush covered Peter's neck and jawline, revealing more than he said.

"It was a terrible decision. You knew it from the start!" She screamed this, frightening away some nesting magpies.

"Probably!" he shouted back at her. "Yes! It was the wrong decision. Seeing you like this, seeing you so upset. Yes. You made a bad choice!"

"I knew it. You thought that all along. And it was me that made you give that evidence; it was me that made you stand up in court like that. You hate me!"

"Of course I don't hate you." A long pause followed. "I love you. You know that. But this is hard for both of us. Your mother is back in prison after you spent so much time getting her out. And you *got* her out, Hedda, you managed that! An utter heroine. Now, she's back inside and you're going to have to live with that."

He was right of course. *He* wouldn't have allowed high-handed judgements to get in the way of family loyalty. Not when the odds were so high.

"My mother only just survived the camp in Germany, she may not do so well a second time round. Oh, what have I done?"

Peter took her hand in his and looked at her directly. "She *will* survive. Your mother is one of the strongest people I've ever met. Truly. She may have her failings, and it was wrong to get tied up with Ray Hardcastle, but she's resilient. And she loves you. Like I do."

He pulled her towards him and held her tightly and she never wanted him to let her go. He forgave her. A huge weight had been lifted from her shoulders. He knew how to turn sadness to happiness, anger to tranquility. She loved him so much.

They walked back to the house in peaceful silence. They entered the kitchen and while he filled the kettle to make a pot of tea, she took off her coat and hat, picked up his, and hung them both in the hallway. She could feel her heart rate slowing and her mood lifting.

"There's something now, that I have to say. Something I need to tell you," said Peter as he waited for the kettle to boil.

Hedda's heart dropped to her stomach. He poured the water into the teapot and brought it to the table. She sat down and waited.

"I've been offered a new role, a new position, just this week. There's not been an opportunity to tell you – we've both been so busy."

A relief. That's fine, she thought. For one moment she had imagined he'd taken a new lover, someone he'd met at the hospital.

"It's an interesting role with the Directorate of Army Psychiatry."

Hedda had no idea what that was.

"There's a clinical project that's currently in development, and they wish me to participate in it."

"Gosh, that sounds fascinating."

"It's about studying how and why the Nazis think as they do. A bit like we were with Hess. Examining his thoughts."

"Yes?" she said, hoping he might explain more.

"Trying to untangle what makes people do evil things."

"Yes."

"It means I would have to go abroad."

"Abroad? Why? How can you be going abroad – you have work to do here."

"They think I would be excellent. If truth be told, there are few who speak German as fluently as I do and that's thanks to you." He smiled. She didn't smile back.

"They commented on my attendance at court on Monday. I'd asked for the morning off and they'd wanted more details. They seemed not to approve. They weren't happy I was providing a reference for a German immigrant. Not when we're at war with the country."

"But she's Jewish!"

"I know that. But it didn't seem to make much difference. In their eyes she's still an Enemy Alien, and a criminal one at that. They felt I had put myself in a difficult position. That I could have embarrassed the efforts of the Army Medical Corps if it got out to the wider public. Supporting the enemy so to speak, you know what our newspapers are like."

"Any more?" she asked.

"I think it will be about six months. They want me to fly out next week. It's a secret location."

"When exactly next week?" she said. Her voice was flat but her hands shook as she put the cup to her lips.

"Tuesday. There's a flight leaving on Tuesday from Northolt. I'll be home before you know it. I think I can be of use out there, so I've accepted the position."

She went upstairs to their bedroom. She opened the wardrobe, then the chest of drawers, removed her clothing and her few personal items. She packed her belongings into her brown suitcase that had sat in the corner of the room for the last two years. She placed the velvet drawstring bag, containing her jewelry, in her handbag: two necklaces, her two brooches and a simple gold bracelet that Peter had given her on her birthday.

She took a final look around, partly to check she'd left nothing, partly to memorize the totality of the room, then went down the stairs and out the front door. No point in saying goodbye. She waited an age for the underground down to King's Cross. When she exited into the daylight, the sun had disappeared entirely. She walked to Collier Street and rang the bell. Lizzie answered.

"Hedda! How are you? How's your mother? We've all been so worried about you. You must feel dreadful."

Hedda didn't reply. How she felt was not for sharing. Instead she said:

"I would like to stay here for a couple of days if that's alright? Just till I'm settled."

Without waiting for her response, she sidled down the corridor past Lizzie and into the kitchen. She lifted the biscuit tin off the top shelf and took out the key to room Number 5. She headed up the stairs, unlocked the door and entered. Alice's possessions were just where she had left them on Monday. The bed was made and the room was tidy. It was pitiful. Hedda placed her suitcase and handbag on the small table and removed her shoes. She took out her toothbrush and flannel and placed these on the bedside cabinet. Then she climbed into her mother's bed and pulled the pink eiderdown over her. She made herself as small as possible and turned towards the wall. She could smell her mother all over the sheets, sweet perfume and salty cooking and the scent of childhood. She felt her mother's arms embrace her in a warm hug. Hedda rested her head deep against her mother's soft chest. She was five years old again.

December 4, 1943

Dear Hedda

Thanks for letting me know where you were. I was worried. I arrived safely on Tuesday. I can't tell you where and they're very clever at not stamping the letters with postmarks, so no guessing either. We are just settling into our digs and getting to know one another. This promises to be a fascinating project and one I hope will change the course of history. I know that's a huge claim to make, but the work is valuable and important. I wanted to write to assure you that I'm safe and let you know that I hope to be home in March for a short visit, and then possibly by June, when we review the project. So not too long to wait, darling girl. Please write back care of Mill Hill. They promise they will forward on your letters.

Your ever loving Peter

P.S. I have a confession to make. Before I told you of my posting abroad, I did something stupid. I wanted something of you. I took the rose brooch. I expect you've noticed and wondered where on earth it is! I have it on the desk beside me as I write this letter. I should have asked first. I hope you can forgive me for this impulsive action and I promise I will return it to you when we are reunited.

March 11, 1944

Dear Hedda

I'm so sorry but it looks like I won't be home this March after all. It's taking much longer to design the scope of the project, let alone get going. We've hardly started. There has been so much professional disagreement. That's what it's like when you get a bunch of psychiatrists together in the same room. Anyway, the project is obviously delayed so it looks like we're planning to be over here till the end of the year at least. I'm so sorry. I do hope you are managing. It won't be long.

Your loving, Peter

October 2, 1944

Dear Hedda

Can you believe it's been nearly a whole year since I arrived here? No, I can't either. We're in a much better place with the project and if things continue to progress with the war effort, it looks like we might be on the way to a conclusion. And that would be splendid. On the other hand, there is now a proposal that we might support the country back on its feet when we defeat the buggers. I think it's going to be a while. And I'm going to say something very difficult. Please don't wait for me any longer. You are so young and it's mad to keep waiting for me. I just don't know when I'll be back. Life is too short.

With very best wishes, Peter

The last letter received by Hedda was in a different handwriting.

December 23, 1944

Dear Hedda

I'm writing to you on Peter's behalf. He has been extremely busy, what with the ongoing research and the new project, and he should have told you how life has changed for him in his last letter. Only recently did I find out that he failed to do so. I didn't like the idea of you still not knowing so I took it upon myself to write to you and he is now aware of this. I know he's very sorry and regrets his poor communication and hopes you are well. The news is this: he and I have been getting to know one another over the last year or so. I'm a doctor of neurology. While we were working together, Peter and I discovered that we had close relatives from Treorchy, the same little village in Wales. It was a delightful coincidence! We had lots to share and lots in common. During the course of our work, we found ourselves becoming close and now believe that we have a future together. I don't doubt this is difficult for you to read and it's difficult for me to write, but what would be worse would be keeping you in the dark and giving you false hope.

Peter wondered whether you might, in the end, return to Germany. Not now of course. If you do, then it would be pleasant to meet up.

With best wishes, Patricia

Well, of course. He was always going to revert to type, to his own kind. The alien Jewish girl from another country was always a dalliance, a bit of exoticism, a chance to demonstrate his wide-ranging cultural tastes but in the end, the woman he would settle for, whom he would marry, who would bear his blue-eyed, pale-skinned children, would be respectable, educated, and thoroughly British, brought up within the chiming bells of a decent country church.

PART III

22

CROSSING CONTINENTS
LONDON

1944–1953

The months that passed following Peter's departure to Germany and marriage to Patricia were pleasant enough, more so than Hedda might have expected. The end of the war was a blessed relief and the celebrations were a sight to behold.

Valerie, finally married to Thomas, and Hedda joined forces with the others from the factory and partied, drinking and laughing, kissing and hugging. Everyone was grateful to Mr. Churchill and the soldiers and sailors and flyers for bringing victory. They tried not to think about the millions of dead in every corner of the world: bodies lying under the rubble of bombed buildings, buried in mud-filled rivers, or resting in unmarked forest graves. Hedda tried her hardest to shut out the images from the news films of Dachau and Auschwitz – skeletal figures, hands reaching out, no longer recognizable as human beings. And if she couldn't prevent those images entering her thoughts and dreams occasionally, she wasn't going to talk about it to Valerie or Thomas or anyone else. During this terrible six-year war, everyone had suffered. Her suffering, and the suffering of the Jewish people was no different; no one, she decided, could claim a monopoly on human tragedy.

That May Day in 1945 was a great big thank you to Mr. Churchill and it was hard for anyone to imagine what would happen next. No one expected that just a few months later, he would be thrown out in favor of Mr. Attlee and his Labour government. Hedda had no vote but was sad that despite Churchill's great victory, the good British people wanted a change. They were exhausted and she knew the saying: "a change is as good as a rest."

She had come to terms with solo living, without a lover, without a mother. She had found herself a small flat in Hammersmith at a reasonable rent, and the pleasure of having her own bathroom and toilet almost made up for the self-pity in which she very occasionally indulged. The landlord was a friend of Mr. Krivitsky. They'd been at school together and Hedda was recommended to him. He provided a character reference and said there would be no problem in paying the rent as she was still employed by KV Clothing. Mr. Faber was happy to oblige a good Jewish girl like her.

Her own place. And preferable to rattling around the abandoned luxury of the Berlin apartment, following the sudden departure of the Kaleckis. She bought a few things to make it homely and ran up a small curtain from a permissible factory off-cut to cover the under-the-sink area. She loved returning after a hard day at the factory, removing her clothes, leaving them where they fell, and jumping into her own bath. Freedom, she thought, as she lay in the soapy lukewarm water. No longer having to depend on others' whims and fancies, not Eric's or Lionel's or even Peter's. Many times, she felt she had arrived. An independent woman about town.

Rationing continued and there was a grayness to life. From time to time, she also felt "gray:" not a brooding charcoal black, just the gray of the grimy, soot-covered pavement. On those days, she indulged in thoughts of Peter, and would descend into a shadowland. She was angry, and angry at still feeling angry, and this tied her up inside. She would rerun the final walk in the woods and how she was lulled into thinking all was well before the hammer blow when he announced his departure. So casually. *I've been posted abroad, darling. They* need *me there.* Of course they did. He was indispensable, wasn't he? He'd been cruel, and she hadn't known that about him. Better to have found out then, she supposed, than later on.

Hedda visited her mother on and off while she was in Pentonville. The first visit was shortly after her sentencing, just before another wartime Christmas. It was thoughtful of them to allow Christmas visits and she was grateful to the authorities but what she saw shocked her, both the state of the prison and the physical deterioration of her mother. Prison noise was overwhelming: the cacophony of metal doors slamming shut, frustrated shouts and screams, reprimands and orders echoing around the thick Victorian walls. Deafness would be a blessed relief in this place.

When she saw Alice, Hedda's gloved hand shot to cover her mouth to muffle her shock. She pretended to be temporarily lost in a fit of coughing. Her mother's hair had turned from light brown to gray and was wispy and thin. There were even some bald patches, maybe the after-effects of the shock of imprisonment. She looked haggard. Hedda had never seen Alice without flesh on her bones, never seen her cheeks other than round and rouged. She had probably looked like this in the German prison camps, but the SS officers hadn't issued reels of Kodak to the inmates. She wondered if she had failed to notice Alice's weight loss before her incarceration, so wrapped up in life with her ex-lover.

On that first visit, they both struggled. Hedda wondered why she had felt compelled to go to the police and could no longer understand what had motivated her to throw her mother to the wolves. They argued. Alice blamed her daughter for her misery, then screamed that Hedda would forget her and that she would die in this foreign land – all alone. When Hedda said that was untrue and unfair, her mother rejected her daughter's reassurances. Hedda had abandoned her before. Hedda told her that was unkind; she had worked ceaselessly to get her out. She *had* been out and free until *she* decided to steal the nylon and sell the stockings, knowing it was against the law. Alice cried and Hedda found that hard. No daughter likes to see their mother crying.

Hedda next visited her mother on a rainy day in early spring when her mother was looking rosier in the face and after that, she took the bus to the prison every few months until Alice's release on another rainy day in November 1945. War was over. Alice had served the full 24 months, not a single day removed from her sentence despite her excellent behavior. In the end she had adapted well to her prison surroundings; she saw the best in people and made good friends, and they liked her cheerful disposition. She was a good cook in the prison kitchen and people liked that too. The prison guards warmed to her, teased her about her strong accent and poor use of English, and got her to repeat rude words and phrases like a pirate's parrot. She had a knack of winning people over and was almost sad the day the giant doors swung open and she was free to go.

They had arranged accommodation for her in a halfway house in Hampstead where she stayed for a few months. They couldn't send her back despite the earlier threat of deportation; Germany had been destroyed, razed to the ground. The authorities knew it was impossible to return Alice along with the many others to a country with no electricity, no clean water, no homes in which to live. Thousands of displaced persons from Poland, Austria, Russia and Germany, refugees in their own countries, required resettling. How could they send her back to the country where the evidence of mass extermination of Jews was apparent for all but the blind to see?

So she stayed. Hedda met up with her mother from time to time and talked about nothing much, until the day Alice announced she was returning to Saarbrücken, thanks to the German Repatriation Fund for German Jews, and would be living in a small house just outside the town. She would be receiving a monthly pension, not a fortune by any means, she told Hedda, but enough to live on. There she could afford some occasional visits to the hairdresser. Maybe they could turn her into a pretty brunette again? She laughed but it was important. And why not? It was those small things that made life bearable.

Hedda traveled with her to Dover. They sat on the bus together from Victoria and watched the fields of Kent pass by, sharing thoughts about the crossing, and were grateful that there was no wind and the waters would be calm. Nearing the end of the journey, Alice took her daughter's hand, stroked it, and planted the gentlest of kisses on her open palm. Then she moved it to her own cheek and held it there, transferring the kiss from flesh to flesh. At that moment Hedda truly loved her mother. She watched as Alice boarded the boat, holding the large carpet bag in one hand and her suitcase in the other. Hedda remembered the day Alice had changed into her finest clothes, preparing for the Gestapo arrest. She had been brave, inventing the story of the wireless to protect her husband and daughter. A time when her mother was capable of a good deed, of doing the right thing. Those times were just too few.

She stood on the deck and waved and Hedda waved back. On the other side, Alice would purchase a ticket that would take her through Belgium and Luxembourg and then onto *Saarbrücken*. Alice Israel was going home.

1953

And so, as in all the best fairy tales told by the Brothers Grimm, several years passed and the young girl grew into a mature wise lady, but unlike in the stories, no handsome prince came to her rescue. Not that she needed saving. She was an independent free-thinking woman who was enjoying her breakfast of porridge and toast when the telephone rang. It came with the rental, but Hedda had few people to call or who called her. She was waiting to hear from Valerie and Thomas as to how they were settling into their home in Redhill, following their move to the Surrey suburbs. She wanted to meet the new baby, Erica, and hold her in her arms. Hedda imagined the soft baby skin and those tiny hands and the way the baby's fingers would curl around hers. But she also worried about the tremendous responsibility of bringing a child into the world and how life would always be defined by the child's needs rather than one's own. How would she manage? How had her mother managed? On the third ring she picked up the phone.

"Hello," she said, "Hedda Israel here."

"Hedda, my darling, it's Betty!" screamed a familiar voice.

Betty? Hedda felt a rush of prickly skin-tingling blood across her face and chest. Betty hadn't been in touch in months. Years had gone by with minimal contact. After Peter's sudden departure and subsequent marriage to Patricia, Betty and Hedda had attempted to remain friendly, but it was awkward. Betty's loyalties were divided, both women unsure whether to avoid all mention of him. Hedda didn't want to express her feelings of anger and hurt as well as her love, afraid that Betty would blab straight back to Peter. Nor did she want news of Patricia, or how his job was going, and Hedda assumed Betty was relieved when their meetings dried up, saving them both the discomfort of these encounters.

Hedda wasn't even sure where Betty was anymore. She knew from previous conversations that her relationship with Viktor was more serious, so much so that she had been considering conversion, despite Viktor's casual attitude towards the religion. She was taking classes at the synagogue in Belsize Park and Hedda was shocked when Betty told her she was learning Hebrew and attending Saturday services. Betty, with her blonde curls and English rose complexion, becoming a Jew! Hedda found the idea hard to accept. But that had been well over a year ago and she hadn't seen Betty or Viktor since. She knew that they weren't living together: Betty had developed the habits of a nun, albeit a Jewish one, and would consider premarital relations inappropriate, so maybe this phone call was an invitation to a wedding?

"How lovely to hear from you," she said, hoping she was disguising her shock. "I was just about to go out for a walk." That was a lie but she didn't want Betty to think she wasn't a busy bee with places to go and friends to meet.

"Oh my darling, it's been far too long. Where does the time go? It flies, it flies. I've got some very exciting news!"

Here it comes, thought Hedda. Wedding bells. "Oh, do tell me," she asked.

"Absolutely not. I want to see your face when I tell you. I'm going to keep you in suspense."

"Oh Betty..."

How Betty loved her drama. She and Hedda's sister would have made perfect companions.

"So. What are you doing today? Can you meet up with me and Viktor?" she asked.

It's definitely wedding news, Hedda decided. She wants to show off the ring.

"Shall we say midday at the Lyons Tea Room? Midday alright for you, darling? We'll be upstairs. Toodle-ooh!" And she rang off.

Hedda spent some time deciding what to wear. She wanted to look her best, for Betty to think, "you look gorgeous, darling, clearly thriving." She didn't want Betty's pity. In the end, not having a huge choice in her small wardrobe, she chose her favorite, a much-worn maroon dress covered in small polka dots, pulled in at the waist with a narrow belt. She'd recently treated herself to a new pair of cream shoes and decided it was the perfect day to try them out despite worries about blisters.

She caught the tube into central London, then sat on the top deck of the bus, enjoying the lions of Trafalgar Square, and marveling at how London life had almost returned to normal. Walking into the tea-room, she was filled with fluttering butterflies. It was going to be hard seeing Betty again in the flesh with her jutting cheekbones and that sweet smile, so like Peter's. She hoped Betty would avoid all discussions of her brother, though knowing her, she would blunder in with stories of his blissfully happy marriage. Hedda didn't even know if Peter had become a father; he had always wanted to start his own family when the time was right. During many long wartime nights, they had agreed they both wanted children once the war was over. It felt like the most natural thing to celebrate their love. They had even decided on names:

Imogen, who would have glorious red hair and pale freckled skin like Peter, and Samuel, who would look like Hedda with a cheeky round face.

She climbed the stairs to the first floor and saw the unmistakable figures of Betty and Viktor in the far corner, leaning forward, their heads almost touching. They didn't spot Hedda's arrival. Were they deep in conversation or kissing? Despite her dread of what lay ahead, Hedda crossed the floor and by the time she reached their table, Betty had seen her and their heads pulled apart.

"Hedda. It's you! After all this time. My dear darling, how absolutely wonderful," she said in a gush of words as if the hot tap had been left to run. "Viktor, isn't it just sweet to see Hedda again, and doesn't she look well, so pretty and what a delightful dress. Sit down," she said and poured Hedda a cup of tea without asking.

As Betty ordered, Hedda studied her friend's face. She looked exactly the same as five years ago, although her hair was darker and on closer inspection Hedda noticed her lipsticked mouth was etched with vertical lines and there were definitely some wrinkles around her eyes. Older. But wiser?

"There's just so much to tell you, I have *no* idea where to start. But how are you, darling? What's your news?"

Hedda told them she was well, still working at KV Clothing but as a senior supervisor now; she had her own flat at a reasonable rent and was quite content. She didn't mention her regular introspection: "Why didn't I just turn away from my mother's wrongdoing and keep my lips sealed?" From the way Betty was fidgeting and throwing looks at Viktor, Hedda knew that Betty was simply dying to move onto her news. As it was, Hedda had little else she wanted to share.

"You both look very well. I think I might have guessed what you might want to tell me..." Hedda's scrambled eggs had arrived, and she picked up her knife and fork, indicating it was Betty's turn to talk.

"Have you really?" Betty said with the old twinkle in her eye. "Go on then. What's our news going to be?"

"I'm sure Hedda doesn't want these guessing games. Shall I tell her or will you?" said Viktor.

Hedda realized she hadn't yet heard him speak; she'd forgotten his strong Viennese accent, reminding her of childhood holidays and happier times. "Are you getting married?" she asked them tentatively.

Betty started to whistle Mendelssohn's wedding march then broke into laughter. As she did, Hedda spotted the thin gold band on her friend's finger and felt a fool.

"No darling! We're already married! Last year. Simple affair, you know, very few guests, but it was all part of my conversion and once that had happened, we did the deed in Finchley Synagogue. Viktor just wanted us to trot off to the local Registry Office but I wasn't having any of it. I've become a 'Jewess', isn't that amazing, and I'm going to make sure we do things properly. The community has welcomed me in; they have been so generous, it would have been a disgrace if we hadn't married under the chupa!"

Hedda was taking her time with her eggs, pleased to have something to focus on rather than the outpourings of Betty.

"Anyway, we're husband and wife now, and are enjoying all the benefits of marriage." She winked at Hedda. "We're moving to Israel! Everything's packed. Most of our possessions were sent on two months ago, so it's just a matter of saying goodbye to our dearest friends and then, whoosh! We will be catching the train right down to Naples where we're going to spend a few days seeing Pompeii and the volcano, and then taking the boat across the Mediterranean. The journey will be magnificent. In a month's time, Viktor will start his new job in Tel Aviv. The hospital has only been open for two years! It's sparkling new. The Sheba Medical Centre. They're only taking the very best doctors, and Viktor is one of them. Isn't it a small miracle?"

Hedda was finding Betty's news hard to digest: first her wholesale adoption of Judaism, learning the scriptures, reading the holy books, getting married in the synagogue, and finally moving to the new state of Israel. Betty was so very English, the English rose with blonde hair and pale skin and red lips, and a provocative wiggle to her hips. And Viktor? He was no zealot, no believer. He was a cynic when it came to matters of religion, someone who looked down his Jewish nose at those who practiced.

"Are you pleased for us?" Betty said, interrupting Hedda's thoughts.

"Betty and Viktor. Huge congratulations," she said. "Congratulations on your wedding news and congratulations on..." She paused, not sure what to call it. "Finding your new home."

"You're absolutely right. I hadn't thought of it that way. It *is* our new home. To be honest darling, this place no longer feels right for either of us. There are people around who have some dreadful attitudes when it comes to," she took Viktor's hand to indicate what she meant, "our sort. As soon as Viktor opens his mouth and speaks in that German accent– "

"Austrian," he interrupted.

"I know that darling, but everyone thinks he's German. Anyway, he's heard his own patients saying he should go back, or that we fought the war against his sort. It's awful," she said. "So we're going. Once we're there and settled, we will write and let you know how we are. Wouldn't it be wonderful if the next time we speak, I will be holding a little baby," she said coyly.

"Are you–"

"No, darling, but we'll certainly start trying as soon as our feet touch the soil of the Holy Land. Thank goodness this government made Israel happen, a safe place for us to be."

The meals were finished and the tea was cold. Hedda thought it was probably time to say her goodbyes. "It's been so lovely seeing you both again. I'll make a move now," she said and got up to leave.

"No!" Betty cried. "There's more. You can't go yet."

They'd had weddings and baby talk and emigration news. It couldn't be bad health news because they were both far too happy. She had no idea what else Betty might say.

Betty was looking meaningfully at Viktor. "Go on, Vicky. You talk to her."

Viktor coughed and cleared his throat as if about to address the assembled customers. "When I was on the Isle of Man I made several friends. One of those friends is also from Vienna. In fact, there were many from there, artists and musicians and scientists and this man, he was training to be an architect. He'd already started his studies in Austria, and was going to continue in London except he, like all of us, got shoved into that wretched camp."

"Vicky, what's that got to do with it? You can't tell Hedda his whole life story."

"I'm getting there, Bets, I'm just setting the scene. I'd better shorten this tale, it seems. His name is Leon. He was married to another refugee but I'm very sad to say she died very recently."

"Oh," Hedda said. She had no idea why Viktor was telling her this and was embarrassed. It was sad but nothing to do with her.

He continued: "Anyway, Leon is father to two little girls. The youngest was born only a few weeks ago, I believe. The older girl is five or six. I'm sorry, I can't remember their names."

"They're called Clarice and Rebecca," Betty said. "Why are men so dreadful with names?"

"The thing is, he's finding it difficult to cope. What with mourning the death of his late wife," he said. Hedda wondered how she had died, but thought better than to ask.. "And Trying to hold down his new job, and managing the girls, well, it's all a bit much."

Hedda said nothing. Embarrassed, she didn't understand why they were telling her this and just wanted to get on with her day. She had decided she would stroll back to Charing Cross and catch a bus to South Kensington – this Sunday was rapidly disappearing.

As Hedda was planning her next moves, Betty burst out: "Hedda, we were all wondering if you'd like to meet him? Leon. Don't be offended! I can see it in your face! We think you would really like him. He's intelligent and handsome and such a good friend of Viktor's, and we love you so much and just think that maybe..." She tailed off.

"Maybe what?"

"Maybe if you were to meet him, you would see what a nice man he was, is, I mean, even though he's very sad right now, that won't last forever, and something, something might develop?"

The pounding heart Hedda had felt at the start of the meeting was there again, twice as fast and twice as loud. She didn't know if she should slam her hands down on the table and exclaim, "How dare you? How dare you think I'm just going to be someone's seconds?" or say, "Well, thank you so much for thinking of me, I could do with a man, I'm not getting any younger, and a ready-made family as well!" Hedda said neither of these things and instead shuffled her feet under the table.

"Leon would be very grateful if you were available to meet him. We said we would talk to you and let him know. His father lives here in London too, and they would happily meet you together, if you would like that? He's in Putney, so not far from you. They were suggesting the Association of Jewish Refugees. Leon's even written down the address with a date and time."

Hedda looked at the piece of paper, two neat lines recorded in an artistic hand. A Sunday morning, 11 o'clock. She just happened to be free. She took the note and put it in her handbag. She was trembling.

"Well, this has been a meeting full of surprises," she said, getting up again, but this time with no intention of indulging further conversation. "Thank you. Let him know that I'll attend." So formal. She felt like she'd been summoned. She started to walk towards the stairs, then turned. "The very best of luck, dear friends. Enjoy your new life." As a final thought, she said, "Do you know, we didn't once talk about Peter." But her friends were lost in conversation, hands grasped across the table, sharing thoughts of Naples and Israel, of Vienna and Putney.

23

REBIRTH

1953–1956

That week, Hedda had trouble sleeping. Her nighttime dreams were filled with strange elderly men, mouths twisted in ugly grimaces and reaching out their blue-veined hands to grab hold of her. In her dreams she evaded their bony fingers, but their desperate hopeless faces played on after she woke up in the early hours. In a damp sweat, she would get up and wash, then pace the room, watching the sky turn gray, then pink, then blue.

She knew she didn't have to meet him. She was under no obligation to this man, this stranger. On the piece of paper was a telephone number and it was just a matter of dialing it and telling the man she was unavailable, this Sunday and every other Sunday. Maybe there was a whole queue of women lined up? Maybe he wouldn't like the look of her, or maybe he'd already met with others and rejected them? More importantly, maybe she would find him ugly and mean. By the time the working week was over and the weekend had arrived, she was a quivering wreck with pasty skin and dark shadows under her eyes. No chance now.

Like so much of postwar Britain, the offices in which Hedda met Leon and his father, Mendel Meier, were gray and featureless. Faded leaflets were strewn on side tables in the meeting room, advertising friendship groups and other useful organizations designed to support the thousands of Jewish refugees who were making their lives in Britain. She remembered the leaflet when she first arrived fresh off the boat, with instructions not to speak German in public, and to be polite and respectful at all times. And now here she was, hoping to become naturalized and sever the very last connections to the country that had stripped her and countless others of their rightful citizenship.

When she first walked into the meeting room, Hedda froze in the doorway; Viktor and Betty had played a mean trick. It was Viktor, sitting on one of the four worn chairs, it was Viktor moving his heavy glasses from one hand to another. Hedda knew Viktor's crouched body shape anywhere. An older man, Viktor's father, sat beside him. They both stood as Hedda unfroze and stepped forward into the room, and shuffled their feet awkwardly. It was then she noticed the man she had taken to be Viktor was a couple of inches shorter but in every other way identical. The same dark hair worn long over the collar, the same olive skin, glasses framing an intelligent moody face, and a romantic stubble across his jaw line. Neither the man nor his father said a word, they just stood there, eyes lowered. Hedda hadn't expected this sort of inhospitable reception.

"Hello," she dived in, breaking the awkward silence, "I'm Hedda Israel. I'm pleased to meet you both."

Unbelievably to Hedda, it was the father who spoke next. "Pleased to meet you too," he said haltingly in a strong Viennese accent. "This is my son, Leon. I think you know a little about our circumstances?"

My son? Hedda felt she had been thrown back in time to old family gatherings where her parents would introduce her and her sister to their new friends and acquaintances: "Here are my lovely daughters, Edith and Hedda. Say hello, children." Edith would curtsey, half mocking the assembled company. Hedda remembered that horrible creeping shyness and how she would hang close to her mother's dress, reluctant to engage with the oily smiling strangers. She could turn on her heel and leave right now, nothing lost. She'd remember another appointment, another event she had stupidly forgotten to put on her calendar, but as she stood there studying Leon and his tragic face, the way he resembled Viktor, and remembering those stirrings she had had for Viktor all those years ago, she decided there was nothing to lose.

"Please, sit down," Leon said, pulling out a chair and joining her. There was a jug of water on the table, and as he poured himself a glass, Hedda could see his hand shaking, drops of water splashing onto the tablecloth. She felt sorry for him. She hadn't considered that he might also be nervous.

"Leon. Offer a glass to Hedda!" said his father, reminding the impolite son to mind his manners.

He poured her a glass and passed it across. His hand still shook. She noticed a thin gold wedding band and wondered whether he imagined he was still married to his dead wife.

"I'm sorry," Leon said. His voice was Viennese but less accented than his father's. "I think Viktor told you my wife died very suddenly, very recently, and I'm not thinking as clearly as I would normally. Please forgive me."

He looked her straight in the eye for the first time since her arrival, and Hedda held his gaze. His face was riven with sadness. It had the look of someone just managing to survive, his head inches above the waterline, breathing in small gasps of air that allowed him to remain living, minute to minute. This man, this helpless, hopeless man, she could look after him, help him, rescue him. She could give him the oxygen he so desperately needed.

"I have two young girls. One is just a few months old. She is being cared for by the council. The older one, she's six years old and my father is helping me, and a neighbor helps as well."

Whilst Hedda was interested in the baby and the little girl, she was even more curious to know how Leon's wife had died, but it would have been rude and intrusive.

"Viktor spoke very highly of you," said Leon.

The thought they'd been discussing her, sharing her personal details, maybe saying nice things about her, filled her with pleasure. She had been the subject of another's conversation. For however short a time, Hedda Israel had been the center of someone else's world. No one ever thought about her, not since her ex-lover had left. She was flattered. She wondered what they might have said: "Pretty and sweet-faced, if you like that sort of thing, but no film star: intelligent, but never finished her education, not very ambitious but works hard. Had a bit of a doomed love affair with an older man. We don't really talk about it."

"Oh, that's nice," she said. "It was good to see Viktor and Betty last week before their move to Israel. They were so excited."

"Yes. Don't really understand it myself. All rather radical if you ask me, this move overseas. Viktor and I had lots of time to share our thoughts on the subject, amongst many other things, and I'm no Zionist. Although it is, of course, essential there's somewhere where Jews can feel safe." He paused and looked off into the distance. "I often wonder what it means to be a Jew. I'm not religious, you see, not like my father."

Mendel, the father, was not looking happy. "Leon, I'm sure Hedda doesn't want to know your views on politics or your inability to embrace the meaning of Judaism."

"No that's fine," she interrupted. "I'm not a believer, either."

"Well, maybe with time I can change both your minds. God directs every thought and action and one day you will come to know Him."

"I doubt it," Leon said and offered her the first attempt at a smile.

Hedda melted.

Over the next several weeks they exchanged more personal details. Leon brought the children to the Jewish Refugee Offices and Hedda fell head over heels in love with them both. Rebecca, the baby, had a shock of dark hair and deep brown eyes, and she liked nothing more than being picked up and cuddled. Her little arms would wave in the air and she would gurgle as she was lifted high. Clarice was a chattering, confident six-year-old keen to hold Hedda's hand and tell her the name of each of her dolls. Hedda thought of Anna's exuberance and her pleasure in sharing her news and views. She thought of Dorothy clutching her hand tightly in the air raid shelter as the German bombers thundered overhead.

Unlike the children, Leon was not a physical man, and studiously avoided handholding and the other small gestures that normally announced the start of a new relationship. Hedda remembered more intimacy during her teenage park walks with Walter. But she put his lack of interest down to grief and loss and was patient and undemanding.

On January 1, 1954, they married in Wandsworth Town Hall and Hedda Israel became Hedda Meier. The small group of guests were dressed in wooly scarves and hats to keep out the bitter winter cold, and there was hardly time to take off the thick coats before the ceremony was over, and Leon and Hedda were announced as "Man and Wife." Mendel was there, along with Mr. Krivitsky who had given the couple two beautiful blue vases which had come all the way from Hungary. They had been in his family for decades and he wanted Hedda to have them. A lady from the council attended and Rebecca slept through the whole affair whilst the kind neighbor was on hand to ensure that Clarice had company.

Betty and Viktor sent a card decorated with a golden menorah underneath the wedding canopy, and Valerie and Thomas rang to extend their good wishes but were too tied up in nappies and washing and household duties to attend. They sent lots of love and promised to visit soon. No one looked particularly happy and it seemed that Leon and Mendel were pleased when it was over.

Hedda moved in that day, into the flat in Drysdale Road, though nothing happened that night. Hedda could sense the ghost of his first wife in every space. When she opened cupboard doors, Wife One stretched out her manicured fingers and stroked Hedda's cheek, soft as a feather. When Hedda pushed the broom underneath the bed she felt Wife One's elegant hand grab hold of the brush and tug lightly. When Hedda turned the tap on fully in the bathroom, Wife One turned it half off. She hid behind the bedroom curtains and waited by the front door. Hedda felt her cold breath on their wedding night, and the next night, and for many weeks after.

Leon would roll away from Hedda, complaining of tiredness and headaches, and she would pull the sheets and blankets around her to make up for his lack of touch. He was not tender. Hedda had little time to think about her new life, or about Leon's lack of feelings. Later, she would examine her motives for marrying him. Little Rebecca shared their room and Clarice slept in the small room next door, only a thin wall away, so it was hardly surprising that intimacy was absent. Hedda's days were filled with feeding, winding, changing, and playing with the baby, walking Clarice to school each morning and collecting her each afternoon, shopping and cooking, keeping the flat tidy and ensuring the dishes were washed and put away after every meal. Her previous experience of babies was limited to her single visit to Valerie and Thomas when she had held Erica who had been asleep, eyes tightly shut and taking the tiniest of soundless breaths. Hedda had somehow imagined that bringing up a baby would always be that simple and perfect.

On a bitter cold February night at 3:13 according to the luminous paint on the clock beside the bed, Leon rolled over, pulling most of the sheets and blankets around him and off Hedda. Rebecca was crying as she did each and every night. Lying there shivering, Hedda ran through all the baby checks. She had fed and changed her, cuddled her, fed her again, but still baby Rebecca carried on wailing. Her dark eyes were red-ringed, her tiny fists screwed into golf-sized balls and her strong back arched in pain. Sometimes Hedda wondered if she cried for her lost mother, but then remembered she had cried loudly as soon as she had entered the world and hadn't stopped since. Hedda didn't take it personally. And anyway, Rebecca was always happy to spend time with her new mother during the daytime. It was just the long desperate nights when her little tears flowed. Hedda lifted her from the cradle, careful not to wake Leon, and rocked her gently. She continued her lament.

"Sshh…" Hedda whispered softly. "Sshh."

The baby sobbed, her back still stiff.

"Please little Rebecca, don't cry, don't cry."

And then a tune Hedda hadn't thought of in years, a sweet song that Ramades would sing about his lover, Aida, filled her head. Egyptian kings and queens, slaves and serving girls passed in front of her like the paintings on an Egyptian frieze. She stood on the desert sand, giant carved pharaohs behind her.

"Celeste Rebecca, queen of my thoughts, you are the splendor of my life..." she sang quietly. Rebecca's name fitted perfectly in place of Aida's. She continued singing the song and as she did, Rebecca's beautiful dark eyes began to close, her body relaxed, and the crying stopped. Hedda watched her fall into a deep Egyptian dreamless sleep.

The bedroom door swung open and Hedda saw little Clarice standing there, framed in the doorway.

"I had a dream," she said in a tiny voice. She rubbed her eyes as if to remove the images.

"Was it a bad one?" Hedda asked.

Clarice didn't answer but sidled into the bed and squeezed herself between the baby and Hedda. With the smallest of movements, Hedda gently placed Rebecca back in her cradle and climbed into bed. Then she wrapped her arms around Clarice's warm body and whispered: "Sweet dreams, dear Clarice, sweet dreams." For the first time since becoming a Meier, Hedda had become a real mother.

***

Leon began work as Chief Architect for Richmond Borough Council six months after the wedding. It was a big step up and testament to his hard work, creativity, and talent. The promotion filled him with pride and as far as Hedda was concerned, he seemed happy for the first time since she had known him. His happiness was contagious, and his pleasure fed her pleasure; they were beginning to feel like a real family. He preferred not to discuss his work with her, and as Hedda's days were filled with childcare, she would have liked some news of the outside world. However sweet and jolly Rebecca was, adult conversations were largely missing. Sometimes she thought she would like to return to work with the chatter and camaraderie of the factory, less tied to every whim of the baby and request of Leon's. On bad days, she felt like a glorified domestic rather than a wife and mother but then Rebecca would break her heart with her fits of giggles, and she felt grateful to be caring for these two wonderful little girls and their father. And finally, they got round to some sort of love life. Rebecca was sleeping through the night and had moved into Clarice's room, and although he rarely showed Hedda much affection in public, he was prepared to show her a little more in private.

It was the end of another busy week, the domestic routine well-established over the last two years, and Hedda was in the kitchen finishing off the chicken soup. She was just about to add the egg which formed those delightful strips of flavor in the hot broth when Leon burst through the door, the most animated she had seen him in ages. He was waving a large piece of paper, folded over several times.

"I've bought some land," he said, his face alight with accomplishment.

"Pardon? What on earth do you mean?"

She turned off the gas and leaned against the table where Clarice and Rebecca, now a sturdy two-year-old, had finished their tea and were playing with the last bits of toast, most ending up on the kitchen floor.

"I didn't want to say anything until it was definite. There's a street in Richmond, well a little place called Petersham, close to the river. It's a very nice area, and the council is selling plots on one side of the road. I've bought one. I got one of the first choices! I've been working on the design for months and I think you'll like it. The girls will have their own bedrooms, with one bedroom spare for when my father comes to stay, then a kitchen, a study and large living room. There will be a garden, front and back. I'm very excited. I hope you will be too."

Excited? Hedda was amazed and shocked and frightened: a great cocktail of emotions. She was going to be living in their very own house. From the sound of it, a proper family house, not just an apartment owned by another. A house big enough for Leon and Clarice and Rebecca and possibly, just possibly, one more occupant, she thought. A garden in which the girls could run around, play games, dress up, read books, and where she could plant flowers and grow vegetables.

"I am, I am. Thank you. I am so very happy. Our own house," she said.

She sat down and Leon unfolded the paper containing the house plans and spread it out on the table.

"Girls," he said, "I've got something exciting to show you."

That night they celebrated. In bed, he made the first move. They made love and Hedda believed he meant it. She felt her life was beginning and that he would put the past behind him. She didn't expect him to ever forget Ena, but now they were planning a future for themselves and the children, and happiness was within her grasp.

She knew Ena's story and she understood how troubled she had been before she died. She had suffered a terrible depression for many months and years, and pregnancy and childbirth had worsened her mood to the point where she saw no options ahead. Otherwise, Clarice and Rebecca's mother would never have done what she did. She would never have left two darling daughters if she were of sound mind. Leon knew this to be true but found it difficult to accept. Or forgive. Sometimes at his most open he told Hedda how selfish he thought Ena had been, leaving him with the baby and with Clarice, not caring how he would feel when he found her lifeless body. But most of the time, he remained silent on the subject, and she was grateful to him for sparing her the horror of listening to his anger and his grief. Now they could move on.

And new life *was* beginning. Six weeks after Leon had come home clutching the plans for the house, Hedda became sick in a way she'd never felt before. She didn't dare leave the flat, consumed by an overwhelming nausea. Poor Rebecca said: "Mummy, what's wrong?" as she rushed to the bathroom yet again.

Leon was never around to support Hedda, far too busy traveling between work, the flat, and the building site of the new house. The foundations were laid and the yellow brick walls went up; Leon had access to a team of council laborers and builders who were quick and efficient.

When Hedda first viewed the site, her belly was round, and the first butterfly wings fluttered inside her. The house was beautiful. At the front he had designed a long window that stretched the full length of the house across the living room to allow in maximum light. It overlooked what would be a front garden filled with tall trees, now just a muddy patch with a digger and stacked bricks. Hedda gazed through an upstairs window and imagined herself standing there, on the other side of the glass, looking at a magnolia tree covered in blooms, her new child in her arms.

In late March when the sun was shining and the daffodils still covered the grassy banks outside the newly built houses, they moved in. Seven weeks later Hedda's mother traveled from Saarbrücken to attend the birth. They hadn't seen each other since her departure from Dover and Hedda thought Alice looked fatter and healthier than when they had waved goodbye. Alice seemed happy to see her younger daughter and pinched the grandchildren's cheeks and tickled them under their chins. She'd brought them little hedgehog toys, Macki and Mucki, and Rebecca and Clarice loved them. They took them on a tour of the house, pointing out every cupboard, every lampshade, accompanied by the wonderful chatter of childhood: "This is my bedroom, Macki, and this is where Mummy and Daddy sleep."

It was the first time Alice met Leon, though Hedda had sent her family photographs and she'd spoken to him on the telephone. Alice had never really got over Peter, whom she had adored, his upright English good looks contrasting so sharply with Leon's semitic features.

Following her long journey, she had made herself comfortable in Leon's chair and when he arrived home from work, Hedda knew he wanted her to vacate it. He was a man of habit.

"Mutti," Hedda said, "Leon's home. Come and say hello."

She got up and they shook hands.

"I hope your journey wasn't too tiring," he said politely, maneuvering himself around her and towards his chair. He wasn't going to revert to the enemy language, even for his mother-in-law.

"No. It was very pleasant." Her thick German accent was a surprise, but she hadn't spoken English in years and was bound to sound German again. "I look forward to helping you both out. I'm sure you look forward to the new baby?"

"Yes. And I know Hedda is. She's very excited. As are the girls. They hope for a baby sister, one they can boss around and dress up. It would be nice to have a boy, too, but I really don't mind as long as the baby is healthy."

That evening Hedda prepared the last bits for their meal, a simple chicken soup, followed by a Hungarian goulash with thick noodles and dark cabbage, and a rice pudding with cream and jam. Each of the courses was easy enough, but by the end she was exhausted, especially with the washing and drying still waiting for her. Her legs ached and the baby seemed determined to use every sharp joint to poke and prod.

She had made up the spare bedroom earlier, placed some sweet-smelling freesias in a vase, and removed all last traces of dust from the bedside cabinet. She was glad when Alice went to bed early, tired after the long journey, whilst Leon remained reading in his beloved Ercol. Once the girls were bathed and asleep, Hedda crept downstairs and into the living room. The full-length curtains across the long window were pulled closed and Leon had on his reading light.

"So what do you think of my mother?" she asked.

He didn't look up, didn't speak.

"Leon! What do you think? Is she how you thought?"

She could feel his reluctance to engage. He swiveled the lamp away and put down his book. "Hedda," he said somewhat wearily, "she's how you described her. You were accurate. She's what I expected. You went through a great deal on her behalf and now she's here to help you. Pay it back, if you like. I just hope she does." It was obvious he wanted to get back to the book. "I'm sorry, I've had one of those days. You must be tired. Sit down. Rest."

His eyes returned to the pages. He adjusted the position of the Anglepoise and continued reading. Hedda stood there for a further moment then returned to the kitchen to put the last few plates away.

The baby was late. Hedda's due date came and went, followed by more days when nothing happened, not even the occasional twinge. Her mother exuded a restless energy and Hedda knew Alice was becoming increasingly impatient. By the beginning of June, Hedda told her mother that if she wanted to return home, she really wouldn't mind. She meant it and Alice was relieved to accept Hedda's kind offer. She packed speedily and Leon drove her into London where she caught the coach from Victoria back to Dover, and then onwards across Belgium and into Germany. For Hedda it was one less body to feed and tend, one less room to dust and tidy.

Before she left, she told Hedda to let her know: "As soon as the baby is born, everything please, and, of course, whether I am to be Oma to a little girl or a little boy!"

On June 4, at around five o'clock in the morning, Hedda's labor pains began with such force that she screamed out in pain, waking both girls who ran into the bedroom with terror in their sleepy faces. Her whole body was stretched tight on a torture rack, and Hedda decided she wasn't giving birth, she was dying. Leon rushed next door to the neighbors and Julia, in dressing gown and slippers, came to mind the children as Leon drove to Kingston Hospital, Hedda wailing and panting on the back seat. As he helped her up the hospital steps, she announced she was giving birth right there, in the corridor, but some nurses rushed over and took Hedda off his hands, guiding her into a wheelchair and towards the labor ward. Thirty minutes later, she held a little baby girl close to her breast, wrapped firmly in a simple hospital blanket. Pulling down the top of the white fabric, Hedda saw the smallest amount of light brown hair. The baby's eyes opened and looked directly into hers.

"Sophie, my little darling baby," she said, "I'm your Mummy. Your only mother. I love you."

Leon entered the room.

"Look, look what we've created. She's a beauty."

He came over and took her hand. Then he leant over and carefully picked up the swaddled baby, holding her very gently. Hedda's heart was full.

"Well done, my dear," he said. "That wasn't easy. She's a little miracle. She's a pretty thing, like you. You've done well."

The first compliment he had ever paid her, she thought, as she lay in an exhausted haze. That would do for now.

24

GRAND DESIGNS
WEYBRIDGE, SURREY

1960

Behind the houses on Sandy Lane, Petersham, was a council estate. It was built after the completion of Leon's house and consisted of a series of red-brick terraced homes, with small front gardens and brick archways leading to the back, dividing house from house. Each day the older girls walked through it to reach their school, whilst Hedda pushed Sophie in the pram.

Leon hated the estate: he hated the way their gardens backed onto his garden, with only the poplar trees dividing them, and would go into one of his darker moods on hearing their noisy get-togethers and inconsequential chatter. Despite his socialism, he showed scant sympathy for those who would never afford their own properties, those who could not appreciate his music, his poetry, his books. He used the word "common" to describe them and the estate. Hedda agreed the houses were not pretty, but these were the families bombed to smithereens during the war, and they deserved to live in homes more substantial than prefabs. He would grudgingly agree but not without criticizing the cheerless designs and cheap building materials. "Uninspired" was what he said.

"We are constrained in everything," he would say. "It's always about price, never vision. How can one practice architecture successfully if limited by small-minded bureaucrats who choose money over art!" He had become increasingly unhappy at work and morose at home.

On this day over Sunday lunch, he was telling Hedda about the house his former work colleague had designed and built a year ago. Francis Goodrich's house was part of a private estate called Saint George's Hill, Weybridge, and the house was a masterpiece he had heard. Francis had his own architectural practice and was working on some exciting projects including a boating lake, part of the Festival of Britain. Hedda knew that Leon's friendship was tinged with envy and he felt bitter that opportunities that had come Francis' way had passed him by. Having once been denied membership of the local golf club because he was a Jew, he concluded the prejudice extended more widely.

"Would you like to go and see the house?" he asked as the children's voices could be heard outside.

The girls were playing dressing-up in the garden, wearing the Davy Crockett hat sent over by Ena's sister from San Francisco. Rebecca was pretending to be Queen Elizabeth, and Sophie was a lady-in-waiting, following her around. Clarice idly supervised on a rug.

"Rosa and Francis have invited us over. They suggested next week. We're not doing anything then, are we?"

"I would love to," she said.

A family trip out. They didn't do many, and this sounded interesting. And it would be pleasant to see Rosa again. She'd only met the other woman once, when she came with Francis after work before heading off to the Old Vic theater to see some Ibsen, something Hedda could only dream of. She remembered because it was a play called *Hedda Gabler* and they all commented on whether the main character would be like her. They promised they'd let her know.

They entered the "Estate" via a private gateway and followed the directions, arriving at an ultra-modern house fronted by long lawns, low spreading conifers and rhododendrons, and a cluster of tall trees. It was stunning. Leon parked the car and ushered the children out, mouths hanging open, in front of the glass palace. Even young Sophie looked impressed. They approached what could only be the front door, and Rosa appeared waving, a wide smile on her face.

They followed her through a concrete courtyard into a space of light and air with white walls and shining glass that extended from the white carpeted floor to a ceiling of polished wood, high above their heads. Francis greeted them warmly. He was a tall distinguished looking man who wore a bow tie with stylish artistry. His appearance exuded success: a man who was his own master, not diminished by the limitations of the local council.

"You obviously found us successfully? Not always easy, we are rather tucked away," he said. "We'll have a coffee and then a house tour. Would you like that, girls?"

The girls nodded, and they followed Francis to another open space where light spilled in from above and through another floor-to-ceiling window that separated the house from the adjoining woodland. On the walls hung vivid pictures. One of a bridge painted in less vivid muddy beiges and browns caught Hedda's eye. She recognized it as the work of one of Leon's fellow interns, Edward Esther.

"You like it?" said Francis as Hedda gazed at the painting. "See out there? Esther's been busy in the garden as well."

She looked out and saw a giant sculpture of jagged metal, a figure of a man, three meters or more, who appeared to stride across the grass with the possibility that he might just crash through the glass and join them on the settee. Esther had outdone himself.

"Look girls, over here!" she said, pointing to the giant metal man.

Rebecca and Clarice ran over and pressed their noses up against the window, their breaths leaving mouth-sized stains. Sophie shuffled closer to her big sister, in case the giant began his assault. They were delighted when Rosa suggested they could go outside and play.

The tour continued. Hedda found the house stunning. There were free-standing walls that separated one space from another with twinkling white lights inset into alcoves, floating shelves that appeared to hang without fittings, and above the polished ceiling like a dark glowing copper sky. Hedda couldn't imagine what it must be like to live on this scale.

"Oh Rosa, what a beautiful place," she said lamely.

"It's very special, isn't it? Did you know we had a horse in the living room last week? A real white horse. They were shooting a picture for a whiskey advertising campaign. It's going to be in the color supplements: 'You can Take a White Horse Anywhere.'"

All Hedda thought of was the mess and hoped the horse hadn't relieved itself on the carpet. "You must be very happy."

"Not really," Rosa said and her face changed. "Actually, I'm quite unhappy. I'm stuck here in this house, by myself from seven in the morning until seven at night, often later. I can go for days and days and see no one. Francis is always working in London and the nearest house is over two miles away. Neighbors don't exist here. Sometimes I even talk to Esther's *Iron Man* for a bit of company. I'm sorry to sound so ungrateful."

"It sounds difficult."

"It is. Do you remember that play we were off to see that night, the one named after you?" Rosa laughed and continued. "She was nothing like you! She was selfish and critical of everything. But she felt trapped. Trapped in her marriage and trapped in her house. I was more like her than you! I'm sorry, I didn't mean to burden you with my problems. But I see you with your lovely girls, living in a street with neighbors either side, and I'm envious. Sometimes you can have everything and still feel you have nothing."

"Does Francis know how you feel?"

"No! He thinks I love the place. And I wouldn't tell him otherwise. It would break his heart. He's worked so hard – it's been a labor of love for years and years, our baby, so to speak."

Hedda knew that would be true. The grand architect would be destroyed if he knew his wife was slowly going mad in her concrete and glass prison. She knew Rosa would never do that to him. "I love the house. It really is beautiful. And you're very welcome to come to Richmond whenever you like. I bake a decent apple cake, you know."

Rosa laughed. "Thank you. I'm rather dependent on Francis, though. No car you see. I don't drive. Never mind. I must stop feeling sorry for myself."

As the wives stood by the window, the husbands walked across the lawn towards the girls. Leon crouched down, glasses carefully positioned on top of his head, camera slung around his neck. He was going to take some family pictures. Carefully crafted shots.

"Stand between the giant's legs," he shouted, "that will look excellent."

On the drive home the girls were finally quiet in the back, tired from their afternoon of running and hiding.

"What did you think?" Leon asked as they turned into Richmond Park. The deer were resting in large family groups at a safe distance from the traffic. "Did you like the house?"

"I did. It was impressive, but it wasn't very homely. Not like ours. I wouldn't want to live in it. And think of all that hoovering and dusting!"

"Ah," he said, "always so terribly practical. But I think on this occasion, I'm inclined to agree. It's a show home, isn't it? Not one to live in with three little girls running around, not one to bring up a family in. And think of the heating bills. What do you think, girls? Whose house do you like best? Ours or Francis's?" He looked in the mirror to see their response.

"Our house!" they shouted in unison. "Our house. Our house is the best! But could *we* have a giant man in the garden?"

On other Sundays, when Hedda prepared the roast lunch, Leon and the girls drove to Bulldon Mansions to visit their grandfather. Sometimes they arranged to meet him in Kew Gardens beside the pagoda and Rebecca and Sophie would slot a single penny in the turnstile and push down the clanking arm. They would sit on a bench in the pagoda's shadow and would offer their Opa some slices of cake baked by Hedda and then they would stroll, sometimes as far as the Palm House, to view the fantastical white creatures known as the Queen's Beasts.

"What are they?" Sophie asked. "Why does that one have wings? Why has the lion got a crown? That one's a unicorn – who invented unicorns?" Endless questions which neither Mendel nor Leon could answer.

But mostly they met at Opa's flat in Shepherd's Bush. Mendel lived on the second floor of Bulldon Mansions and Hedda had only ever visited him twice, enjoying the rare weekends when she had the house to herself. On her first visit she was transported back to the apartment in Saarbrücken. There were the same wide concrete stairs and the dusty smell of aging plaster. She remembered the young Nazi boys, who had stood so arrogantly outside the entrance to the shop, memories she thought she'd erased. She saw her mother with the sign hanging around her neck, head held low, and the man who had tricked them, pretending to ask for directions, and the arrival of the Gestapo, and Hedda was filled with blessed relief that she was resident in West London and not in North Germany.

The children enjoyed their visits; he made a fuss of them and smuggled them bars of Nestle's chocolate to take home. But once they visited him on a Saturday, which they didn't like at all.

"He wears a funny white shawl on his shoulders," said Rebecca.

"It's not a funny shawl, Becca," Clarice said, "it's a prayer shawl. He was praying."

"Do *we* pray?" Sophie asked.

"No," said Leon. "But Opi does. He likes to pray on a Saturday – it's important to him."

"Why don't we pray on a Saturday, Daddy?" Sophie continued.

"We don't believe in stupid stuff like that," Clarice said, and that closed the topic of conversation.

And it was true. They didn't believe. Although the children

knew they were Jewish, they'd never attended synagogue or talked about Jewish festivities, and they enjoyed bacon and pork chops. The fridge was too small to separate the meat from the dairy. Hedda occasionally wore a silver necklace with a small menorah attached which she imagined she would give to one of the girls when they were older, but they didn't light candles at Hanukkah. Leon and Mendel would occasionally discuss the children's upbringing, speaking in German so the girls wouldn't understand their grandfather's disappointment and the son's defiance of organized religion.

"Why can't you do this for me?" Mendel would ask.

"Because, dear father, if there were such a thing as a God and a God who cared for the Jews, then I don't think he would have allowed the destruction of millions, do you?"

"We have free will. God gave us brains to make decisions."

"Yes and look at how people use those brains. Not very successfully. Most people can just about manage to complete their weekly football pools."

"One day, God will bring you faith."

"Not if I have anything to do with it."

Visits to his father would often result in a bleak mood. Following lunch, he would retreat into his darkroom and surround himself with film negatives and boxes of photographic paper. In the blackout, surrounded by gadgets and glass bottles, he would watch the images appear ghost-like from the blank paper. He would spend all afternoon there and when he emerged the smell of the chemicals made all their eyes run.

Darkroom moods. Hedda sometimes wondered what images filled his head. His internment? His late wife? His frustrations at work? Her? Did Hedda depress him? Did he even think about her? She had little time to dwell on his internal world with the children arguing upstairs and preparations for tea.

One evening, a couple of weeks after the visit to the Weybridge estate, he said:

"My father irritated me today."

"He does that to you, I know that. But he's your father. We only have one."

"That's true."

"The children love you."

"I love them," he said. "I developed a picture this afternoon of you and the girls at the house in Weybridge. I'll show you tomorrow. It's one of my better photographs."

She faced him and took his hand. "I look forward to seeing it. I'm sure it's beautiful."

The moon shone bright through the bedroom window and she could hear Sophie quietly snuffling next door. She felt content.

25

LOVE CONQUERS ALL
REDHILL, SURREY

1963

Friday evening. The girls were in bed and husband and wife were settling down to watch a drama, written by a favorite playwright, that Hedda had looked forward to all day. Leon had been quiet since returning from work, which she put down to end-of-the-week blues and ongoing distaste for the dull architectural projects he'd been allocated.

For the last few years, with all three girls at school, Hedda had found some independence from purely domestic and maternal duties. She had built a small sewing business, altering clothes that had become too tight, taking up hems in line with the fashion for shorter skirt lengths, sewing on buttons, and replacing broken zippers. She enjoyed welcoming her customers into their home and had developed a community of friends and acquaintances. Some of the women stayed for a cup of coffee, even a slice of cake, and her days were busy with conversation as well as shopping, cooking and housework. By Friday she was ready to down tools, remove the thimble from her finger, take the pins from her mouth, and relax in front of the television.

The program was just about to start when Leon said, "Hedda, can we talk?"

There was something about his tone of voice and the deadly serious look on his face that convinced Hedda "the talk" was not going to be good. She felt her skin prickle, the same feeling as when Peter announced his relocation over 20 years ago.

"What is it?" she said.

He got up and switched off the television. It really was serious.

"You're worrying me."

"Hedda." A short pause, then: "I've met someone."

Oh God, oh God. Hedda's solid world was turning into a liquid mess. "You've met someone?" All she could do was repeat his words. Did he want her to ask who she was, *where* she was, how they had met? What did he expect Hedda to say?

"Yes. We love one another. I suppose you might say we're in love."

Oh my God. He was cruel, she thought. What did he think he was, some sort of love-struck teenager? Grow up. "You are?" she said.

"Yes. We've been seeing each other for a while now. Actually, the last three months. I met her through a colleague."

"You did?"

"She's a psychologist – a child psychologist."

Oh God. The irony. So close to the profession of Hedda's one and only love. They had never discussed Peter. Leon had never asked. When he found out she had lived with a man, he disapproved. He had made her feel second-hand, as though she should be grateful to him for accepting damaged goods.

"I must tell you that it's like I've found the key to the door that, up till this point in my life, has been locked and is now finally open. She *is* the key."

What sort of romantic fiction had he been reading?

"I'm sorry," he said. "I wasn't looking for love, but it happened. It's made me realize that my feelings for Ena weren't love, not like this. I cared for Ena, I really did, but we were young and immature. And you know I've always cared for you, as my wife and as the mother of my children. This is different. It's a meeting of minds as well as hearts. I know now, I didn't love Ena. Not like I love Katya."

Oh. Another immigrant. Probably Austrian, probably from Vienna. At that moment, she felt such protective loyalty to the memory of Ena and such utter contempt for this woman who had sauntered into their fragile lives, destroying the past and the future, that she wanted to place her hands around her skinny Austrian neck and throttle her.

"I'll move out," Hedda said. "You'll have to give me a few weeks to find somewhere to live, and we have to consider how we tell the children."

She left the room, her head filled with wire wool pain, scratching every nerve ending. She couldn't think or breathe. Upstairs, she lay on the bed and shut her eyes to the new world he had forced her to enter. When she opened them again, nothing had changed. Even with her eyes shut, she saw flashes of white light that dazzled.

Later that evening, after the program they would have watched was finished, and the news over, he came up. "Do you have any questions you want to ask me? I know this must be difficult for you."

She had a million questions, but hearing the answers would be to insert a blade into an already open wound. She wanted to know when he'd met her, where he'd met her, how long they had been sleeping together. She wanted to know what the lover looked like, dark or light, tall or short, round or bony. She wanted to know more about her parents and whether they'd brought her up to steal the husband of another. She wanted to know if the husband-stealer was serious. She wanted to know everything.

"No, Leon. I don't have any questions for you."

During the course of the week they managed to avoid each other. She prepared his lunchtime and evening meals as usual but left the room whilst he ate them. Any future arrangements were discussed after the children were in bed or in German. Clarice hated this.

"What are you talking about?" she asked. "You know I don't like it when you speak German. I don't like people knowing that you're from another country."

By Friday, Hedda had organized to spend the weekend with Valerie and Thomas. She didn't tell her friend the reason, only that Leon and her needed a little time apart. She prepared food that she thought Leon would manage to warm up for himself and the girls and said she would leave Clarice and Rebecca with him for the weekend but take Sophie.

Valerie was delighted by the news of Hedda's visit, eager to show off the new baby. "And Erica can't wait to play with Sophs," she said. "She hasn't stopped talking about her ever since I told her you're visiting."

Hedda took the train to Redhill, and Thomas met her at the station. She had hoped she was capable of hiding her emotions, but a giant lump in her throat rose up as soon as she saw him. She tried to swallow it down. It was the thought of their sympathy and hugs, and she didn't want Sophie to see her crying.

Sensing Hedda's fragile state, Thomas asked no questions on the drive, instead chatting about the baby, his sweet laughter, what a little mother Erica was to him but of course, like all babies, what a dreadful sleeper he was. They hoped he wouldn't keep Hedda or Sophie awake. She reassured him: these days she slept through anything, she was that exhausted. At the house, Valerie was preparing a late tea, and when she saw Hedda, she wiped her hands on her apron and wrapped her in a huge hug. Hedda burst into tears, sobbing onto Valerie's comforting shoulder while trying not to let Sophie hear.

"What's wrong, Mummy? Why are you crying?"

Valerie bent down to Sophie and pulled her into her body. "Mummy's just a little tired, she's fine, honestly." Valerie, always so sensitive and thoughtful.

Hedda wiped away the tears before Sophie could see them.

"Erica!" Valerie shouted up the stairs. "Guess who's here? Downstairs. Come down!"

A mini-Valerie, dressed in floral pajamas, bounced down the stairs and into the kitchen. "Sophie, Sophie, Sophie!" she shouted. "Let's go upstairs and play. What do you want to play? I thought we could play Mummies and Daddies," she said, and grabbed Sophie by the arm, pulling her towards the door.

"You have one hour exactly," said Valerie, "and then it's books and bedtime."

After the girls were out of earshot, Valerie turned to Hedda. "This isn't just about needing a bit of time apart, is it? It's worse. What's happened?"

Valerie led Hedda into their neat sitting room and though she had stopped drinking years ago, Hedda gratefully accepted a gin and tonic. Thomas joined them and she described Leon's confession, his sickening metaphor of finding the key that opened the lock, and how this woman was spending the weekend with him.

"Do the girls know?" Valerie asked.

"Not really. I think Clarice understands that things aren't right at the moment. She feels the atmosphere but these days she spends most of her time in her room, anyway. If Rebecca and Sophie have noticed anything, they haven't said, but we've tried really hard not to speak about it in front of the children."

"What about this weekend? What have you told them about her?"

"Leon said that a new friend of his will be staying for a couple of days. A friend from work. That seemed to satisfy them although I think Clarice will realize there's more to it once Katya arrives. She's not stupid."

"Oh Hedda. It's so typical of you. Always doing the right thing for others," Valerie said, pouring another drink. It was helping.

"But that's not true. I don't do the right thing. You of all people know that. If I'd done the right thing I 'd never have gone to the police about my mother," Hedda answered, taking a large sip and enjoying the way the alcohol seemed to soften the hard edges in her head.

"You did what was morally right, lawfully right. It was probably the most difficult thing you've ever had to do."

Not listening to the reassurance, Hedda interrupted, "And I'd still be with Peter and not that bastard of a husband."

"Maybe. Maybe not. His work was taking him abroad anyway."

"He didn't have to go, though."

"He did. It was important work, vital, and knowing Peter, he wouldn't have been able to turn it down. For him it was the morally right decision to make at the time."

"But surely emotions are more important than morals? Morals are what we teach children. And they don't work! What kind of morals does Leon have? His emotions are no better than a baby's – 'whah, whah, whah, I want to be in love' – no thought for me or the children or anyone else!"

From upstairs, they heard the sound of baby Daniel crying out. Hedda hoped her angry rant hadn't woken him.

The girls pattered down the stairs saying that Daniel was awake.

"Thanks," Valerie said. "Well, he's awake, but now it's your bedtime, so teeth and bed and Thomas will be up to read a story in five minutes."

She followed their groans up the stairs and came back with the baby in her arms, putting him to the breast which he nuzzled greedily. "What will happen with the girls?" she asked.

"I don't know. We haven't spoken about it yet. It's too horrible. I suppose the plan will be that she takes on the mothering of Clarice and Rebecca, and Sophie and I will find somewhere to live close by so that schools won't be disrupted and she can see her sisters from time to time. The girls will be so sad. She will be their third mother. It breaks my heart. I've been Rebecca's mother since she was just a tiny bit older than Daniel is now, and Clarice was Sophie's age. I love them both so much. But in the end, Leon is their real father and I'm just a pretend mother. A surrogate." The drink had loosened her tongue.

"You do the best pretend job of anyone I know."

Hedda laughed. "Thanks Valerie. Actually, I think the girls

would agree – there's always food on the table and they have everything they could want." Hedda took another long sip. "Do you know, I have no idea whether she's got children, though she should be a bit of an expert, given her job." Hedda explained that Katya was a child psychologist, an eminent one at that, with published books citing new ways of developing children's creativity and intellect. "She'll have two little ready-made research samples to work on. She can try out all her new-fangled ideas on them! You know, when I met Leon all that time ago, I stupidly thought that was it, my life laid out for me for the next 50 years. I knew he didn't love me, that for him it was simply a marriage of convenience. But I think *I* loved *him* and I assumed he would want me around to bring up his children and take care of him. I never imagined his 'beating heart' would be stirred by another."

"I'm so sorry."

"Don't be, I'm going to be alright. I needed to talk. And I needed this drink! Thank you. And now, I'm going upstairs to give those darling girls two sloppy, wet goodnight kisses."

"We've been playing lots of games, Mummy," said Sophie, reaching out her little hand and waving it at her mother. "We played with Erica's dolly and we were both Mummies and the dolly was Daniel, and Mummy, can we have a baby?"

"Not at the moment, darling, I only have one baby and that's you. Sweet dreams," she said and shut the door behind her.

***

The weekend passed easily. A 15-minute walk past the parade of small shops and towards the common was the recreation ground, with its long metal slide, paint chipped roundabout, a few worn swings and a seesaw. It also possessed two sets of monkey bars at differing heights onto which Erica immediately climbed. She swung effortlessly across the full length of them, executing a perfect jump and landing, arms extended. Sophie struggled to hold onto the very first bar, let alone manage to travel. Her little face looked crestfallen.

"It's too hard, Mummy, I can't do it," she said crossly. She tried again and failed. "It's impossible," she said, her lower lip trembling with childhood disappointment.

"I don't think Sophie will be making the Olympic gymnastics team any time soon," Hedda said as the two girls raced each other to the slide. "I sometimes wonder if it's the Jewish gene. When do you hear about Jewish athletes? Writers? Yes. Musicians? Yes. Psychiatrists? Certainly! But sportsmen?"

"Hedda! That's a dreadful generalization! It's just that different people are encouraged to pursue different career paths," Valerie said diplomatically.

"Can I ask you something?" said Hedda, as they wandered away from the impossible monkey bars.

Valerie nodded her head.

The girls were now happily sliding down, running back round and up the metal steps, sliding down in perpetual motion.

"Did you ever think of me as a Jew?"

Valerie looked appalled.

"No, what I mean is, did you ever think that maybe there's something in the Jewish character that lends itself to being a victim? That we need to suffer. That we bring these things on ourselves?"

"Never!" she said. "That's just awful! What *do* you think of me?" She was clearly upset, her face furrowing and her mouth turned down.

"I'm sorry, I don't know why I thought that. Maybe it's what I think about myself, that it's what I deserve. That feeling of never quite belonging, always on the outside looking in. I had a boyfriend in Germany..."

She tailed off, remembering his blond hair, his blue eyes and friendly face, and how love-struck she had felt.

"When we first started meeting I found it difficult to feel comfortable when he put his arm around me or when he held my hand. And when he kissed me! I just wanted it to stop. I now wonder whether I'd thought he couldn't possibly find a Jewish girl attractive, that he was just humoring me, that he felt sorry for me.

So instead of accepting his nice words and his advances, I made sure I didn't enjoy it. I rejected *him,* rather than letting him reject *me.* If that makes sense?"

"Not really." Valerie stood up from the bench they were sharing and pushed the pram back and forth. Daniel was fast asleep.

Hedda continued. "It's like now. I keep thinking that maybe if I was more Jewish or less Jewish, or less German and more Austrian, or maybe I'm just not pretty enough or clever enough for him. Ena was beautiful, dark eyes, long slim nose. Me? Look at me."

Valerie had had enough. "Stop it! It's got nothing to do with you. It's him. Whatever's going on right now is about his needs and his wants and his sadness. And he is a sad man. But you're not. A sad woman, I mean. You have every right to feel angry and upset and all those things, but I know you – whatever happens next, you'll turn it round and you'll make the best of it. And I've never thought about you as anything other than my dear friend. Who sometimes says her words wrong and still can't pronounce her 'W's."

The girls were back, squeezing together on the bench. "We're starving," they moaned in unison.

They walked back, the girls skipping ahead, Daniel smiling and gurgling in his pram.

"How do you think Leon's weekend is going, Val?" Hedda asked when they were nearly home.

"Not well," she answered immediately. "I've just got this feeling, not very well."

Hedda arrived back late that afternoon. Leon looked exhausted, which gave her immense pleasure. *Schadenfreude,* they called it.

The place was a mess. There were plates on both tables with the remains of some sort of smeared children's food, along with an open packet of biscuits and two dirty glasses containing half-drunk milk. The living room curtains were partly drawn even though it was sunny outside.

As Hedda walked through the front door, Rebecca ran towards

her shouting, "Mummy, I've missed you. I've missed you." She ran over to Sophie who was unbuckling her shoes. "We had a nice lady here, but she's gone now so let's play dressing-up."

They skipped off into the back garden and standing on tiptoes, Rebecca opened the shed door to retrieve the box of assorted clothing and hats assembled over the last years. Sophie would miss that most, Hedda thought.

"Where's Clarice?" she asked Leon. She wasn't ready to hear about his weekend.

"She's upstairs in her room. I haven't seen her for a couple of hours."

Clarice was sitting on her bed, flicking through a magazine. Her bedroom was awash with pictures of cats that she'd either cut from various publications or had drawn herself. She would have loved to care for one herself but knew her father was not an animal lover. Hedda wondered if Katya was a Cat Lady and would persuade Leon to change his mind once she took over.

"How was your weekend?" she asked, gently sitting down on the bed. She could see Clarice was in a terrible mood from the set of her head, and the way she rubbed her hands together. Her nails were bitten.

Clarice didn't look up.

"What did Daddy say about Katya?" Hedda asked her. She wondered whether Leon had shared the next steps. She knew Clarice wasn't stupid and would have worked some things out.

"Not a lot. She's a friend, he said. They shared your bedroom, so funny sort of friend. I heard them arguing this afternoon. I heard the door shut about an hour ago, so I suppose she's gone. She didn't say goodbye. I was pleased about that."

Interesting.

"You're upset. I can see that." Hedda put her arms around Clarice, who started to silently weep. Hedda held her closer. "Do you want to tell me about her? Was she pretty?"

"No! She was old!"

"Was she nice to you and Rebecca?"

There was a long silence and Clarice stopped crying. "She

spoke to us as if we were morons. As if we didn't speak English properly." She imitated Katya's slow speaking voice, putting on a heavy accent: "Hell-oo, chill-da-ren, myy naame is Kat-e-ya, and youu muss-bee Clar-reece."

Hedda hid a smile. What a wonderful imitation. "Maybe she was trying to get to know you," she said in Katya's mock defense.

"I didn't like her," Clarice said.

"From what you have said, I'm not really surprised," Hedda replied, smiling at Clarice who smiled back, encouraged to say more.

"She was stuck up. Like she was a teacher. She reminded me of our geography teacher looking down her nose at us."

"Like Miss Campbell – she must have been bad!"

"Mummy?" Clarice's voice had changed. "Mummy, she's not Daddy's girlfriend, is she? She's not going to move in with us, is she? You're not leaving us, are you?" Clarice burst into tears again and pushed her whole body against the wall, wrapping her arms around her knees.

"Oh darling," Hedda said. What else could she say? Leon hadn't considered the impact on his daughters for one moment, especially how Clarice would feel, who so clearly remembered her birth mother. "I'm going down to talk to Leon, and then I'll know more. Things will work out. You'll see."

Clarice didn't look up or speak. She'd said everything she had wanted to say.

Leon was sitting in his usual chair, his skin a strange shade of gray, when Hedda entered the living room. He attempted a smile which she didn't return. "How was your weekend?" he asked.

"Really? You want me to describe *my* weekend? Oh come on, you can do better than that."

"Yes," he said dully. "Rather crass of me. I suppose I should tell you about mine."

"I think that would be a good idea."

There was a silence which Hedda didn't fill. She enjoyed his discomfort. She could wait all night.

"I don't think it's going to work," he said eventually. "We love each other but that's not enough. Love will only get us so far. There's the children to think of."

"Oh really? And you only realized that this weekend?" she asked, amazed at how his "love" had obviously eradicated all common sense. "You hadn't thought about how Clarice and Rebecca and Sophie might feel? Never mind me. I'm a grown-up, I've been through enough to cope with pretty much anything, but your daughters!"

The truth of what she said shone in his eyes, now filled with tears. Of self-pity, Hedda thought.

"She didn't want to take on full-time mother duties. She's successful in her professional life and wants to continue. She can't make space for the girls as well."

Hedda considered everything she had done for him, from that very first day they had met in that grim office, his father by the son's side. "She's obviously a very distinguished psychologist who would much rather write about children in her academic books than deal with them in real life, wipe their noses and give them kisses and cuddles," Hedda said, beginning to enjoy Leon's failure at new love.

"Probably," he said.

"Probably? You're pathetic! Pathetic. What were you thinking? Living in some Mills and Boon romance where true love was going to solve everything. Except it doesn't, you know, because in the end, we need to grow up and do our duty and look after our family. And maybe, just maybe, that's what you will start to do from now on!"

She'd never spoken to him in this way and it felt good. He was silent, then got up and left the room. After a moment, she walked out and to the back door where she stood and watched the girls clad in long crepe dresses down to their ankles, squashed hats on their heads, marching around the garden and holding hands.

"It's time for bed, children," she shouted.

"Five more minutes, Mummy?" they shouted back.

"Five more minutes," she said, a tingling relief flooding every cell.

26

ONE STEP AT A TIME
KINGSTON, SURREY

1967–1971

Katya's name was never mentioned again. Hedda had no desire to discuss his love-madness. She refused to use her name as a grenade to lob over the barricades during their infrequent arguments or return to the scene of the crime and pick over the evidence. Put the offender back in the dock. Hedda did not harbor grudges or seek revenge. And if he did talk with others, revisiting the gory remains of his failure at love, Hedda had no knowledge. She believed he looked back with shame. Maybe he wrote about the ex-lover in the poems he occasionally composed but Hedda never found the verses. They didn't discuss her or the events that led up to the weekend, and none of the girls asked, especially not Clarice. The Woman was in their house, and then she wasn't. She had slept in the parents' bedroom and then Hedda had returned home, changed the sheets and The Woman was gone. Much later on, when Hedda saw the name of Katya Friedmann in an article on parenting in a Sunday newspaper, suggesting she was now residing in Scotland with a partner, Hedda didn't point it out and Leon wouldn't have read an article on childhood tantrums, anyway.

Domestic life had returned to normal in the Meier household. Birthdays had been celebrated, the latest one being Sophie's 11th, and now she was off to join her sister at the local grammar school! International life with its frequent conflicts had also resumed. The latest war between Israel and an Arab alliance lasting a mere six days was over. The tissue thin airmail letter from Leon's younger brother lay on the coffee table between them. Arie described commandeering a heroic group of Israeli soldiers in the Golan Heights and fighting a bloody battle, and the whole nation was celebrating their success in defeating their combined Arab neighbors. The letter was punctuated with exclamation marks and underlining proclaiming victory against Nasser: "He wanted us Jews pushed into the sea!" "The enemy wanted us dead!" He wrote that the Arab countries were broadcasting tremendous victories against the Israeli military which were lies. "We fight for our very survival as a Jewish State, and we hold on and fight back!"

And it was clear from the headlines appearing in the papers and on the radio that Israel *had* secured massive victories against Egypt and Syria and Jordan despite joint efforts to destroy the very existence of the country, and they could be nothing if not proud.

"Whilst it's a great relief," Leon said, "one has no idea how this will develop. I can't see this being an end to the conflict. There's just too much history of hatred."

Hedda agreed.

"I think we're only approved of when we are the victims; when they send us to the gas chambers," he went on.

"That's a bit extreme," she said. "I think there are lots of people who believe in a country for the Jews, even if they don't understand the politics. And why should they? I don't think I do."

He picked up the letter and scanned the first page. "Do you know, I'd never have thought my baby brother would have turned out this way, the big army man, the proud nationalist."

"Do you ever think you'd like to go out there, see him again after all these years, and see what the country's like?" she asked.

"Never!" he said. "I have no interest in traveling to Israel.

Uncultured, lacking in charm and caring more for flag-waving than the exploration of who we are, what makes us Jewish."

"Your father would love to see your brother again before he dies," she said, trying to keep the conversation focused on the personal, not the political. Mendel had been unwell with a variety of undiagnosed complaints over the last couple of years. He had stayed with them when at his worst and she had nursed him.

"Arie will have to come over here, then, as I'm certainly not making the trip there, either by myself or with my father in tow."

Hedda was secretly relieved. She would rather not lose Leon to an overseas trip and imagined his brother had better things to do than take a foreign holiday.

"I'm sure Betty and Viktor are relieved. And the children," she said, moving the focus away from their family.

Betty had occasionally written to Hedda with news of their growing brood of three boys and one little girl, as well as proud descriptions of Viktor's rapid promotion to senior consultant in the Tel Aviv hospital. With his considerable earnings they had bought a large estate not far from the beach and the park, next to sweet-smelling orange and lemon trees. Betty sent pictures of their inner courtyard surrounding a fishpond, bejeweled with tiny blue glass tiles. Hedda passed on any news to Leon, who had never quite recovered from Viktor's emigration, and the betrayal he felt of their shared middle-European history and artistic temperaments.

"I imagine they are," he said, and then entirely unprompted, continued: "It was Betty's brother, wasn't it, the one that you had the bit of a thing with. I know you told me at the time, but forgive me, I wasn't in the right frame of mind back then. Betty's older brother. Your live-in partner?"

The English have a turn of phrase for every circumstance and the perfect one here was "Hedda nearly fell off her chair!" They had moved from Arab-Israeli politics to holidays to Leon's father and brother and then to an apology for his failure to inquire about her previous love life. To say she was amazed was an understatement.

"You look shocked. Peter? He was a doctor and he went to work in Germany to support war-damaged soldiers. I believe that's what you told me at the time. Do you want to tell me more? Would you like to talk about him?"

Hedda froze in disbelief. Married for over 13 years, this was the first time that her husband had encouraged her to share something so personal.

"If you would rather not," he said, already regretting the offer.

"No, no. I'm just surprised."

She told him about their very first meeting, the trip to the British Museum and the Bloomsbury pub. She told Leon how Peter had stood outside the telephone box as she called Herman's telephone number, and how he wrote down the employer's details and at the same time suggested they might meet again. She spoke of his psychiatric research at the Maudsley, and the studies the doctors made on Rudolf Hess, to which Leon said: "Why have you never told me this before?"

"Because you never asked."

She left out great chunks of time, including the small domestic day-to-day intimacies, as well as their night-time love, and skipped over the arguments that led to her mother's imprisonment. She explained he was sent abroad by the hospital military, and that's when the relationship ended.

"Where is he now?" he asked.

"I really don't know." Hedda had decided long ago to seek no news or updates from Betty, and that way he would gradually fade from memory like a supporting actor in an old Hollywood film whose name appears two thirds of the way down the credits. "He married a colleague, another doctor out there, and I imagine they have children. I think he's still in Germany."

"That's kind of ironic, isn't it? He's made his home in the land which you should rightfully still be living in, and you're over here."

"I would hate to live in Germany now!" she said. "I'd be looking at everyone and thinking, what did you know back then? What did you do? What secrets do you hide in your hearts? No, I love this country and the way it took us in, and this feels like my forever home."

"Well, that's good then, as I have no intention of relocating!" Leon laughed and at that moment, she felt genuine love. He'd listened and not judged and made a small attempt at suggesting he saw a future together. It was the closest she'd felt to him in a long time.

———

Friday nights were sometimes film night, a favorite time when Hedda, Leon and Sophie would watch old family cine-films that would be projected onto a screen, ceremonially removed from its wooden housing and cranked upright. Last week they had watched one of Leon's earliest attempts at stop-frame filmmaking, complete with magic titles that appeared letter by letter, shuffling into place across the screen. Little Chinese figures sent by Ena's sister from San Francisco sailed over the fabric water. Leon loved to experiment and the whole family would be roped into dressing up as witches and fairies and then – whoosh – with a crafty edit on his editing machine, one of the children would disappear and reappear in another part of the garden.

The following day Sophie suggested they work on another stop-frame effort and he surprisingly agreed. She collected a series of little figurines and ornaments together, brought them downstairs, and set them up on the dining room table. Hedda found some blue fabric which they draped over the table, and Leon piled up books at the back, discreetly covering them in pieces of brown corduroy and green velvet from Hedda's sewing room, always full of offcuts and samples. Soon they had created a three-dimensional landscape of hills and forests and a mountain lake at the edge of the table. Leon positioned the tripod and mounted the Super 8 on its cradle. He was the director, Josef von Sternberg, and Sophie, his lovely assistant, manipulating each figure half an inch at a time. Hedda's scenery production complete, she headed for the sun-filled garden to enjoy the rare luxury of time with her book.

She'd been there no more than 20 minutes when Sophie rushed out shouting: "Mummy, Mummy! It's Daddy! He's not well!"

Hedda followed her through the kitchen and into the living room where Leon lay collapsed on a chair, clutching and clawing at his chest. His face was white and screwed up with some dreadful pain.

"Hedda, please! It feels like someone's sitting on my chest, I think I'm having a–"

"A heart attack," she said to the operator on the line after calling 999.

Sophie remained calm, not pestering her with the obvious question of "Will he be alright?"

Within minutes a blue light flashed outside, and two burly men ran down the garden path. Leon continued to push at his own chest and was sweating profusely.

"We'll take over from here, love," they said, assembling a stretcher on wheels and then putting their arms under his, raising him up to a half-sitting, half-standing position before placing him on the bed. They strapped him down and wheeled him out, past the large magnolia tree and into the ambulance. Sophie and Hedda followed.

"Now you're not to worry about him, ladies," they said. "He's in good hands. We'll take care of him. Give the hospital a ring in a couple of hours, not before then." One of them handed Hedda a small card with the telephone number of the Accident and Emergency Department, Kingston Hospital.

When they returned inside, Sophie started to cry. "I think it was my fault," she said.

"Of course, it wasn't, why would you say that?" Hedda wrapped her arms around Sophie, her whole body shaking.

"I said the material had moved, so he was stretching over the table, careful not to knock down all the other figures, we'd spent ages positioning them, you see, and we'd already taken about ten shots and he just shouted out like he'd been stabbed and if I hadn't said anything, he'd be okay."

"It was nothing to do with you. He's been complaining of chest pains for a while, but we never mentioned it. It's his heart. It's sending him a message to slow down, take things easy. I think he'll be okay. But I need to call Rebecca and Clarice and let them know what's happening." Hedda gently released her hold of Sophie's body.

He remained in hospital for a couple of weeks and during that time she visited him on the weekends and once during the week. Hedda had never learnt to drive, never been given the opportunity, though she had often thought she would enjoy the freedom it allowed. She took the bus and walked the last bit. It was the hospital where Sophie was born but then she hadn't noticed how shabby and unwelcoming it was – she hoped his stay would not be long. When Hedda saw him on the ward he promised he would give up cigarettes, except for maybe the odd cigar and occasional pipe which didn't count. She remembered her father's love of pipes, the Dutch one especially, with its pretty blue and white china bowl. She would welcome the return of that earthy, grassy smell of childhood.

The doctors told them that years of stress had contributed to his damaged heart and that the attack could have happened at any time; there was no rhyme or reason to why it happened at that moment.

Leon agreed the time had come to retire and with the combination of sick leave and remaining holiday, he never returned. Hedda knew it was the right decision but her precious days, with customers calling in for fittings and chats and coffee, disappeared. He was always there in the house, reading, listening to music, playing the guitar or just there in the Ercol. He needed feeding three times a day.

So life went on. One day at a time. Another four years passed. The sweet melancholic songs of Joni Mitchell echoed down the stairs from Sophie's room, replacing the nasal rasp of Bob Dylan who'd left the house in Rebecca's arms when she'd packed for Sussex University, following in her big sister's footsteps. Clarice lived in a tower block that looked directly on to the other towers in Tower

Hamlets, the big architectural idea of the early 1960s, pursuing a career in social work, sorting out the discarded children of the East End. Hedda could never decide whether Clarice was happy, but she'd at least managed to flee the nest and start shaping her own.

And Hedda talked again to ghosts, both living and dead. Long ago she had decided she would have liked Ena, so different from Hedda; fiery where Hedda was calm, determined where she lacked ambition, and romantic and poetic where Hedda was practical. Hedda and Ena would often share their thoughts and observations on Leon: how he never washed up his own plates, why he believed so strongly in artistic freedom but not the freedom of his wives. Ena would occasionally confide the struggles she felt before and after the girls were born. Hedda listened to Ena's desires to find fulfillment in work, brought short by housework and nappies. She sympathized with the beautiful dead woman and held her translucent hands, secretly thankful that any ambition she had felt ended the day she took on motherhood. From then on all she wanted was to be the best mother she could to Clarice and Rebecca and Sophie, defying Alice's template of impoverished maternal love.

Sometimes the little figure of Anna would sit next to Hedda at her sewing machine, asking questions, picking up the thimble and placing it on each of her bony fingers, and even though Hedda had no news of Hanna and Borys or of Anna, the child-ghost suggested the path taken after their return to Poland.

Very occasionally she saw the bone-thin bodies of those who didn't make it to a place of safety, to England, or Argentina, or America, or Israel, who boarded the cattle trucks and made their hopeless journeys within the borders of Germany or Poland, Czechoslovakia or Hungary. And she felt such guilt. Such shame. Her abandonment of them. She asked herself the question they all did. Why them and not us? What did they do wrong, what did we do right? And then the ghosts, their faces pressed against the long living room window, looked at her and told her it was not her fault and it was not their fault, that they were not right or wrong. Their lips crinkled in half smiles and they waved weak arms before floating away through the magnolia leaves and white saucer blooms and out through the garden gate.

———

With Leon spending his days at home, taking the occasional recuperative walk to Ham House and visiting his friends in the locality, he had become more familiar with the community in which he lived. He resented the number of Germans who had moved into the area, employed by Deutsche Bank or the German Embassy or the multitude of big businesses that had blossomed in the last decade. Britain had encouraged them, requiring West Germany to build itself back up and divest itself of the crutches of Allied support. Now these people wanted an idyllic English suburban life, combined with a first-class education delivered in German, the best of both worlds. Leon found it hard seeing "the Germans" drive around their streets in their fancy Mercedes and BMWs until Hedda pointed out that he owned an Audi and was as much a fan of German engineering as they were.

On the surface these newer immigrants were delightful and friendly new neighbors: "Oh you speak German, where are you from?" they would ask. Nonetheless they remained the children of Nazis, born to parents filled with poison against Hedda and Leon and every other Jew, and those parents had swallowed thirstily. Susanna, one of Hedda's many German customers, had confided that her parents had tried their best and her father had resisted military work thanks to poor eyesight. Hedda believed her, but Susanna still couldn't provide stories of parental heroism, hiding Jews or feeding them; her parents had remained passive bystanders.

On a cold wet morning, February rain slashing against the picture window, Leon sat downstairs recuperating after a second, unexpected stint in hospital two weeks previously. Sophie was at school and Hedda was upstairs with Susanna, altering several of her dresses, taking them in at the waist or bust. As Susanna stood there in her slip and tights, the dress halfway over her extended arms, they heard a terrible thump on the wooden floor downstairs.

"Excuse me, Hedda said, "I just need to see what that was," already knowing. She ran downstairs where Leon lay on the living room floor, groaning in pain. His face was facing the floor and she didn't want to move him, but placed her hand on his back so that he knew she was there.

"Leon, it's Hedda," she said. "I'm going to call the hospital. Someone will be here soon. It will be alright."

He groaned to indicate he had heard and understood. Susanna was coming down the stairs, back in her own clothes and she crouched down and touched Hedda's hand still on Leon's back. Then she moved to the phone and called the ambulance which arrived just as quickly as before. This time Leon was unable to help the men lift him onto the stretcher. The groaning had stopped and he was unconscious. They stretched out his limbs, rolled him over and gently lifted him on. They checked his breathing and his heart, but the signs weren't good. They asked Hedda if she had a car and could follow the ambulance. Susanna offered to drive her to the hospital and she accepted gratefully. It took another 20 minutes before the ambulance pulled out of Sandy Lane, blue lights on, and once it had left, Susannah held open the passenger door to a Mercedes. Leon would have laughed.

"It will be fine," Susanna said.

"Thanks," Hedda said, "but it won't be fine. I don't think he will be coming home. I think he's dying."

"You don't know that!"

Hedda thought her matter-of-factness had shocked Susanna. But how else could she be? It was Hedda's nature. They drove in silence and arrived at the hospital shortly after the ambulance. Susanna dropped Hedda in the Casualty department, checking that Hedda didn't want her to stay. "Thank you but that won't be necessary." She'd done more than enough. A good German. Susanna planted two small kisses on each of Hedda's cheeks and left.

Hedda entered the waiting area and let an unsmiling

receptionist know that Leon Meier had been rushed in about 15 minutes ago, having suffered a heart attack. The receptionist looked down at her notes, called through and within a minute a young, white-coated doctor appeared. "Mrs. Meier?" he asked.

"Yes, that's me," she answered.

"I'm afraid the news is not good," he said.

Hedda could see his discomfort and imagined he'd not been working long enough to be practiced in the art of delivering bad news. "Is he dead?" she said.

The young doctor looked shocked at her bluntness. He cleared his throat. "He didn't come round. I'm very sorry." He paused, waiting for a response and when there was none he continued: "We gave him cardiac resuscitation but I'm afraid he must have suffered an irreversible attack at home. He wouldn't have suffered. He would have felt nothing. Would you like to see him?"

She followed the white coat along the corridor, through plastic flapping doors and into a small side room.

"Will I be allowed to touch him?" she asked before entering.

"Of course. I'll be outside if you have any further questions."

She quietly pushed at the door so as not to disturb him, and there he was, lying flat on his back, eyes shut. It was hard to believe he wasn't in a calm, dreamless sleep. She was sure his chest slowly rose and fell under the thin blanket. She reached out her hand to his forehead, unsure how it would feel and gently placed first her fingertips and then her whole hand on his brow, sweeping away the too long hair from his eyes. His skin was warm and clammy, and accepting that he was dead was that much harder. She bent down and planted a soft kiss on his forehead. She waited for the right words to come, the last words which he would hear from her.

"I'm not quite sure what to say, Leon. I loved you, and I think, in your own way, you loved me too. You've been a good companion. You've been a good father to our children and they loved you dearly. You made us all laugh. I pray that you are now at peace. I think you are. Goodbye."

The words were inadequate to express the complexity of her feelings, but they were sufficient for now. She planted one more kiss on his forehead, which was just beginning to lose its warmth, and stroked his cheek. One final goodbye and then she left the room.

"Is there anything else you would like to know, Mrs. Meier?" the young doctor asked.

"Not really," she said. "He looks very peaceful. I suppose you will tell me what I have to do next?"

He looked embarrassed. "Someone will call you with information about the procedures following death. I have to ask you whether you are able to formally identify that that man was your husband, Leon Meier?"

She smiled. "Yes, that's Leon," she said. "Thank you doctor and please pass on my thanks to the other staff, the ambulance men as well."

She left the hospital and walked slowly to the bus stop. She wondered what would happen to the clothes he was wearing; he had loved that shirt with its frayed collar and shabby cuffs. She wondered when to tell the girls, how to tell them, what music she would play at the funeral. He had wanted a cremation. It was a relief his father was dead, she thought, she couldn't have dealt with caring for him.

The 65 bus arrived and she stepped on, found a seat upstairs, and looked around. No one knew that she'd just lost her husband. Maybe she should tell the nice-looking woman two seats ahead who looked a little like Valerie: "Oh, can I tell you my husband's just died? Yes, dead. Passed away. He is no more." For all Hedda knew, maybe the nice-looking woman had just heard of the death of *her* best friend, or her mother or a child. No one ever knew the thoughts or feelings of the person sitting next to them, on the top deck of a bus. All little islands of isolation. She looked out at the Kingston shoppers and the street cleaner and the children starting to emerge from school, oblivious to her world. And that was somehow a comfort. The world went on, regardless.

PART IV

27

WHAT A COINCIDENCE!
RICHMOND, SURREY

Spring 1979

Since Leon's death eight years before, Hedda had adjusted with ease if not pleasure to single status. When she looked in the mirror she saw a woman well past middle-age with hooded eyes and sagging skin but few wrinkles and a friendly smile. Hedda knew she was no beauty, but she liked the comforting familiarity of her round cheeks and upturned nose. Her face was a safe anchor. And Radio 3, the perfect sewing companion, a steady stream of Bach and Brahms, Schubert and Schumann, and her beloved Beethoven, increased her sense of security. She re-tuned if they broadcast one of those avant-garde pieces and listened to the afternoon play instead. She was never lonely.

She had ensured a steady stream of customers through the doors; her trusty all-electric Elna whizzed through hems. She took out darts and seams to make room for extra inches, and she pinned and tacked the never-ending supply of alterations sent from the dry cleaners. She was skilled in maintaining friendships with her fellow refugees and Leon's work colleagues. Friends enjoyed her excellent home baking, with crumbly vanilla *Kipferl*, apricot *Streusels*, and lemon cheesecake being particularly in demand.

On this unseasonably warm day for the beginning of May, Pearl

Geller took a bite of the freshly baked almond slice as she and Hedda sat in the garden discussing children, husbands, and Jim Callaghan. Whilst Hedda was irritated by Pearl's constant need to describe every failing of her dead husband, she enjoyed their wide-ranging conversations and common cultural understandings.

"The baby is how old now?" asked Pearl.

Clarice was the proud mother of little Dillyn born 18 months previously, and already expecting her second child.

"He's a year-and-a-half and a sweetheart. I enjoy having a grandson. It's a novelty after bringing up the girls. I try to be a good grandmother but I'm not sure whether I am. What's a good grandmother anyway?"

"You don't look old enough to be one!"

"What should I look like then? Like the old lady in Hansel and Gretel?"

Hedda thought about how she had taken on the role of mother without rehearsal, thrust straight onto the stage of family life. She sometimes wondered what the three girls thought of her; what they had thought of her then, and what they thought of her now. Hopefully they were grateful and appreciative of her efforts, but whether that was the same as love, she couldn't decide. Sometimes she felt their pity for how her life had turned out and what had gone before, but they never asked questions and she never provided details. Children don't want to believe their parents ever had a past.

Having finished the first slice, Pearl looked longingly at the plate of cakes, then back to her empty teacup, then towards Hedda.

"Another slice, Pearl? Another cup of tea?"

Pearl agreed and whilst Hedda was refilling the pot, she took out her copy of the *AJR,* the publication of the Association of Jewish Refugees, and turned to a page she wanted to discuss. A mass grave of 8,000–9,000 Jews killed by the Nazis had recently been discovered in a forest near Lambach in Austria. The grave was near a wartime labor camp and included documents that the victims were Hungarians marched to the area by the Germans in 1944.

"I think they might be some of my family," she said as Hedda sat down again with the fresh pot.

Hedda looked appalled. "What will you do?" she asked, her hand shaking as she poured the milk and handed Pearl the plate of cakes.

"I haven't decided. I may go out there this summer with my sister although she is not so well these days."

"I'm not sure you should. What would it achieve?"

"I would pay my respects and say my goodbyes. It says that the bones will be reinterred at the Mauthausen Memorial site." She paused. "Would you consider coming with me?"

Since the family holidays, Hedda hadn't stayed away from the house for even a night. The idea of spending two weeks away with her friend on such a grim venture filled her with horror. "I don't think so, I'm not ready."

"I'm not sure I am either." Pearl laughed and ate her second almond slice in two bites.

Hedda picked up the paper and scanned the pages for a change of subject.

"There's an article here about a new museum that's opened in Poland. A place called Poznań commemorating Polish Jews and others. It says the incarcerated Jews were made to build a motorway. Why does that place sound familiar?" Hedda said.

"Well, that's one country I certainly won't be visiting!" said Pearl. "Miserable place! Gray buildings. Nothing in the shops. We are certainly the lucky ones."

Hedda nodded. She had been lucky in so many ways. Poznań. Why did it ring a bell?

Since 1948, the Cassel Hospital had occupied an attractive Georgian building overlooking Ham Common. Presumably the trustees thought the pretty village atmosphere of Ham, the open space on the common, and the tranquil pond surrounded by willows and chestnut trees would benefit the patients. The idea of the founder was radical: the patients would actively participate in their own treatment, including the running of the hospital itself, and create a new type of therapeutic community. Rather than remain passive victims of their mental distress, they would actively design the solutions, working hand in hand with the doctors and nurses.

Once or twice, Leon and Hedda had attended typically English garden parties in the beautifully laid out grounds at the back of the house. Gravel patios fronted large Georgian windows which were thrown open to the summer air. Children would roll down neatly mown grass slopes, covering themselves in stains. Sometimes a traditional jazz band featuring clarinet and trombone played "When the Saints Come Marching In," sometimes pretty long-haired girls dressed in black dresses formed a more sedate string quartet.

The patients were mainly indistinguishable from the guests and staff and manned tombola stalls, served chilled lemonade, or drifted around the grounds, chatting to the new arrivals. The parties were the epitome of English country life and although Hedda enjoyed the Mozart sonatas and the occasional win on Hook the Duck, she never overcame her sense of being an outsider, an interloper, that her presence made others feel uncomfortable. She would envy her girls, their accentless voices, their sure sense of homeland, and sometimes wondered if she would benefit from exploring her inner world within the hospital. But then the feeling would pass and by the time she was home, with a pile of washing to get through and meals to prepare, her sense of alienation would have vanished into the warm summer air from which it came.

For many years now, Hedda had made it her habit to take an afternoon cycle to the local shops. She would shop for a few items, a packet of sugar, possibly some coffee beans, the occasional chocolate treat, and pack the purchases into the wicker basket fixed to the front of her Raleigh Shopper. Then she might continue to the pond on Ham Common where she would prop the bike up against the cherry tree, stretch out her legs on her favorite bench opposite the pond, and enjoy the ease of calf muscle. Douglas

House, home to the German School, sat squarely behind her and the Cassel Hospital was located further down the lane.

That afternoon, following Pearl's morning visit, she cycled to her usual spot. She watched the light breeze catch the blossom petals and toss them upwards. Some landed in her hair, then formed a pink carpet around her sensibly clad feet, non-slip on the bicycle pedals. The world went by: mothers held the hands of their children, waddling like the ducks they'd come to feed, and Hedda waved at occasional people she knew.

When the sun began to fade behind gray clouds, she decided it was probably time to make a move. There were items still to wash up and she had forgotten her cardigan. It was at that moment a familiar figure walked across the Common from the direction of the Cassel. Even from that distance, he looked familiar. Maybe one of her customers' husbands? Maybe an old work colleague of Leon's? There was something about the set of his head and the way his shoulders pushed back as he walked that reminded her of someone. She watched as he reached the far side of the pond and took out some bread from his jacket pocket. He surveyed the scene before she saw him break the bread into smaller pieces and scatter it. The greedy pigeons, always waiting and watching, swooped down before being joined by a couple of smaller birds. Little black moorhens grabbed their share before returning to the water. Once finished, he sat on the bench and took out a cigarette. Hedda continued to watch until he threw down the stub and strolled back towards the hospital.

It was him. Thirty-five years older, but still, she was convinced that the man was Peter Carter, lover of Hedda Israel, husband to Patricia, and presumably now working at the Cassel. Her stomach knotted tight, a sensation not felt in years. Her head throbbed.

As she cycled back, she tried to piece it together and once home had convinced herself it was another foolish apparition she conjured up, just like the time she boarded the ferry and thought it was her sister Edith performing the flamenco moves. She put the teabags in the caddy, the bar of soap in the bathroom dish, and washed the plates and teacups from the morning. So unlike her to have left them; she wondered if there had been a reason. If she had spent those extra minutes clearing, washing, and drying she would not have seen the man. He would have gone by the time she arrived. The man. She wanted to tell someone, talk to someone. She wanted to tell Leon.

"Leon, you'll never believe it! Guess who I saw today, I'm sure it was him, Peter, the man I told you about? I think it's him. He must be working at the Cassel. What an incredible coincidence, don't you think? I thought he was in Germany. Shall we have him over for coffee and cake?"

And Leon would say, "Of course, Hedda, he loved you, didn't he? It would be good to meet someone who loves you. Like I never could...."

So she told him, and then wondered whether she should telephone Clarice or Rebecca or Sophie and let them know what had happened. But Clarice was far too busy with the new baby and Rebecca and Sophie would be in lectures or with their university friends and she never called them anyway.

That night she dreamt she was back in Mill Hill with Peter and Eric. They were in the woods behind the house, and Peter was running away towards another figure, a woman who looked like Betty but wasn't, and Eric grabbed Hedda and tried to kiss her and she didn't resist. She woke up feeling dirty and disturbed. After breakfast she started work on some new repairs sent from the dry cleaners. She even considered sharing the news with Gary, the van driver who delivered the clothes, then thought better. She waited until roughly the same time as the previous day, then left the house for the short cycle to the Common. She sat on the bench and waited. When she saw him, he was walking with someone else, a shorter man who looked younger from his full head of hair. The taller man took out the packet of cigarettes and offered it to the shorter man, who shook his head in refusal.

Hedda watched as they talked. At one point the short man took out what looked like a notebook from his breast pocket and appeared to be reading from it. This seemed to engage them in greater discussion and then the tall man got up and for one awful moment it looked like he would walk around the pond in her direction. Her stomach lurched again, and she dropped her head to become invisible.

She now knew the taller man was Peter; every part of her knew it. The set of his jawline and cheekbones, the way he held the cigarette and placed it for just too long in his small mouth, the way his shoulders sat on his body, his lazy walk, the remaining red hair that was cut close to his receding hairline. She didn't want him to see her – she wasn't ready. She sat still and without looking up could just see the two of them walking back across the Common, away from her. Life was good. She lived in the present tense and had no wish to revisit the past.

That evening Sophie called. She was having a hard time at Manchester, boyfriend difficulties. It seemed she'd got herself too involved with a nice young man whom she didn't want to be with anymore, but nor did she want to hurt his feelings. She felt trapped.

"Explain to him how you feel," Hedda said.

"He'll be devastated."

"You're only 20, too young to get stuck in a relationship that's not working."

"I'll think about it."

They were talking about relationships and feelings and love and Hedda ventured an opening. "Have you got a bit longer to chat?"

Sophie was quiet on the other end. "Yes, Mummy. Is everything okay? Are you alright?"

Hedda heard her daughter's concern and was touched. "Oh darling, I'm fine. But something's happened, something strange and I just want to tell someone."

"Go on. I'm intrigued."

"I've seen someone in the last couple of days that I think I recognize."

Sophie sounded almost disappointed. "I thought it was going to be something exciting," she said.

"I think it might be. He's from quite a long time ago. Actually nearly 40 years ago. Before the war started."

"And? So was he someone special?"

"He was. Someone very special."

"Is he someone you had a thing with?" she asked as diplomatically as she could manage.

"Yes, I suppose so. That's a modern way of putting it. I lived with him for about five years, actually."

"What? You lived with a man? Why didn't I know?"

"No reason for you to know," Hedda said.

"But that's such a big part of your life."

Hedda felt Sophie's shock as well as her annoyance at her withholding such vital information.

"And who is he? Are you going to see him again?"

"He was a doctor. A psychiatrist."

"Oh no, not one of those," she groaned. "Is he German? Or Austrian? I bet he's Viennese, isn't he? He's got to be Jewish."

"None of that. Actually he's very English. Very well spoken. And he has red hair. Though when I saw him yesterday, there wasn't much of that left."

Sophie was quiet. She was obviously trying to process this new idea of her mother having a former love life with a young English man.

"What do you think? What should I do? Should I say hello?"

"And I thought it was me that was calling you for advice," she said. "I don't know, Mummy. Yes. Say hello, otherwise you will be wondering about it all."

"And what if it's not him? If I've mistaken this man for Peter?"

"Was that his name?" She really knew nothing of Hedda's past.

"Yes, Peter Carter. I was friendly with his sister first. Betty. That's how I met him. She was a pen friend. Say hello? Introduce myself? He probably won't recognize me otherwise. I'm so much older, fatter, and wrinklier."

"You're still beautiful, Mummy."

"Thank you, my little Sputz," said Hedda. "I'll sleep on it and if your wise words are still ringing in my ears in the morning, I'll pluck up the courage to say hello. Now you also need to be courageous, and tell Andrew that your time together has come to an end."

"You're right, but it's hard," she said, not wanting the conversation to return to her problems.

"Whoever said life and love were easy," Hedda replied.

The following afternoon, she cycled to the bench at the same time as the previous two days. It was cloudy with the sort of skies that indicated future drizzle, just waiting until the bike was propped and she was on sentry duty. The rain didn't arrive and nor did he. She waited nearly an hour but he didn't materialize.

The next day she repeated this and the day after and even though the sun now shone, he didn't make an appearance, not to feed the ducks or chat with his friend or just have an outdoor smoke. She wondered if she had made the whole thing up. Or maybe it *was* him, visiting the hospital as part of some research work and now he was back to where he'd come from. Back to Germany? She decided to give it one more go. It was Friday, another beautiful day, and she rode down Back Lane, past Douglas House and on to the Cassel. She walked through the metal gates across the gravel driveway, pushing the bike by the handlebars, and stood in front of the door straddled by two pillars. There was an ornate knocker in the shape of a lion's head. She took a deep breath, knocked, and within a few seconds, a woman opened the door wide.

"Hello, what can I do for you?" she asked with a welcoming smile. She was either a hospital receptionist or a nurse or even a patient pretending to be one of the two.

"Well, it's a bit of an odd request," Hedda said. "I believe you might have a doctor working with you that I know." That was insufficient information. "His name is Peter Carter and he's in his sixties."

"I'm afraid I'm not allowed to provide information about our staff or our patients," the woman in white said. "I'm sure you understand."

"Yes, of course. It's just that, well, he's an old friend from a very long time ago and I think it was him I saw at the beginning of the week. If it was him, I think he would like me to say hello."

The receptionist or nurse or patient seemed to alter as if a cog of understanding had clicked into place. "Can you give me one moment?" she said, and Hedda watched her walk further into the house.

Her heart thumped so loudly she was sure it could be heard from the depths of the hospital.

The white coat returned, a broad smile lighting up her face. "Peter *is* working here. He wondered who you were, but said I was to ask you if your name was Hedda?"

Oh my God. It's Peter. She felt her knees go weak and reached out her hand to steady herself on one of the pillars.

"Yes. Hedda Meier but he will know me as Hedda Israel."

"He's in a group session but wondered whether you are free to pop over later this afternoon. Say about five o'clock?"

She nodded and whispered, "That would be fine."

"I'll let him know. Hedda. That's a really pretty name. Are you Norwegian? I can hear you have a bit of an accent and the only Hedda I've ever heard of is from that play, *Hedda Gabler*. He was from Norway, wasn't he? The writer, I mean."

But Hedda was already wheeling her bike across the gravel, unable to reply.

She changed into a fresh blouse and skirt and caught the bus to the Common. This time when she knocked the door was answered by Peter, who stood there in the doorway looking exactly like himself. Less hair and a face that was no longer in its thirties, but it was Peter, all over again. Every muscle in Hedda's face strained in the wrong direction in her efforts to keep calm.

"Hedda. Hedda Israel, no less. It really is you. Come in, come in."

He turned and she followed him down the hallway to the large drawing room that backed onto the manicured gardens. She'd been in the room before but only when the young musicians swept their bows across the strings in earnest concentration. Then, she had allowed herself to think of the possibilities she had missed at their age when she was stuck in the noisy factory or scraping the dried egg off the plates in the Simmons' household. She thought that life takes us on an infinite number of paths and we have almost no control over which ones we follow. She certainly had had no choice. Her path had been laid out by her mother before she was born, by her mother's insecurities and weaknesses, her vanities and foolishness.

The large French doors were open and the net curtains stirred ever so slightly. He stepped through to a small table laid out with a floral tablecloth and teacups.

"Sit down. I can't tell you what an utterly wonderful surprise this is. We have so much catching up to do."

She had lost the power of speech and if he saw how nervous she was, he didn't say.

"I've called for tea."

Still she said nothing.

"Look. It is genuinely wonderful to see you again after all this time. And what an incredible coincidence to find ourselves in the same place at the same time. Of all the gin joints in all the towns, she walks into mine!"

Hedda smiled.

"I assume you are married? With a family? You must have snapped up a husband immediately."

She didn't interrupt, partly because she was still dry-mouthed and tongue-tied, partly because she was curious to hear his speculations.

"Well, *I'm* not married, not anymore," he continued. "I was, as you know. To Patricia. She was a lovely woman. Lovely. Beautiful. Clever. And very Welsh! But it wasn't love. We just had so much in common. So much to talk about and share. Anyway, we divorced about four years after we married, which was very easy in Germany. Didn't have to prove anything. And we didn't have children so no nasty decisions over child rearing. Both of us were so preoccupied with our work that children were not even considered. I don't regret it. My work has been everything to me."

As he talked, Hedda formed the impression he'd worked on his speech, planned out the words and the sequence, and she felt flattered that he'd obviously put in the preparatory work for her benefit.

"After the divorce, Patricia remained in Germany and she met someone else pretty damn quickly. A very pleasant German who had resisted the Nazis and been imprisoned for a short time. A good German. We managed to meet a few good ones while we were there but not many, I'm afraid. She carried on her work and I came back to England. And she had children, four of them. They write to me, you know. We've kept up a delightful friendship and the children used to practice their English on me. I suppose a bit like you and Betty, pen friends, bonding over words."

The tea arrived and with a shaky hand, Hedda poured whilst he talked.

"And you? What about you? You live around here, I imagine. It's a beautiful part of the world. I've not been here long. I'm renting a flat not far from the hospital."

She told him the bare headlines: how she was married but no longer, her husband having died several years ago of a heart condition, and how she had three grown-up daughters, two from her husband's first marriage, and one the product of him and her. Oh, and she was a grandmother.

"You've been very busy by the sound of things," he said, and she agreed.

She told him she lived close to the Cassel, on her own. She had a lovely house although the kitchen was far too small, and some good friends.

"It's been a pleasure catching up," he said. "Thanks for making the effort. You were always so thoughtful. And I know this sounds daft, but I feel ridiculously nervous right now, not at my best. A bit of a wobbling jelly, if truth be told. Maybe I could take your telephone number? I could call you to arrange another time for a further catch-up?"

Peter. So honest and kind and vulnerable, she thought. Just one of the reasons she fell for him so deeply.

"Yes, of course. It's all a bit of a shock, isn't it," she answered. She pulled out a small notebook from her handbag, kept there for jotting down shopping lists and other domestic matters. She took out a biro and wrote her number and as she wrote, the image of him standing by the phone box scribbling down Herman's number, and his invitation to "meet again" came to her in full technicolor. Thirty-five years later. And here she was, writing her number down on another torn piece of paper.

28

RETURN OF STOLEN GOODS
RICHMOND PARK

Spring 1979

They arranged for him to come over for lunch on the Sunday two days after their first meeting. She'd prepared a simple buffet style meal of cold meats and cheeses, German bread, cucumbers and tomatoes, followed by some creamy trifle with a homemade custard. As she sat in the living room focusing unsuccessfully on her book, the sound of the garden gate swinging open alerted her to his arrival. She watched him walk down the path, his long-legged stride unchanged, those shoulders still pushed back as if held in place by a coat hanger. She tried to swallow the ball of anxiety in her throat and went to the door. He stood there and broke into that smile, deep wrinkles around his eyes. "Ha! Hedda! The right house."

He was nervous too, she thought. There was only one number 34 on the street.

"Come in," she said.

He stepped through and she indicated a chair to him, the Ercol now replaced by a swivel chair of Danish design, very comfortable and fashionable. She offered him a coffee, which he accepted, and left him to browse the bookshelves and record collection.

"What a library," he said as she came back in with their drinks. "Was it both of yours?"

She explained that Leon had been a voracious reader, everything from Tolstoy to Trollope, and that books had been an essential part of their lives. When Leon became unwell, books were even more important as he tried to find the answers to the philosophical matters that concerned him.

"You must have had some powerful conversations," he said.

"Not often," she replied. "He was always reading and thinking about what he read, and noting down ideas, but he didn't really share those thoughts with me. He was very 'internal.' He didn't trust that I would be able to engage in his intellectual conversations. He probably would have liked talking to you, though. You could have done a great job in psychoanalyzing him!"

He sat down and looked steadily at her. Then his gaze traveled the room. "The room is beautiful. Well-organized. Thoughtful. Lived in. It feels like a family inhabits this place – a family which has lived a good life."

Hedda thanked him. She thought it was a compliment. Maybe he felt some envy? He had missed out on family life: the pleasures and the pain.

They were silent for a moment, then he asked, "How is your mother? I hope she's still with us."

Hedda nodded.

"And well? I imagine she made a life for herself after her release?"

Hedda explained that she had barely seen her mother in the last 20 years: once when she came to help with the birth of Sophie and once when they traveled to Germany after she returned.

"So she went back? I'm surprised. I would have thought that was the last place on earth she'd want to be after everything they did."

Hedda smiled. "She went back as soon as she could. She never really felt anything other than German, despite it all. German-ness just ran through her. She missed everything about the country, the mountains and the lakes and forests, the language and the music and even the people themselves."

Hedda resisted saying more about Alice, about how she'd been made to feel over the years, about her mother's inability to see that her actions were wrong, a betrayal of England's generosity. Her mood would have soured.

"Your mother was always a surprise; she never quite seemed to do what any of us expected. She was so concerned with the opinions of others, and her desire to please was obvious, but then, on the other hand, she was rebellious. She hated being told what to do. Underneath it all though there was a sweetness, a kindness..."

"I disagree!" said Hedda. Peter in professional mode again. She'd forgotten that about him. "I think she was, and still is, selfish. Unable to ever see things from another's point of view. Certainly not mine. Don't get me wrong. I'm glad she returned to Germany. It meant that I no longer had to have her in my life. How could she so easily forgive everything the Germans had done and live amongst them? I will never understand."

"So you're glad she's in Germany but you're not able to accept her going back home? A bit contradictory, don't you think?" he said and proffered a small smile.

"Yes. Of course. Nothing we feel is simple. But she's a difficult woman. And there are too many things she's done that make it hard for me to like her or forgive her. Definitely not forgive her! She made my father's life a misery, she pushed Edith away, and of course there are all the things she said and did to me!" The mood *was* changing and Hedda stopped herself. "Peter, let's eat." She indicated he should move to the dining table whilst she calmed herself in the kitchen.

When she returned, he said, "Please understand I'm not for one moment suggesting your opinions of your mother are wrong. How could I possibly barge into your life and start lecturing you on what you should and shouldn't think and feel. It's none of my business. I have spent the last 30 years working with patients who are tied in knots with pain and anger towards their parents or their partners or their employers or the country that behaved so savagely to them and their loved ones. We try to consider the nature of forgiveness and what it means. Maybe it's believing that forgiving isn't forgetting, or excusing or saying that everything that took place, everything that happened in the past is to be forgotten, that it's okay. It's not about that. But maybe it's about managing our internal world, preventing the events of our past from influencing our future."

Hedda felt like one of his students in a dusty lecture hall. One of his crazy patients at the Cassel. She hadn't invited him round for a sermon. She wished he was gone. Her face said it all.

"I'm so sorry. I've climbed onto my soapbox and you need to tell me to get down."

She took a small sip of the sweet white wine she had poured. "I'm not ready to talk about this, certainly not today."

"I can't believe my insensitivity. No excuses! Mad!"

"It's fine, really it is. Now eat. You always liked my food."

They shared some easy stories about their married lives, and Hedda talked about her grandson, and what the girls were up to, and the comforting routine of her daily life. He touched on his work in Germany after their break-up but kept it brief, knowing that the topic was far too big for today.

By late afternoon, she was exhausted. They agreed to meet again: mid-week for a coffee somewhere local to the hospital. He would phone her after he had finished his work. As they said goodbye at the front door, he took Hedda's hand.

"So much more to discuss and share. So much more. I've so enjoyed seeing you again, being in your company. Where have the years gone? Honestly, it feels like only yesterday that we were..."

"We were what?"

"We were together."

"And then we weren't?"

"Yes. I'm sorry. Am I forgiven?"

Hedda smiled. "Oh Peter, that's funny. Forgiveness isn't about forgetting though, is it?"

"You *were* listening to my lecture then?"

Hedda leant forward on tiptoes, placed a small kiss on his cheek, and said, "I always listened to you."

She watched him walk back up the path, past the magnolia, its petals now turning brown on the overlong grass, and when he reached the gate he turned and waved, knowing she would still be there.

They next met in a little café on Ham Parade and, following a coffee and a currant bun, they decided to walk across the Common into Richmond Park. The air vibrated with a thousand insects and the gentle heat warmed the skin – a perfect day. They passed the pond and took the long road that led up to Ham Gate. Peter talked about his work at the Cassel but Hedda's thoughts were focused on his work in Germany, long past the Official Secrets Act by now, she assumed.

"When I first went over, I worked with traumatized soldiers," he said as they walked side by side. "They'd seen and done unimaginable things. We were still applying methods we used after the First World War, hypnosis and similar deep sleep treatments, to address their severe anxiety. We also trialed new treatments. The men were encouraged to express their deepest feelings in a group setting, in a community of sufferers where they would feel safe, knowing that the others had experienced similar sights and sounds. Some of the men responded very well to this treatment so when it came to those officers who..." He trailed off.

"Who what?" she asked, knowing what was coming next.

"...who were the first to go into the camps." Another pause. "I'm not sure how much you know."

She was surprised at his question, wondering if he thought she was still that naive 20-year-old, but conversation temporarily stopped as they navigated their way through the tall turnstile gates and into the park. There was a small cottage on the other side and Hedda had sometimes imagined living in this idyllic place, the whole park becoming your garden, complete with deer and rabbits. She pointed it out to him and indicated a bench where they could watch the wildlife from a distance.

"Of course, I know, of course I do," she said, picking up the conversation as they sat down. "I know everything. And every day there's more horrors. Why just a few weeks ago, we were reading about a new mass grave found in Austria of Hungarian Jews. And there's a new museum opening in Poland, Poznań, to remember all their victims and the terrible things done to the Poles."

"I'm sorry. How could I think you *wouldn't* know? I don't want to upset you. The work we were doing with those men and women, the first to go into Belsen, the first to see the bodies of the dead and the living, well, I think our work may have been of some help. We had to bear witness and allow them to describe in the greatest of detail what they saw, what they heard, and what they felt. And now I carry those testimonies within me."

"I think about it, see it every day," she said, trying hard not to cry. "So did Leon. Our guilt for getting out. It's our punishment."

"We both carry a heavy load," he said.

"Yes," she said, and looked at him. "What you did in Germany, your work, it was powerful, meaningful. Terrible but vital."

Peter reached out and took her hand. "Thank you. That means a great deal to me."

Not noticing the handholding, a sudden look of discovery formed on Hedda's face. "I've remembered. It's finally come back to me: Poznań."

Peter was finding it difficult to follow her line of thought.

"It's where the Kaleckis came from." She had that look of smug satisfaction, when the answer to a riddle is finally solved. "That's where they were returning to that night." Her expression had changed. "I often think of them. Of course, they must be dead. But maybe I could find out, someday, what happened." She looked down. "You're holding my hand! How funny. Like the old days."

"Would you like to go back to the old days?"

"Certainly not. I'm not that young girl anymore," she said more primly than she intended, "and wouldn't want to be."

He cleared his throat. "You're right. Although there's much that could be improved about this country and this government, life is so much better now than back then. And we can look forward to even better times, I hope."

There was something in the way he had said "we," that made her feel an implication. It was a hint, a suggestion. At that moment she felt herself a teenager, a young woman, an older woman. Ageless. But she wouldn't allow herself to indulge in fantasy; she was a practical and sensible grandmother.

"I'm not sure I agree. I'm not sure times are getting better."

Peter let go of Hedda's hand and took out a cigarette. He lit it and inhaled deeply.

"What I'm about to say, I've been thinking about since you came to the Cassel. I wanted to find the right moment. It's this: I want to say I'm sorry."

Hedda opened her mouth to speak but he gently touched her lips.

"Let me speak. If I don't say it now, I don't think I ever will. I'm sorry I abandoned you. Blocked out any thoughts of your suffering. I had to, with everything else I was dealing with. But it was unforgivable. You were so young and so vulnerable and had already experienced so much. I am really so very sorry. Please, let me finish. Now I feel I have a second chance – to put things right, if you will. I'm no believer in fate, but I do enjoy a good coincidence and that's what we have here – you and I existing in the same geographical space and time, after all these years – there's got to be some reason for that, don't you think?"

He waited for her response. She shifted her position, moving further down the bench so she could face him without touching him.

"I was on my own. Utterly. I was so young. And you knew when you told me you were going abroad that you had no intention of returning to me. You just couldn't be honest." She was surprised by her own directness. She hadn't planned to confront him. His face showed pain.

"I don't know any more. That's the truth. I don't know what I intended. But I know I loved you. Deeply. That I do know. And I don't think I ever stopped loving you."

Hedda gasped. This she wasn't expecting. She got up and walked towards a small cluster of trees where some young deer were grazing. She waited, watched him finish the cigarette, then walked slowly back. "I don't know what to say. I don't know how I feel. About any of this, I'm 59 years old, for goodness' sake!" she said as if that explained her confusion. "Nearly 60!"

"And I'm 67 and drawing my pension," he said, laughing. "Look, I promised myself I would 'declare my feelings' and then, if you thought I was ridiculous, or this was impossible, then we would agree to go no further. Is there something for us? To go forward? Don't even speak. Nod or shake your head."

She didn't move. Not an inch. Then she nodded. And nodded again. He reached into his jacket pocket, for a celebratory cigarette she thought, but instead he pulled out a small jewelry box of blue cardboard. She looked appalled. "You're not going to do anything completely crazy, are you now? We're both far too old for that!"

He let out a huge peal of laughter. "Oh Hedda! I'm not that presumptuous. But I can see what it must have looked like. But I want you to open it. Go on." He handed her the box and at that moment she guessed the contents.

"It's my brooch, isn't it? The one you stole from me. Well, my mother's brooch really. Or Anna's brooch. You were a thief. I'd forgotten that." She carefully lifted the lid and there on a small piece of cotton wool was the gold brooch shaped like a rose, with its six-pointed petals and the small red ruby at its center. "You've brought it back. After all this time."

"Well, if truth be told, I wouldn't have returned it," he said, "if you'd responded in a different way. I'd have kept it. My keepsake of you. My souvenir of what might have been."

"So now you are forgiven and you're no longer a thief!" She cupped her hands around his sharp jaw and kissed him fully. "Thank goodness I haven't forgotten how to," she said. "It's been quite a while!"

Sophie was back from university and working in the pub beside Petersham Meadows, enjoying the freedom of a few months away from her studies and getting up to goodness knows what. All three girls had discussed their mother's news. They had wished her luck and teased her for not telling them more about the wartime love affair.

Peter and Hedda had arranged to meet for a drink on Sophie's next shift and when they entered, she was chatting with the punters sitting on the stools around the open bar. Sophie gave them a friendly wave and they found a table. There was the usual clatter of glasses and babble and laughter, conviviality of the true British kind. Hedda watched her daughter reach out her hand to shake his before scooting off to pour their drinks. When she came back, he said something which made her laugh and she looked over, smiled, then waved again. She likes him, Hedda decided. She could see her daughter liked him.

They sat at a small corner table by the window that looked out towards the river beyond the meadows, and Hedda felt transported back to the pub by the canal where Peter first met Alice, and then further back to the place in Bloomsbury where it all started. The time when she was the daughter caring for her mother, and now – what a wonderful reversal – it was her daughter, providing the drinks, caring for her mother.

"What a lovely girl. You must be very proud. She seems delightful. And she looks like you."

"Oh, I hope not!" she said.

"You make being a mother look so easy. And after your experience with Alice, she hardly provided you with a model to live up to, did she?"

"She was always wrapped up in her own needs," she said. "She and my father – I'm not sure why they married really. But I think that's true for many couples – you can't imagine they've ever really cared about each other."

"Do you think she loved you?"

"I suppose so. In her own way. She gave us lots of lovely clothes and toys and she never punished us or treated us badly. But I don't think she gave us much thought – we were just there in her life. It was fun to dress us up and show us off, but it could have been any two children. There was nothing special about us."

"I did like her, though."

"I know you did!" Hedda exclaimed. "That's how she worked! She had a charm that even the most insightful and intelligent of men would succumb to. Some women have it and some certainly don't."

"Well, I think you're very charming," he said and kissed her there in the pub in front of her daughter.

"One day I'll be able to think of her with more kindness, but not yet. I'm not yet ready. Forgiveness. It's vastly overrated."

"You don't have to forgive. You're under no obligation. You wouldn't forgive the Germans. Why should you? What purpose would that serve?"

She thought it would serve a purpose: of banishing the ghosts and the anger and the turmoil that remained, but now Sophie was standing over them, collecting their empty glasses.

"We are all dying to get to know you more," she said.

"I think your daughter has inherited your mother's charm," Peter said as Sophie walked away, balancing the glasses in one hand.

"Maybe, and I hope some common sense and good judgment as well. You can only get so far fluttering your eyelashes."

"Your judgment is impeccable, my darling. You couldn't have chosen a finer man to see out your final years."

She gave him a light shove. "Final years? I intend to be around for a long time yet, with or without you."

"With me, always. With me."

29

LOOSE ENDS

SAARBRÜCKEN, WEST GERMANY

Summer 1980

They flew above white pillows of cloud, the brightest azure sky outside the oval window, against which Hedda's nose was pressed. Just past her sixtieth birthday, her first ever flight and she was loving it. With seat belts buckled and safety procedures demonstrated by the elegant air hostess, she thought she would die when the deafening roar of the engines started and the plane accelerated down the runway.

"And just when I've found you," she said, squeezing Peter's hand so tight he thought his bones would break.

"Don't be afraid. Look down," he said and she wondered at the marvels below, at the cars and the trees and the houses, transformed into tiny replicas for Lilliputians to inhabit. The exhilaration she felt to no longer be earthbound; she could get used to this flying.

They were off to Germany to visit Alice. She expected them in a few days, after a short holiday in the surrounding countryside of Saarbrücken. They had considered visiting Berlin where Patricia still lived, but decided it was too much for their first

314

foreign trip together. When Hedda wrote to Alice that Peter had returned, she showed little interest. Hedda was grateful for her mother's apathy. It meant no wasted time and energy in describing their new lives together and answering irrelevant questions. Maybe she was pleased her widowed daughter had found a partner in later life, but her interest was minimal. She didn't know they lived independently and continued their working lives to maintain financial independence. She didn't know they shared a bed frequently and held hands in public places. She was ignorant of the tender, mature love they showed each other.

"How long will it take before we're back on the ground?" Hedda asked, feeling every air current deep in her stomach as the plane made its descent, not quite believing the huge metal aircraft would land on those tiny wheels or stop speeding down the runway. But when it did and she'd walked down the metal steps, she felt like a film star and wished she had dressed the part in sunglasses and headscarf like Jackie Onassis.

They collected the hire-car Peter had organized and drove to a small farm in a pretty village where they would be staying. On arrival, a large aproned lady greeted them, rosy cheeks and hair tied in a traditional plait and bun. Hedda immediately decided she must have been one of those blonde girls the day of that very first procession, waving her arms frantically, blowing kisses to the goosestepping Nazi youth who had marched through her town.

"We can't stay here," she whispered to Peter, "she's one of them."

Peter chose to ignore Hedda and followed the lady through to a picture-postcard farm kitchen, with saucepans and frying pans and every possible wooden spoon and cooking utensil hanging from a timber frame above the large pine table. The woman grabbed Hedda's hand and shook it vigorously, happy to welcome her English guests. She insisted on carrying both suitcases up the two flights of stairs to an airy landing with a window looking onto a field of grazing cows. There were two doors, one to a pretty blue bathroom and one to their bedroom, perfectly made with two fresh white duvets folded in half German style on a comfy looking double bed, a vase of country flowers on a wooden dresser, and a plate of freshly baked biscuits.

"*Wenn du fertig bist, komm auf Kaffee und Kuchen runter,*" she said ["Come down for coffee and cake when you're ready."]

"Still think we can't stay here?" Peter asked, sitting down on the bed, grabbing Hedda and pulling her down too.

"I know, I know. She's obviously a nice woman. Kind. And it's a beautiful room. It's just hard to think that she was one of them. One of those who cheered and waved, who were so in love with Hitler and the Nazis. She's about my age. Her parents could have sent me to the camps. Her parents probably worked there."

"Possibly. It's also possible that she or her family tried to resist but weren't brave enough. Are you going to ask her? Ask her to account for her actions nearly 40 years ago? You will kill yourself if you see everybody this way. You will become another of their victims."

He was right. They had discussed the trip for months. As well as visiting Alice, the trip was an opportunity to put the past behind her and let go of her scalding rage when reminded by events in the news. They unpacked, hanging the few clothes they'd brought in the carved pine wardrobe that smelt of mothballs and childhood. Hedda washed her face and touched up her lipstick in the small bathroom mirror before joining Frau Bartz downstairs.

The table was laid with three different kinds of cake and she poured steaming black coffee from a metal jug. She spoke no English but Peter responded to most of Frau Bartz's questions: was the room satisfactory, what was the purpose of the trip to the area? She was delighted to welcome foreign guests, it was such an overlooked part of Germany and would they wish her to point out local attractions? The more she talked, the more Hedda relaxed.

"I went to school in Saarbrücken," Hedda said finally.

Frau Bartz looked immensely pleased. "You did? That's wonderful. I don't think I realized you're German?" she said, beaming at her.

"I'm not," Hedda replied, "I was once, long ago, but I'm British now. I got out, you see. I was one of the lucky ones. Others weren't.

My sister did. Get out, I mean. And so did my mother. My father
died. And my favorite family went back to Poland. I doubt they
made it. The daughter, her name was Anna, she was only 12. And
she was really good at mathematics. "

Frau Bartz threw up her hands in horror and held them
hanging in the air. "Oh my dear, my dear," she cried, "I am so truly,
deeply sorry, a thousand times sorry, a million times sorry. We
didn't know. Really, we didn't."

Peter looked at Hedda. He wondered if now she would speak
her mind but Hedda kept silent. She wasn't going to argue with
Frau Bartz. Even if she was one of the very few who "didn't know,"
Hedda had heard that excuse proclaimed too often. And they did
know. They all did. They absorbed the message through every pore
in their bodies, believing every word that came from Berlin and
from the mouths of Goering and Goebbels and Himmler and
Hitler, every word from every Nazi, from every speech and every
film and the lessons in schools and the newspapers and their
parents. Every word contaminated their bodies and their brains.

Hedda crossed the kitchen to where Frau Bartz stood by the
sink, staring out at the chickens in the yard. She was weeping and
using the edge of her large apron to dab her face. Hedda placed her
arms on her shoulders and felt the woman's body shake. She let out
a noisy sob.

"Frau Bartz," Hedda said. "Whether you knew or you didn't
know, we cannot change the past. What's gone is gone. But we can
learn from it and make a good life for ourselves and for others. I do
not hold a grudge, Frau Bartz. You are a good German. I can see
that. Please. Stop crying."

Wiping her eyes she turned and looked at Hedda with what
could only be described as genuine apology and regret.

In German, Frau Bartz said, "You are a good German also. And
I'm very, very sorry for what happened to you and your family. But
we all must make the best of what is left of our lives. And I hope
you are happy in England and happy with your husband and will
be able to enjoy your time in the country of your birth. Please, sit
down and take some cake. And more coffee?"

Hedda caught Peter's eye and smiled, though whether that was to acknowledge his new status as her husband or to reassure him that she was alright, he wasn't quite sure.

Four days later, they drove a short way out from the farm, parked the car and walked down a tree-lined avenue of swaying birches. They were approaching Alice's house and Hedda could feel her heart rate increase at the thought of the meeting. The afternoon was perfect, soft warmth and birdsong all around. They passed several small, detached homes before they reached number 14, a gray concrete exterior of a single-story dwelling with shuttered red windows. There was a small front garden with apple trees and flower beds edging a gravel path, which crunched under foot.

From around the side of the house appeared a handsome man in his late twenties, with a clean-shaven face and fine features. This must be one of the tenants. Alice was living with two young men who rented rooms in her house, and shopped and cooked for her. They provided her with company and in return they paid a minimum rent; it would not cover a basic shopping basket. But the service they offered Alice, of two men in love, chattering over chocolate cake, helped her feel less lonely in her final years and maybe that service was worth the accommodation and meals they received in return.

"Hello, hello, you're Hedda and this is Peter? I'm Stephan," he called in a friendly voice. "Alice has been talking about you non-stop for the last few days. She talks of nothing else. Come through. We're all in the back."

He spoke English as fluently as Peter spoke German. He led them around the house into a garden filled with more fruit trees in full leaf, tall hollyhocks and daisies, and there was Alice sitting at a table with another young man, the shade keeping the worst of the afternoon sun off her face and body. She didn't get up. Hedda saw how large her mother had become, and imagined she restricted her movements to a minimum. She looked like a very old lady, which Hedda had also not been expecting.

"Mutti, how are you? I hope you're well?" She bent down and kissed her mother on the cheek.

Richard, Stephan's partner, got up. "We'll leave you to it. Shall we bring out some refreshments? Alice?" Richard seemed to be nudging her to speak. "Alice, they've come to see you, you've been so excited, haven't you?" The men walked off towards the house, chatting enthusiastically.

"Hello, Alice," Peter said.

She responded to his voice. "Peter?" she asked. "Peter! How lovely to see you after all these years." Her giant face rounded even further into an ingratiating smile.

"And you, Alice, and you too," he replied. "But you must be so pleased to see your daughter. It's been a long time."

She turned to face her daughter. "Hedda dear. You look older. It's lovely to see you. Are you well?"

Hedda avoided looking at Peter for help or explanation. She couldn't decide if her mother was senile or completely indifferent, even after all this time. "I'm fine. Very happy to have been reunited with Peter."

"He was always such a handsome man. Better looking than Leon. And clever. You were a doctor, weren't you?"

"I still am."

"Ha. Lucky patients."

She hadn't changed. Except she had. Suffering from the disease of old age.

"Mother, I've come over to see you, to see how you are, but also because–"

"Because you want to see if your old mother is dying?"

Hedda chose to ignore her mother's unkind remark. "Because I want to say something to you, something's that important to me."

"That sounds interesting. You always were a mystery. I don't think we ever quite understood each other."

"I think you are probably right."

Richard returned with three glasses of apple juice and a plate of biscuits. They were silent as he placed the tray on the table.

"He's such a nice boy, so considerate and thoughtful," Alice said as he returned to the house.

"Mother," Hedda said. Peter knew she was nervous and placed a reassuring hand on her arm. "I want to say, I want to tell you that I forgive you."

Alice looked puzzled. She took a long sip of her juice, then picked up a biscuit and broke it in half.

"I'm not sure you heard? I've come here today to say I forgive you. *Ich vergebe dir.*"

Alice smiled and chewed. "Yes, I heard. I'm not deaf yet, but I don't understand. *You* forgive *me*? For what?" She looked at Peter, expecting him to be nodding in agreement. "For bringing you up to be a good girl? For my being a good wife to my late husband? For surviving those dreadful camps they put me in whilst you were fancy free? For getting on with life in England? Working hard, despite the fact that I was a foreigner, an outsider. I think it is *I* that should be forgiving *you*. Don't you think so, Peter?"

Hedda turned to Peter who very gently shook his head, but Hedda had no intention of responding further. An early apple dropped from the branch landing with a tiny thud on the grass. A wood-thrush sang and another answered. The subject was closed. Hedda made a move to go and Peter got up.

"Hedda, you almost forgot! You brought something for your mother," Peter said.

Hedda reached into her handbag and pulled out a small box. She placed it on the table in front of her mother. "Open it," she said.

"My hands, my fingers, they're not as they were."

Hedda opened the lid.

"A brooch?" Alice said, "My brooch!" Her face broke into a smile. "I remember this. Why do you have it?"

Hedda explained she had taken it when she went to Berlin as a memory of her mother but left out the rest of the brooch's journey from England, then back to Germany and finally back in her possession.

The men joined them when they saw Peter and Hedda preparing to leave. "It's beautiful," said Richard, "may I look at it?" He held it up in the late afternoon sunshine and the stone caught the light, twinkling red streaks across his face.

"Beautiful," said Stephan.

"It's a trinket," said Alice. "I remember your father buying this when we were first courting. He couldn't afford much. Cut glass and gold plate. Please have it. Or maybe Stephan would like it for his collection? Have it. Don't argue boys."

Richard and Stephan looked to Hedda who nodded her head in agreement with her mother – why not? The brooch had served its purpose and the boys appeared to like it. Her mother's offer was both generous and selfish. They said their goodbyes, kissing Alice once on her cheek and shaking the men's hands. The sun was less bright and the shadows cast fading shapes on the yellow grass as they left.

"That went well," said Peter.

"I think you're teasing," she said slowly. "But actually, maybe it did. I wasn't expecting anything from her and that's what she delivered. Why would she have changed? People don't."

"Some people do. I hope you think I've changed," he replied and opened the passenger door.

"So what now, my little darling? Home?"

"No," she said, "not yet. Now I've seen Alice and said what I needed to say, I'm ready to do the final bit."

"It will take some time," he said, "and the journey won't be much fun."

"Everything's fun with you, and we have all the time in the world."

30

BURYING THE GHOSTS
POZNAŃ, POLAND

Summer 1980

As Peter had predicted, the journey wasn't much fun. It had taken three full days to travel from Saarbrücken to Poznań, crossing the border between West and East Germany then onto Poland, where they had stayed in basic Soviet-style accommodation and eaten tasteless meals of overcooked cabbage and tough meat. First they had driven to Bad Hersfeld, a faded spa town, and had clambered over bits of the old city wall. It was raining when they first saw the signs of the hammer and sickle at Marienborn, the border between the Federal German Republic and the German Democratic Republic, and as they approached the many checkpoints that straddled the road, there were frequent commands to '*Halt!*' and '*Halt hier!*' and '*Halt hier, Grenze!*' There was no doubt they were entering Soviet territory. Most of the cars in front and behind them were siphoned into a lane called 'Allied Traffic', traveling from west to east. There were few cars crossing the other way.

"I'm not sure this was such a good idea," said Hedda. It was bringing back memories of previous frontier crossings.

322

"I think they like visitors. They want tourist money. They need our dollars and Deutschmarks."

"All the same," she said as they pulled to a halt in front of the young border guard.

He was wearing a long brown coat, peaked hat and leather boots and gloves, and Hedda thought he must be far too hot. He looked like he should be in school, not breathing in the foul air of 100 idling engines, spewing fumes from their exhausts. It made her cough and she kept the window closed.

"Passports please," he said in German, flicking his fingers back and forth in a gesture he had made innumerable times before.

Peter handed him their open passports and the guard looked at each photo, then checked the faces of the travelers before him.. "English?"

"Yes, both English," Peter replied.

"And the purpose of your visit?"

"We will be traveling to Poland. It's a leisure trip, a holiday."

The border guard laughed. "There's not much in Poland to detain you," he said. "It's not where I'd go on my holidays. What's England like, then? Where do you live?"

Hedda was surprised at his desire to enter into conversation. She looked over her shoulder to see if the car behind was impatient but the sole occupant, his head partially masked in cigarette smoke, was reading a newspaper.

"We live not far from London," Peter replied.

"Ah London! Big Ben. The Queen! I'd like to see London one day."

"I hope you will," Peter said.

The guard was still holding their passports and Peter reached out his arm, the conversation concluded. The guard leant in, his hands on one end of the documents, Peter's on the other.

"You know, some of us would be glad if we could travel. See the world." He released his grip and flicked his fingers again, indicating they could go.

"The British Museum is my favorite!" Hedda shouted as they drove off in the direction of Berlin.

They avoided the difficulties of further border crossings by staying south of Berlin in a small riverside town in an inconspicuous hotel. It wasn't a place to linger so following a simple breakfast of dark bread and jam, they continued, hoping to make Poznań by lunchtime. The drive was mainly featureless, with long stretches of gray road lined with tall trees, beyond which were fields, small villages and, as they skirted round the larger towns, block upon block of drab apartment housing. Hedda had agreed with Leon that many of the British towers and 'villages in the sky' were ugly, but nothing compared to these.

It was lunchtime by the time they arrived in Poznań after crossing another border between the GDR and Poland. In shop windows, on billboards and wherever a photograph could be hung, the face of Pope John Paul II beamed down radiantly. It was not what Hedda had expected. She had forgotten his appointment to the Vatican the year before and was pleased that the Polish people were clearly so proud of their new pope, born Karol Józef Wojtyła in the town of Wadowice.

"I didn't think it would be allowed," she said to Peter as they drove south of the town, to where the new museum was located.

They had stopped at another of the food shops with almost empty shelves and bought themselves some sausage and rolls to eat for their lunch. The town looked a little brighter in comparison to others they had passed through. There were fewer queues outside shops and generally a feeling of more color and movement. Maybe this was a good sign for the new museum they were about to visit. It was on the site of a wartime labor camp which explained why it wasn't in the middle of the town. It was a place called Zabikowo and Hedda had brought the news article from the *AJR* magazine to remind her of its history.

"It was used as a prison for communists and Polish resistors in the last years of the war, but before then as a labor camp for Jews," Hedda read out. "They were brought there to build a new autobahn between Berlin and Warsaw. I hope it wasn't the one we were driving on!"

"What happened to them?" asked Peter. "Did they die there?"

"I don't think so," Hedda said. "It wasn't an extermination camp. It says the Jews were sent to Chelmno."

They followed some small signs to an entrance where a young woman was locking the outer door. She turned at the sound of Peter and Hedda's voices.

"Hello," Hedda said. "I wonder if you can help. We've come from England to visit your museum. We are most interested and are keen to see any archives, if possible?"

The young woman looked delighted at her visitors from abroad. She was a pretty girl, probably the same age as Sophie, with hair so blonde it was almost white tied in a simple ponytail.

"Of course. I'm just closing for lunch but if you would care to return in about an hour or so, then I can help you. Were you looking for anything in particular?" She spoke in English, just like the young border guard; a Polish education was clearly of a high standard.

Hedda explained they were here to see whether the museum had any records on a family called Kalecki.

The girl pulled out a small notebook and pen. "What were their first names? I can start to look when I'm back."

"The father was Borys Kalecki, the mother was Hanna and the daughter was called Anna."

Hedda felt a large lump in her throat as she said the daughter's name. It was too soon to become emotional.

The young woman wrote the names down, then said, "Please feel free to wander the outer grounds – I think you will find them very interesting. I'll see you in an hour." She walked to her car, one of the many Trabants that they'd seen since entering the East, and waved.

On her return from lunch, the girl unlocked the museum doors and ushered them in to an office adjoining the small reception area. She sat opposite them, turning the pages of a large leather-bound book containing photographs, documents, papers, and newspaper articles from long ago. Beside her were similar bound volumes containing more archive materials. They were arranged alphabetically and by date.

"You know this place was mainly a prison camp for Soviet POWs and enemies of the Nazis?" she said, her white-gloved hands taking care not to spoil any of the aging evidence.

"Yes, but I thought that because the Kaleckis came from Poznań, this might be a good place to start."

"K. Kalecki. Kalecki. Ahh... Kalecki!" She was pointing at a register of names written in faded black ink on one of the papers in the book.

"They're here?" Hedda asked too loudly.

"Let me see," the girl said. She read through the listed entries, then turned the page and examined what looked like a letter from an office in Lodz. The silence was dreadful. "From what I can understand, it looks like there are two names here: Borys and Hanna. I can't see the name of Anna, I'm afraid."

"What does it say?"

"Like with so many others, it is not good. It says they died. They were killed. At Chelmno. It's dated April 1942."

"In a gas chamber? Or shot?"

"Neither." She looked up. "Do you know about the place?"

"I'm not sure," Hedda replied.

"Many Jews in this area were taken to Chelmno, a small village not far from here, and told to wait at either the church or the castle courtyard. They had no choice. When the Nazis arrived they had to get into these huge trucks and though they were scared, at least thought they were being taken to a labor camp. Instead, they were killed from being pumped full of carbon monoxide, the vans' exhaust fumes, and were all dead when they arrived."

Hedda cried out.

"I'm so sorry to have to share this grim news with you," said the girl.

They were quiet for a while, trying to comprehend the incomprehensible.

"And Anna? Is her name there?"

The girl looked again. "No, it's not. How old was Anna when the war started?"

"She'd just had her birthday. We'd been to see *Snow White*. That was in 1938, so 13 or 14?"

"She may have managed to leave Poland. There's no record of her here."

"Maybe," said Hedda softly. It was a lot to take in.

"So your questions are answered, darling, however sad the answers may be," said Peter. "And maybe not knowing what happened to Anna means you can write your own ending to her story. For all we know, she's happily living in Tel Aviv, down the road from my sweet sister!"

"That would be funny," Hedda said, grateful to Peter for lightening the mood. She wriggled her shoulders to try to shake off the past and return to the present. "We mustn't take up any more of your time. Thank you so much. You have been so helpful. Are you a historian?"

"I'm still at university studying Modern European History, but yes. This is part of my third-year studies. You may want to take away this small booklet I've written about the area." She handed Hedda a small, stapled booklet which Hedda took and then laughed.

"I'm so sorry, I don't mean to be rude, but I don't speak any Polish." She looked at the cover with its title and author name. "That's funny. Your name is Dabek?"

"Karina Dabek. I'm sorry, I didn't introduce myself before now."

"Is it a popular name in Poland?" Hedda asked. "Are there many Dabeks?"

"Yes, I think so." The girl looked bemused.

"I knew some Dabeks once," said Hedda, noting Karina's puzzled expression. "The boy was called Walter, my first boyfriend. And the mother was called..." she paused, trying to remember.

"Barbara?" said the girl slowly. "And was the father's name Pawel?"

Hedda nodded her head and smiled. "Pawel. That's right. He

was a distinguished looking man. I think he was an engineer. His voice was beautiful. And his wife was so kind. A doctor?"

"Oh, my goodness! Yes! They were my grandparents!"

"Unbelievable!" they both said together. "You can't be. Are you Walter's daughter?"

"Yes! My father is Walter. And my mother is Agnieska. I've got an older sister who's just had a baby boy."

"Incredible," said Peter, "but didn't I say I believed in the magic of coincidence and here it is again, happening right now in Poznań."

The two women ignored Peter's musings.

"My sister lives here. Would you want to meet her? And my parents. My father's in Warsaw right now. He's still working, an engineer, but if you could stay for a few days? He'd love to meet you and Hedda could show off her baby."

Hedda looked puzzled. "Sorry, what did you say?"

"My dad would…"

"No, you said Hedda, your sister's name?"

"Yes, she would love to meet you."

"It's just that your sister's name is the same as mine. I'm Hedda Meier, previously Hedda Israel."

And with that she burst into tears. The realization that not only was Walter alive and well, he had called his first-born after her was both wonderful and deeply moving. While the purpose of their visit was to discover more about the Kalecki family, she now had been granted knowledge of the family who had engineered her move to Berlin and her eventual escape to England. Walter Dabek, her first love. She must have been important to him too. She should never have doubted his feelings.

"May I ask how long your father has lived in Poland?" she said to Karina, wiping her face with a handkerchief she had retrieved from her handbag.

"Of course. He and his parents returned shortly after the start of the war. My grandmother worked in the hospital and my grandfather continued his engineering work. Walter went to university here in Poznań. That's where he met my mother. They've been here ever since. He should be retired now but he won't hear of it!"

"And did he ever say why your sister was called Hedda? It's an unusual name."

"Not really. I think he said it was a pretty name that he and my mother both liked but nothing else. I hope you don't mind?"

Hedda was relieved. "Actually, I'm pleased. I would hate to have been cast as some long-lost love! He was such a nice boy, but it was a difficult time. He was a good friend to me."

Through the office window, Peter could see the sky beginning to turn a golden pink.

"Hedda. Karina. That's a wonderful note on which to leave. It really is time to go."

They stood outside the museum entrance to say their goodbyes, hugging Karina close, and drove back to the center of town. They found a bar, ordered some beers and the daily special.

"What now? We have the car for another week. You decide."

"Yes. I think I'm finally old enough to make my own decisions." She smiled at him. "So, what I would like to do is go home."

"You would? Not wait to meet Walter?"

"I don't need to."

The waiter had brought their beers and they both drank greedily.

"This journey has been everything I wanted. I've seen my mother, said what I needed, even returned her brooch. I know the fate of the Kaleckis, and even though we don't know about Anna, it gives me something to keep working towards. And to find Walter here in Poznań, with a daughter who shares my name. Those ghosts of mine are well and truly buried."

She drank again, quenching a deep thirst. "Good beer. I think this is better than the cider I used to drink."

The waiter arrived with a beige-looking stew and a basket of bread.

"Thank goodness I'm not hungry," Hedda said.

"Do you think you'll want to come back? Not here, but to Germany one day?" Peter asked.

"I think so," she said. "Visit the mountains and the lakes and the forests and the pretty towns. Yes, I would. And Poland as well. It feels like it's changing. But for now, I want to sit beside you in our wonderful red Golf, close my eyes and listen to some Beethoven on the radio while you drive me home."

"Only as far as Saarbrücken. You don't mean that home, I hope?"

"Home. England. Close to my girls. And my grandson. And my sewing machine."

She raised her glass. "To buried ghosts and future lives," she said.

"And to you, my survivor, my darling Hedda, and to you."

AUTHOR'S NOTE

Now that you've read the story, there are questions that need to be answered. Which parts of the story are true? How does the novel reflect the facts as told by Ruth Meller (née Israel) in her video testimony? Which parts are embellished or enhanced? And what is fiction?

Part 1 is almost all true. The shop's advertising poster shows some stylish ladies who are modeling coats, hats and handbags. Black greatcoats in all sizes and pure wool velvet coats in all colors with detachable fur collars are promoted. Interestingly, the prices are in French Francs, clearly showing the advertisement was produced before the area returned to German governance.

The Israels employed staff including a cook and a chauffeur and the shop was successful. Like so many Jews, Paul was subject to antisemitic sentiments during World War I and the incident of being refused service in a popular eating venue occurred.

Ruth had an early romantic interest which went no further and Edith went to the Argentine.

Following Paul's death and Alice's incarceration in Moringen, Ruth relocated to Berlin where she was responsible for securing the necessary paperwork. All the events in that section are based on testimony, including the phone tapping and the many visits to the offices of the Gestapo. Kristallnacht marks the escalation of violence, intimidation and arrests of the Jewish population across Germany. At the tender age of 18, on a stormy night, Ruth traveled to England to start work.

In Part 2 almost all of Ruth's employment history is correct, including the details of the Simmons' unhygienic living arrangements! Many Jewish females initially worked in domestic service before transferring to war work. Ruth worked in a factory as described in the story and it was here that she made many lifelong friendships with other refugees.

Now what about Peter Carter? We know that our mother had a relationship during the course of the war and we think that she lived with a man during this time. We believe he was a political cartoonist possibly working for the Daily Herald, a left-leaning newspaper. From the very sketchy details, I recall her saying he was a fair bit older than her. But the reality is she didn't discuss such matters and wasn't encouraged to do so. Thus, Peter is my work of fiction, my gift to my mother for the love she deserved. He is based on Henry Dicks who I discovered in my research for the novel and who later wrote a book based on his work on de-Nazification. The arrival of Rudolf Hess in Scotland provided rich fodder for the psychiatrists and psychoanalysts at the time. The details about The Maudsley Hospital, as well as The Cassel Hospital which features in Part 4 are true.

I also remember my mother telling me that her mother had been jailed for black market racketeering! Not surprisingly she didn't go into much detail but I'm confident that if the records could be found of those immigrants serving custodial sentences after 1940, the name of Alice Israel would be there! Alice returned to Germany after the war was over.

Part 3 is true and is based on my memories. Ruth married Josef Meller on January 1, 1953, following a swift courtship and a small registry office marriage. Rachel and Claudia, their young daughters, had briefly been taken into care following the sudden death of their mother, Ilse Epstein, and it must have been a great relief to Josef when Ruth agreed to become his wife. He was a fantastic and funny father and I have wonderful memories of him clowning around in the garden, both in front of and behind the camera. He was a terrific photographer and I loved the ambitious cine films and animations he so enjoyed producing. He could also be gloomy and depressed and I can't say I remember much affection between him and Ruth.

The visits to my grandfather Opi in West London, the trip to the wonderful house on the St George's Estate in Weybridge designed by the architect Leslie Gooday, friend of the family, and the making of the animation with the wooden figures and ornaments are all true.

In 1985 Josef died at the age of 64 from another heart attack. He was due to come out of hospital that day.

Part 4 becomes mainly fiction again and I've played around with Ruth's age to allow her to be younger when she is reunited with Peter. She was 65 when Josef died and lived in Petersham alone until her death at the age of 87 although there were always many friends who visited and enjoyed her delicious *hausgemachte Kuchen*.

I once met my grandmother in Saarbrücken. I have memories and a photograph of a very large lady and by that time she was living with two male lodgers. Ruth was not particularly fond of her and I don't think they had much communication following her final visit to England after my birth. Ruth did stay in touch with Edith who stayed in South America but again, it was a distant relationship.

Finally, if any readers wished to view the footage, I would be happy to send them links to the film files. There are four of them and it would be helpful to know which parts of the story were of particular interest. Following Ruth's death, it took me a while to view my mother recalling her childhood and teenage years but was so very glad when I did. I hope that somewhere she is enjoying both the truth and the fiction of her story in *Burying the Ghosts*.

ACKNOWLEDGMENTS

During the course of researching the story I found the following books extremely helpful:

The Secret History of the Blitz by Joshua Levine, **DATE**, Simon and Schuster allowed me to understand attitudes towards black market profiteering and criminality on the home front.

Living through the Blitz by Tom Harrison, DATE, Penguin Books was another useful guide to Londoners' experiences of coping with blackouts and more.

Jewish Refugees from Germany and Austria 1933 -1970 by Anthony Grenville, DATE, Vallentine Mitchell was an invaluable reference book for understanding parliamentary legislation and public attitudes towards Jewish refugees both before and during the war.

The Pursuit of the Nazi Mind by Daniel Pick, DATE, OUP Oxford, examined how psychoanalysis was used during the war to understand the Nazi mind.

The broadcast, "The Psychiatrist and the Deputy Führer" available on BBC Sounds, was the inspiration for Peter Carter, his profession and his involvement with Rudolf Hess. Thanks to Daniel Pick of Birkbeck College who wrote and produced the programme.

There are many people I wish to thank: of course Daniel Meller for kickstarting the project, Rachel Meller, my older sister, and my eldest sister, Claudia Pim, for allowing themselves to appear in the book.

I also wish to thank the following friends who agreed to read my first draft and provide me with invaluable feedback. Thank you to Sharon Baxendale, Pam Case, my two sisters, Caroline Macqueen, Lynda Parker, Maire Jappy and Nancy Wayman.

Sharman Steel was another of my readers in that first stage but then kindly agreed to become my sub-editor when Amsterdam Publishers gave me precise instructions as to how to pull it into shape. Sharman spent many hours on intelligent feedback and on sub-editing duties and I listened to all her suggestions. Thank you Sharman!

Of course, a huge thank you to Liesbeth Heenk of Amsterdam Publishers who told me in an email: "I like your book", simple but powerful words of affirmation.

This book is dedicated to: my wonderful, beautiful, hardworking, courageous, self-effacing, determined mother, Ruth Helga Meller (nee Israel) and my extremely patient husband, Brian Case, who read the story many times and at several stages, always encouraging me to believe that it was good. It is also dedicated to Claudia (Clarice in the story) who so sadly died before she knew the book would be published.

And of course to my darling daughters, Daisy Kelly and Molly Macallister, and my gorgeous granddaughters, Dotty, Mabel, Ruth and Pearl who will now understand the long line of strong women that they belong to.

ABOUT THE AUTHOR

Sonia is the youngest daughter of German/Austrian refugees who arrived in England shortly before the outbreak of war. Born in the 1950s, the first child of Ruth who married Josef, a new widower and father to two young girls, she grew up knowing little of her parents' harrowing experiences.

She developed an early love of theatre and pursued acting in her mid-twenties before entering the world of advertising during the heady 1980s. Stories remained central and a long teaching career allowed her to share a love of literature, theater and the rich world of the imagination.

Burying the Ghosts is Sonia's first novel.

My mother Ruth

AMSTERDAM PUBLISHERS HOLOCAUST LIBRARY

The series **Holocaust Survivor Memoirs World War II** consists of the following autobiographies of survivors:

Outcry. Holocaust Memoirs, by Manny Steinberg

Hank Brodt Holocaust Memoirs. A Candle and a Promise, by Deborah Donnelly

The Dead Years. Holocaust Memoirs, by Joseph Schupack

Rescued from the Ashes. The Diary of Leokadia Schmidt, Survivor of the Warsaw Ghetto, by Leokadia Schmidt

My Lvov. Holocaust Memoir of a twelve-year-old Girl, by Janina Hescheles

Remembering Ravensbrück. From Holocaust to Healing, by Natalie Hess

Wolf. A Story of Hate, by Zeev Scheinwald with Ella Scheinwald

Save my Children. An Astonishing Tale of Survival and its Unlikely Hero, by Leon Kleiner with Edwin Stepp

Holocaust Memoirs of a Bergen-Belsen Survivor & Classmate of Anne Frank, by Nanette Blitz Konig

Defiant German - Defiant Jew. A Holocaust Memoir from inside the Third Reich, by Walter Leopold with Les Leopold

In a Land of Forest and Darkness. The Holocaust Story of two Jewish Partisans, by Sara Lustigman Omelinski

Holocaust Memories. Annihilation and Survival in Slovakia, by Paul
Davidovits

From Auschwitz with Love. The Inspiring Memoir of Two Sisters'
Survival, Devotion and Triumph Told by Manci Grunberger Beran & Ruth
Grunberger Mermelstein, by Daniel Seymour

Remetz. Resistance Fighter and Survivor of the Warsaw Ghetto, by Jan
Yohay Remetz

My March Through Hell. A Young Girl's Terrifying Journey to Survival, by
Halina Kleiner with Edwin Stepp

Roman's Journey, by Roman Halter

Beyond Borders. Escaping the Holocaust and Fighting the Nazis. 1938-
1948, by Rudi Haymann

The Engineer, by Henry Reiss

Memoirs by Elmar Rivosh, Sculptor (1906-1967). Riga Ghetto and Beyond,
by Elmar Rivosh

The series **Holocaust Survivor True Stories** consists of the following biographies:

Among the Reeds. The true story of how a family survived the Holocaust, by Tammy Bottner

A Holocaust Memoir of Love & Resilience. Mama's Survival from Lithuania to America, by Ettie Zilber

Living among the Dead. My Grandmother's Holocaust Survival Story of Love and Strength, by Adena Bernstein Astrowsky

Heart Songs. A Holocaust Memoir, by Barbara Gilford

Shoes of the Shoah. The Tomorrow of Yesterday, by Dorothy Pierce

Hidden in Berlin. A Holocaust Memoir, by Evelyn Joseph Grossman

Separated Together. The Incredible True WWII Story of Soulmates Stranded an Ocean Apart, by Kenneth P. Price, Ph.D.

The Man Across the River. The incredible story of one man's will to survive the Holocaust, by Zvi Wiesenfeld

If Anyone Calls, Tell Them I Died. A Memoir, by Emanuel (Manu) Rosen

The House on Thrömerstrasse. A Story of Rebirth and Renewal in the Wake of the Holocaust, by Ron Vincent

Dancing with my Father. His hidden past. Her quest for truth. How Nazi Vienna shaped a family's identity, by Jo Sorochinsky

The Story Keeper. Weaving the Threads of Time and Memory - A Memoir, by Fred Feldman

Krisia's Silence. The Girl who was not on Schindler's List, by Ronny Hein

Defying Death on the Danube. A Holocaust Survival Story, by Debbie J. Callahan with Henry Stern

A Doorway to Heroism. A decorated German-Jewish Soldier who became an American Hero, by Rabbi W. Jack Romberg

The Shoemaker's Son. The Life of a Holocaust Resister, by Laura Beth Bakst

The Redhead of Auschwitz. A True Story, by Nechama Birnbaum

Land of Many Bridges. My Father's Story, by Bela Ruth Samuel Tenenholtz

Creating Beauty from the Abyss. The Amazing Story of Sam Herciger, Auschwitz Survivor and Artist, by Lesley Ann Richardson

On Sunny Days We Sang. A Holocaust Story of Survival and Resilience, by Jeannette Grunhaus de Gelman

Painful Joy. A Holocaust Family Memoir, by Max J. Friedman

I Give You My Heart. A True Story of Courage and Survival, by Wendy Holden

In the Time of Madmen, by Mark A. Prelas

Monsters and Miracles. Horror, Heroes and the Holocaust, by Ira Wesley Kitmacher

Flower of Vlora. Growing up Jewish in Communist Albania, by Anna Kohen

Aftermath: Coming of Age on Three Continents. A Memoir, by Annette Libeskind Berkovits

Not a real Enemy. The True Story of a Hungarian Jewish Man's Fight for Freedom, by Robert Wolf

Zaidy's War. Four Armies, Three Continents, Two Brothers. One Man's Impossible Story of Endurance, by Martin Bodek

The Glassmaker's Son. Looking for the World my Father left behind in Nazi Germany, by Peter Kupfer

The Apprentice of Buchenwald. The True Story of the Teenage Boy Who Sabotaged Hitler's War Machine, by Oren Schneider

Good for a Single Journey, by Helen Joyce

Burying the Ghosts. She escaped Nazi Germany only to have her life torn apart by the woman she saved from the camps: her mother, by Sonia Case

American Wolf. From Nazi Refugee to American Spy. A True Story, by Audrey Birnbaum

Bipolar Refugee. A Saga of Survival and Resilience, by Peter Wiesner

Before the Beginning and After the End, by Hymie Anisman

The series **Jewish Children in the Holocaust** consists of the following autobiographies of Jewish children hidden during WWII in the Netherlands:

Searching for Home. The Impact of WWII on a Hidden Child, by Joseph Gosler

See You Tonight and Promise to be a Good Boy! War memories, by Salo Muller

Sounds from Silence. Reflections of a Child Holocaust Survivor, Psychiatrist and Teacher, by Robert Krell

Sabine's Odyssey. A Hidden Child and her Dutch Rescuers, by Agnes Schipper

The Journey of a Hidden Child, by Harry Pila and Robin Black

The series **New Jewish Fiction** consists of the following novels, written by Jewish authors. All novels are set in the time during or after the Holocaust:

The Corset Maker. A Novel, by Annette Libeskind Berkovits

Escaping the Whale. The Holocaust is over. But is it ever over for the next generation? by Ruth Rotkowitz

When the Music Stopped. Willy Rosen's Holocaust, by Casey Hayes

Hands of Gold. One Man's Quest to Find the Silver Lining in Misfortune, by Roni Robbins

The Girl Who Counted Numbers. A Novel, by Roslyn Bernstein

There was a garden in Nuremberg. A Novel, by Navina Michal Clemerson

The Butterfly and the Axe, by Omer Bartov

To Live Another Day. A Novel, Elizabeth Rosenberg

A Worthy Life. Based on a True Story, by Dahlia Moore

The series **Holocaust Heritage** consists of the following memoirs by 2G:

The Cello Still Sings. A Generational Story of the Holocaust and of the Transformative Power of Music, by Janet Horvath

The Fire and the Bonfire. A Journey into Memory, by Ardyn Halter

The Silk Factory: Finding Threads of My Family's True Holocaust Story, by Michael Hickins

The series **Holocaust Books for Young Adults** consists of the following novels, based on true stories:

The Boy behind the Door. How Salomon Kool Escaped the Nazis. Inspired by a True Story, by David Tabatsky

Running for Shelter. A True Story, by Suzette Sheft

The Precious Few. An Inspirational Saga of Courage based on True Stories, by David Twain with Art Twain

The series **WWII Historical Fiction** consists of the following novels, some of which are based on true stories:

Mendelevski's Box. A Heartwarming and Heartbreaking Jewish Survivor's Story, by Roger Swindells

A Quiet Genocide. The Untold Holocaust of Disabled Children in WWII Germany, by Glenn Bryant

The Knife-Edge Path, by Patrick T. Leahy

Brave Face. The Inspiring WWII Memoir of a Dutch/German Child, by I. Caroline Crocker and Meta A. Evenbly

When We Had Wings. The Gripping Story of an Orphan in Janusz Korczak's Orphanage. A Historical Novel, by Tami Shem-Tov

Jacob's Courage. Romance and Survival amidst the Horrors of War, by Charles S. Weinblatt

Want to be an AP book reviewer?

Reviews are very important in a world dominated by the social media and social proof.

Please drop us a line if you want to join the *AP review team* and show us at least one review already posted on Amazon for one of our books.

info@amsterdampublishers.com